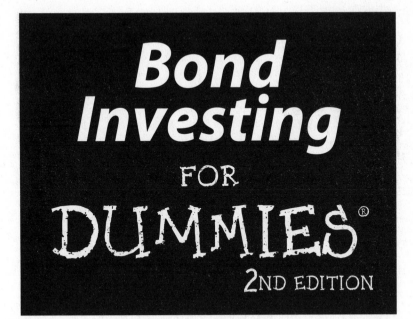

Bond Investing FOR DUMMIES®

2ND EDITION

By Russell Wild, MBA

WILEY

John Wiley & Sons, Inc.

Bond Investing For Dummies®

Published by
John Wiley & Sons, Inc.
111 River St.
Hoboken, NJ 07030-5774
www.wiley.com

Copyright © 2012 by John Wiley & Sons, Inc., Hoboken, New Jersey

Published by John Wiley & Sons, Inc., Hoboken, New Jersey

Published simultaneously in Canada

For general information on our other products and services, please contact our Customer Care Department within the U.S. at 877-762-2974, outside the U.S. at 317-572-3993, or fax 317-572-4002.

For technical support, please visit www.wiley.com/techsupport.

Wiley publishes in a variety of print and electronic formats and by print-on-demand. Some material included with standard print versions of this book may not be included in e-books or in print-on-demand. If this book refers to media such as a CD or DVD that is not included in the version you purchased, you may download this material at http://booksupport.wiley.com. For more information about Wiley products, visit www.wiley.com.

Library of Congress Control Number: 2012942106

ISBN 978-1-118-27443-9 (pbk); ISBN 978-1-118-33053-1 (ebk); ISBN 978-1-118-33134-7 (ebk); ISBN 978-1-118-33335-8 (ebk)

Manufactured in the United States of America

10 9 8 7 6 5 4 3 2

WILEY

About the Author

Russell Wild is a NAPFA-certified financial advisor and principal of Global Portfolios, an investment advisory firm based in Allentown, Pennsylvania. He is one of only a handful of wealth managers in the nation who is both fee-only (takes no commissions) and welcomes clients of both substantial *and* modest means. He calls his firm Global Portfolios to reflect his ardent belief in international diversification — using mostly low-cost index funds to build well-diversified, tax-efficient portfolios.

Wild, in addition to the fun he has with his financial calculator, is also an accomplished writer who helps readers understand and make wise choices about their money. His articles have appeared in many national publications, including *AARP The Magazine, Consumer Reports, Details, Maxim, Men's Health, Men's Journal, Cosmopolitan,* and *Reader's Digest.* He writes a regular finance column for *The Saturday Evening Post.* And he has also contributed to numerous professional journals, such as *Financial Planning, Financial Advisor,* and the *NAPFA Advisor.*

The author or coauthor of two dozen nonfiction books, Wild's work includes *One Year to an Organized Financial Life,* coauthored with professional organizer Regina Leeds, published by Da Capo Press. He also wrote two other *Dummies* titles in addition to this one: *Exchange-Traded Funds For Dummies,* now in its second edition, and *Index Investing For Dummies.* No stranger to the mass media, Wild has shared his wit and wisdom on such shows as *Oprah, The View, CBS Morning News,* and *Good Day New York,* and in hundreds of radio interviews.

Wild holds a Master of Business Administration (MBA) degree with a concentration in finance from The Thunderbird School of Global Management, in Glendale, Arizona (consistently ranked the #1 school for international business by both *U.S. News and World Report* and *The Wall Street Journal*); a Bachelor of Science (BS) degree in business/economics *magna cum laude* from American University in Washington, D.C.; and a graduate certificate in personal financial planning from Moravian College in Bethlehem, Pennsylvania (America's sixth-oldest college). A member of the National Association of Personal Financial Advisors (NAPFA) since 2002, Wild is also a longtime member and past president of the American Society of Journalists and Authors (ASJA).

The author grew up on Long Island and now lives in Allentown, Pennsylvania, where he is a board member of Friends of the Allentown Parks. His son Clayton attends George Washington University in Washington, D.C. His daughter Adrienne is in high school. His dogs, Norman and Zoey, collaborate to protect their home from squirrels and other potential dangers. His website is www.globalportfolios.net.

Dedication

To the people I've known in this crazy world who somehow manage to keep proper perspective on money and have helped me to do the same: Arun, Auggie, Joe, Marc, Michael, Mitch, Susan, Vicki, and the inhabitants of southern France.

Author's Acknowledgments

This being my latest in a number of *Dummies* books, I'd like to thank once again all the good people at Wiley for, well . . . being good people. I'm so glad that you guys assigned Joan Friedman once again as the project editor. If Moody's gave editors ratings, as it does bonds, Joan would be rated Aaa — right up there with Swiss government bonds.

Thanks to some of my colleagues in the investment world, including bond gurus Bill Conger, Bill Bengen, Dan Fuss, Chris Genovese, David Lambert, Kevin Olson, and Steve Pollock. Special thanks to Neil O'Hara, official tech consultant on this book, who knows bonds like Scarlett O'Hara (no relation) knew curtains.

My great appreciation to Helen Bartley, ace wordsmith of Michigan, for her identification of clunky prose and suggestions for its remediation.

I also appreciate the help of all the number-crunchers and analysts at Morningstar, such as Annette Larson and Eric Jacobson, as well as some very helpful folks at the U.S. Treasury, the Securities Industry and Financial Markets Association, and the Financial Industry Regulatory Authority. Special thanks to Rebecca Cohen at Vanguard.

And thanks to my literary agent, Marilyn Allen, for her continued good representation in the tangled and complicated world of book publishing.

Some others who provided very helpful input are mentioned throughout the pages of the book. I appreciate your help, one and all. Oh, I almost forgot . . . Thank *you*, my beloved daughter Adrienne, for your cool illustrations!

Publisher's Acknowledgments

We're proud of this book; please send us your comments at `http://dummies.custhelp.com`. For other comments, please contact our Customer Care Department within the U.S. at 877-762-2974, outside the U.S. at 317-572-3993, or fax 317-572-4002.

Some of the people who helped bring this book to market include the following:

Acquisitions, Editorial, and Vertical Websites

Project Editor: Joan Friedman

Acquisitions Editor: Stacy Kennedy

Assistant Editor: David Lutton

Editorial Program Coordinator: Joe Niesen

Technical Editor: Neil A. O'Hara

Senior Editorial Manager: Jennifer Ehrlich

Editorial Supervisor: Carmen Krikorian

Editorial Assistant: Alexa Koschier

Art Coordinator: Alicia B. South

Cover Photos: © iStockphoto.com / Mark Jensen

Cartoons: Rich Tennant (`www.the5thwave.com`)

Composition Services

Senior Project Coordinator: Kristie Rees

Layout and Graphics: Carrie A. Cesavice, Jennifer Creasey

Proofreader: John Greenough

Indexer: Sherry Massey

Publishing and Editorial for Consumer Dummies

    Kathleen Nebenhaus, Vice President and Executive Publisher

    David Palmer, Associate Publisher

    Kristin Ferguson-Wagstaffe, Product Development Director

Publishing for Technology Dummies

    Andy Cummings, Vice President and Publisher

Composition Services

    Debbie Stailey, Director of Composition Services

Contents at a Glance

Table of Contents

Introduction

*P*erhaps you bought this book online, either in text or digital format. But if you are still the kind of reader who prefers to browse through aisles and handle books before you buy them, you may be standing in the Personal Finance section of your favorite bookstore right now. If so, take a look to your left. Do you see that pudgy, balding guy in the baggy jeans perusing the book on getting rich by day-trading stock options? Now look to your right. Do you see that trendy young woman with the purple lipstick and hoop earrings thumbing through that paperback on how to make millions in foreclosed property deals? I want you to walk over to them. Good. Now I want you to take this book firmly in your hand. Excellent. Finally, I want you to smack each of them over the head with it.

Nice job!

Wiley (the publisher of this book) has lawyers who will want me to assure you that I'm only kidding about smacking anyone. So in deference to the attorneys, and because I want to get my royalty checks . . . I'm kidding! I'm only kidding! Don't hit anyone!

But the fact is that *someone* should knock some sense into these people. If not, they may wind up — as do most people who try to get rich quick — with nothing but big holes in their pockets.

Those who make the most money in the world of investments possess an extremely rare commodity in today's world — something called patience. At the same time that they're looking for handsome returns, they are also looking to protect what they have. Why? Because a loss of 75 percent in an investment (think tech stocks 2000–2002) requires you to earn *400 percent* to get back to where you started. Good luck getting there!

In fact, garnering handsome returns and protecting against loss go hand in hand, as any financial professional should tell you. But only the first half of the equation — the handsome returns part — gets the lion's share of the ink. Heck, there must be 1,255 books on getting rich quick for every one book on limiting risk and growing wealth slowly but surely.

Welcome to that one book: *Bond Investing For Dummies,* 2nd Edition.

So just what are bonds? A *bond* is basically an IOU. You lend your money to Uncle Sam, to General Electric, to Procter & Gamble, to the city in which you live — to whatever entity issues the bonds — and that entity promises to pay you a certain rate of interest in exchange for borrowing your money. This is very different from stock investing, where you purchase shares in a company, become an alleged partial owner of that company, and then start to pray that the company turns a profit and the CEO doesn't pocket it all.

Stocks (which really aren't as bad as I just made them sound) and bonds complement each other like peanut butter and jelly. Bonds are the peanut butter that can keep your jelly from dripping to the floor. They are the life rafts that can keep your portfolio afloat when the investment seas get choppy. Yes, bonds are also very handy as a source of steady income, but, contrary to popular myth, that should not be their major role in most portfolios.

Bonds are the sweethearts that may have saved your grandparents from selling apples on the street during the hungry 1930s. (Note that I'm not talking about high-yield "junk" bonds here.) They are the babies that may have saved your 401(k) from devastation during the three growly bear-market years on Wall Street that started this century. In 2008, high-quality bonds were just about the only investment you could have made that wound up in the black at a time when world markets frighteningly resembled the Red Sea. And in 2011, when stocks went just about nowhere during the course of the year, bondholders of nearly all kinds were richly rewarded.

Bonds belong in nearly every portfolio. Whether or not they belong in *your* portfolio is a question that this book will help you to answer.

About This Book

Allow the next 340 or so pages to serve as your guide to understanding bonds, choosing the right bonds or bond funds, getting the best bargains on your purchases, and achieving the best prices when you sell. You'll also find out how to work bonds into a powerful, well-diversified portfolio that serves your financial goals much better (I promise) than day-trading stock options or attempting to make a profit flipping real estate in your spare time.

I present to you, in easy-to-understand English (unless you happen to be reading the Ukrainian or Korean translation), the sometimes complex, even mystical and magical world of bonds. I explain such concepts as bond maturity, duration, coupon rate, callability (yikes), and yield; and I show you the differences among the many kinds of bonds, such as Treasuries, agency bonds, corporates, munis, zeroes, convertibles, strips, and TIPS.

Because this book is the all-new and thoroughly updated second edition, I'll also be filling you in on some very important goings-on in the bond world over the past half-decade. Notably, I cover the stock market collapse of 2008 and the "rush to safety" that made bonds, especially U.S. Treasury bonds, the belle of the ball.

I also discuss the total collapse of the municipal bond market . . . you know, the total collapse that Steve Kroft announced ahead of time on *60 Minutes* in December 2010. That would be the total collapse that never happened — or perhaps (gulp) hasn't happened yet.

And who can forget the much-ballyhooed Standard & Poor's downgrading of the U.S. government in mid-2011 — and the rather bizarre advance in Treasury bond prices in the months that followed?

Since I wrote the first edition of this book, the number and types of bond funds in which investors can now sink their money has virtually exploded . . . for better or worse. Many of these new funds (mostly exchange-traded funds) are offering investors slices of the bond market, often packaged in a way that makes bond investing trickier than ever.

And perhaps the biggest change in the six years since the first edition of this book was published is this: Interest payments — the main reason that bonds exist — have plummeted to historic lows. Never in our lifetimes — or our parents' lifetimes — have we seen the negative "real returns" (after-inflation returns) that some bonds have been offering.

In this book, you discover the mistakes that many bond investors make, the traps that some wily bond brokers lay for the uninitiated, and the heartbreak that can befall those who buy certain bonds without first doing their homework. (Don't worry — I walk you through how to do your homework.) You find out how to mix and match your bonds with other kinds of assets — such as stocks and real estate — taking advantage of the latest in investment research to help you maximize your returns and minimize your risk.

Here are some of the things that you need to know before buying any bond or bond fund — things you'll know *cold* after you read *Bond Investing For Dummies,* 2nd Edition:

> ✔ **What's your split gonna be?** Put all of your eggs in one basket, and you're going to wind up getting scrambled. A key to successful investing is diversification. Yes, you've heard that before — so has everyone — but you'd be amazed how many people ignore this advice!
>
> Unless you're working with really exotic investments, the majority of most portfolios is invested in stocks and bonds. The split between those stocks and bonds — whether you choose an 80/20 (aggressive) portfolio (composed of 80 percent stocks and 20 percent bonds), a 50/50 (balanced) portfolio, or a 20/80 (conservative) portfolio — is very possibly *the single most important investment decision you'll ever make.* Stocks and bonds are very different kinds of animals, and their respective percentages in a portfolio can have a profound impact on your financial future. Chapter 12 deals with this issue directly, but the importance of properly mixing and matching investments pops up in other chapters, as well.

✔ **Exactly what kind of bonds do you want?** Depending on your tax bracket, your age, your income, your financial needs and goals, your need for ready cash, and a bunch of other factors, you may want to invest in Treasury, corporate, agency, or municipal bonds. Within each of these categories, you have other choices to make: Do you want long-term or short-term bonds? Higher quality bonds or higher yielding bonds? Freshly issued bonds or bonds floating around on the secondary market? Bonds issued in the United States or bonds from Mexico or Brazil? I introduce many different types of bonds in Part II, and I discuss which may be most appropriate for you — and which are likely to weigh your portfolio down.

✔ **Where do you shop for bonds?** Although bonds have been around more or less in their present form for hundreds of years (see a brief history of bonds in Chapter 3), the way they are bought and sold has changed radically in recent years. Bond traders once had you at their tender mercy. You had no idea what kind of money they were clipping from you every time they traded a bond, allegedly on your behalf. That is no longer so. Whether you decide to buy individual bonds or bond funds (Chapter 14 helps you make that thorny decision), you can now determine almost to the dime how much the hungry middlemen intend to nibble — or have nibbled from your trades in the past. Part IV is your complete shopper's guide.

✔ **What kind of returns can you expect from bonds, and what is your risk of loss?** Here is the part of bond investing that most people find most confusing — and, oh, how misconceptions abound! (You can't lose money in AAA-rated bonds? Um . . . How can I break this news to you gently?) In Chapter 4, I explain the tricky concepts of duration and yield. I tell you why the value of your bonds is so directly tied to prevailing interest rates — with other economic variables giving their own push and pull. I give you the tools to determine just what you can reasonably expect to earn from a bond, and under what circumstances you may lose money.

If you've ever read one of these black and yellow *Dummies* books before, you know what to expect. This is not a book you need to read from front to back, or (if you're reading the Chinese or Hebrew edition) back to front. Feel free to jump back and forth in order to glean whatever information you think will help you the most. No proctor with bifocals will pop out of the air, Harry Potter–style, to test you at the end. You needn't commit it all to memory now — or ever. Keep this reference book for years to come as your little acorn of a bond portfolio grows into a mighty oak.

Conventions Used in This Book

To help you navigate the text of this tome as easily as possible, I use the following conventions:

> ✔ Whenever I introduce a new term, such as, say, *callability* or *discount rate,* it appears (as you can clearly see) in *italics.* You can rest assured that a definition or explanation is right around the corner.

> ✔ If I want to share some interesting tidbit of information that isn't essential to your successful investing in bonds, I place it in a *sidebar,* a grayish rectangle or square with its own heading, set apart from the rest of the text. (See how this whole italics/definition thing works?)

> ✔ All web addresses are clearly formatted so they're easy to pick out if you need to go back and find them.

Keep in mind that when this book was printed, some web addresses may have needed to break across two lines of text. Wherever that's the case, rest assured that we haven't put in any extra characters (hyphens or other doo-hickeys) to indicate the break. So, when using one of these web addresses, just type in exactly what you see in this book. Pretend as if the line break doesn't exist.

What You're Not to Read

Unless you're going to become a professional bond trader, you don't need to know everything in this book. Every few pages, you'll undoubtedly come across some technical stuff that is not essential to becoming a successful bond investor. Read through the technical stuff if you wish, or, if ratios and percentages and such make you dizzy, feel free to skip over it.

Most of the heavy technical matter is tucked neatly into the grayish sidebars. But if any technicalities make it into the main text, I give you a heads up with a Technical Stuff icon. That's where you can skip over or speed read — or choose to get dizzy. Your call!

Foolish Assumptions

If you feel you truly need to start from scratch in the world of investments, perhaps the best place would be the latest edition of *Investing For Dummies* by Eric Tyson (published by Wiley). But the book you're holding in your hands is only a smidgen above that one in terms of assumptions about your investment savvy. I assume that you are intelligent, that you have a few bucks to invest, and that you have a basic education in math (and maybe a very rudimentary knowledge of economics) — that's it.

In other words, even if your investing experience to date consists of opening a savings account, balancing a checkbook, and reading a few Suze Orman columns, you should still be able to follow along. Oh, and for those of you who are already buying and selling bonds and feel completely comfortable in the world of fixed income, I'm assuming that you, too, can learn something from this book. (Oh? You know it all, do you? Can you tell me what a *sukuk* is, or where to buy one, huh? See Chapter 9!)

How This Book Is Organized

Here's a thumbnail sketch of what you'll be seeing in the coming pages.

Part 1: Bond Appetit!

In this first part, you'll find out what makes a bond a bond. You'll discover the rationale for their very existence. I take you through a portal of time to see what bonds looked like decades, even centuries, earlier. You'll get to see how bonds evolved and what makes them so very different from other investment vehicles. I give you a primer on how bonds are bought and sold. And I introduce you to the sometimes very helpful but sometimes very misleading world of bond ratings.

Part II: Numerous and Varied Ways to Make Money in Bonds

Anyone, well practically anyone, who wants to raise money can issue a bond. The vast majority of bonds, however, are issued by the U.S. Treasury, corporations, government agencies, or municipalities. This section examines the advantages and potential drawbacks of each, and looks at the many varieties of bonds that these entities may offer. I also introduce you to some rather unusual breeds of bonds — not the kind your grandfather knew!

Part III: Customizing and Optimizing Your Bond Portfolio

All investments — including bonds — carry their own promises of returns and measures of risk. Some bonds are as safe (well, almost as safe) as bank CDs; others can be as wildly volatile as tech stocks. In this part of the book, I help you to assess just how much investment risk you should be taking at this point in your life, and how — by using a mix of different bonds — you can minimize that risk for optimal return.

Part IV: Bonds Away! Navigating the Fixed-Income Marketplace

Here, I address the role of bond brokers; discuss the pros and cons of owning individual bonds as opposed to bond funds; explain how to buy and sell bonds without getting clipped; and offer ways to protect yourself so that you don't get stuck with any fixed-income dogs. (The kennel has lately become overpopulated.) I reveal ways for you to blow away the black smoke that has long shrouded the world of bond trading.

Part V: Bonds as Replacements for the Old Paycheck

Many people think of bonds as the ultimate retirement tool. In fact, they are — and they aren't. In this section, I discuss bonds as replacements for your paycheck. As you'll discover, many retirees rely too heavily on bonds — or on the wrong kinds of bonds. Reading this section, you may discover that your nest egg needs either a minor tune-up or a major overhaul, and that your bond portfolio needs beefing up or paring down.

Part VI: The Part of Tens

This final section — a standard feature in all *Dummies* books — will wrap up the book with some practical tips and a few fun items.

The web offers much in the way of additional education on bonds, as well as some excellent venues for trading bonds. Let the Appendix serve as your web guide.

Icons Used in This Book

Throughout the book, you'll find little cartoons in the margins. In the *Dummies* universe, these are known as *icons,* and they signal certain (we hope) exciting things going on in the accompanying text.

Although this is a how-to book, you'll also find plenty of whys and wherefores. Any paragraph accompanied by this icon, however, is guaranteed to be at least 99.99 percent how-to.

Read twice! This icon indicates that something important is being said and is really worth committing to memory.

The world of bond investing — although generally not as risky as the world of stock investing — still offers pitfalls galore. Wherever you see the bomb, you'll know that danger — of losing money — lies ahead.

If you don't really care how to calculate the after-tax present value of a bond selling at 98, yielding 4.76 percent, maturing in 9 months, and subject to AMT, but instead you're just looking to gain a broad understanding of bond investing, feel free to skip or skim the denser paragraphs that are marked with this icon.

The world of Wall Street is full of people who make money at other people's expense. Wherever you see the pig face, you'll know that I'm about to point out an instance where someone (most likely calling himself a bond broker or perhaps a bond mutual-fund manager) is likely to be sticking a hand deep in your pocket.

Where to Go from Here

Where would you like to go from here? If you wish, start at the beginning. If you're mostly interested in municipal bonds, hey, no one says that you can't jump right to Chapter 8. Global bonds? Go ahead and jump to Chapter 9. It's entirely your call. Maybe start by skimming the index at the back of the book.

Part I
Bond Appetit!

The 5th Wave   By Rich Tennant

"I thought rental properties were the way to go, but the bond market is looking better and better."

In this part . . .

In the first three chapters of this section, you find out what makes a bond a bond. You discover the rationale for their being and what makes them different from other investment types. You can begin to assess whether bonds belong in your portfolio (chances are they do!). I take you on a trip back in time to see how bonds looked in yesteryear and show you how and why they evolved into the most popular investment vehicle on earth today. You also find out how the bond markets work, and about some relatively recent developments that have turned those markets more or less on their pointed heads.

In Chapter 4, you get a preliminary education on the complicated pricing of bonds and the myriad (and often confusing) ways that bond returns are measured. You pick up some very important bond concepts (and much of the bond jargon) that could help you to operate more effectively as an investor in the bond market.

Chapter 1

So You Want to Be a Bondholder

*L*ong before I ever knew what a bond is (it's essentially an IOU), I agreed to lend five dollars to Tommy Potts, a blond, goofy-looking kid in my seventh-grade class. This was the first time that I'd ever lent money to anyone. I can't recall why Tommy needed the five dollars, but he did promise to repay me, and he was my pal.

Weeks went by, then months, and I couldn't get my money back from Tommy, no matter how much I bellyached. Finally, I decided to go to a higher authority. So I approached Tommy's dad. I figured that Mr. Potts would give Tommy a stern lecture on the importance of maintaining his credit and good name. Then, Mr. Potts would either make Tommy cough up my money, or he would make restitution himself.

"Er, Mr. Potts," I said, "I lent Tommy five bucks, and — "

"You lent *him* money?" Mr. Potts interrupted, pointing his finger at his dead-beat 12-year-old son, who, if I recall correctly, at that point had turned over one of his pet turtles and was spinning it like a top. "Um, yes, Mr. Potts — five dollars." At which point, Mr. Potts neither lectured nor reached for his wallet. Rather, he erupted into mocking laughter. "You lent *him* money!" he bellowed repeatedly, laughing, slapping his thighs, and pointing to his turtle-torturing son. "You lent *him* money! *HA . . . HA . . .HA . . .*"

And that, dear reader, was my very first experience as a creditor. I never saw a nickel from Tommy, in either interest or returned principal.

Oh, yes, I've learned a lot since then.

Understanding What Makes a Bond a Bond

Now suppose that Tommy Potts, instead of being a goofy kid in the seventh grade, were the U. S. government. Or the city of Philadelphia. Or Procter & Gamble. Tommy, in his powerful new incarnation, needs to raise not five dollars but $50 million. So Tommy decides to issue a bond. A bond is really not much more than an IOU with a serial number. People in suits, to sound impressive, sometimes call bonds *debt securities* or *fixed-income securities.*

A bond is always issued with a specific *face amount,* also called the *principal,* or *par value.* Most often, simply because it is convention, bonds are issued with face amounts of $1,000. So in order to raise $50 million, Tommy would have to issue 50,000 bonds, each selling at $1,000 par. Of course, he would then have to go out and find investors to buy his bonds.

Every bond pays a certain rate of *interest,* and typically (but not always) that rate is fixed over the life of the bond (hence *fixed-income* securities). The life of the bond is the period of time until maturity. Maturity, in the lingo of financial people, is the period of time until the principal is due to be paid back. (Yes, the bond world is full of jargon.) The rate of interest is a percentage of the face amount and is typically (again, simply because of convention) paid out twice a year.

So if a corporation or government issues a $1,000 bond, paying 6-percent interest, that corporation or government promises to fork over to the bond-holder $60 a year — or, in most cases, $30 twice a year. Then, when the bond matures, the corporation or government repays the $1,000 to the bondholder.

In some cases, you can buy a bond directly from the issuer and sell it back directly to the issuer. But you're more likely to buy a bond through a broker-age house or a bank. You can also buy a basket of bonds through a company that sells mutual funds or exchange-traded funds. These brokerage houses and fund companies will most certainly take a piece of the pie — sometimes a quite sizeable piece. More on that (and how to limit broker and fund-manager gluttony) in Part IV.

So far, so good?

In short, dealing in bonds isn't really all that different from the deal I worked out with Tommy Potts. It's just a bit more formal. And the entire business is regulated by the Securities and Exchange Commission (among other regulatory authorities), and most (but not all) bondholders — unlike me — wind up getting paid back!

Choosing your time frame

Almost all bonds these days are issued with life spans (maturities) of up to 30 years. Few people are interested in lending their money for longer than that, and people young enough to think more than 30 years ahead rarely have enough money to lend. In bond lingo, bonds with a maturity of less than five years are typically referred to as *short-term bonds*. Bonds with maturities of 5 to 12 years are called *intermediate-term bonds*. Bonds with maturities of 12 years or longer are called *long-term bonds*.

In general (sorry, but you're going to read those words a lot in this book; bond investing comes with few hard-and-fast rules), the longer the maturity, the greater the interest rate paid. That's because bond buyers generally (there I go again) demand more compensation the longer they agree to tie up their money. At the same time, bond issuers are willing to fork over more interest in return for the privilege of holding onto your money longer.

It's exactly the same theory and practice with bank CDs (Certificates of Deposit): Typically a two-year CD pays more than a one-year CD, which in turn pays more than a six-month CD.

The different rates that are paid on short, intermediate, and long bonds make up what is known as the *yield curve*. *Yield* simply refers to the annual interest rate. In Chapter 4, I provide an in-depth discussion of interest rates, bond maturity, and the all-important yield curve.

Picking who you trust to hold your money

Let's consider again the analogy between bonds and bank CDs. Both tend to pay higher rates of interest if you're willing to tie up your money for a longer period of time. But that's where the similarity ends.

When you give your money to a savings bank to plunk into a CD, that money — your principal — is almost certainly guaranteed (up to $250,000 per account) by the Federal Deposit Insurance Corporation (FDIC). You can choose your bank because it is close to your house or because it gives lollipops to your kids, but if solid economics be your guide, you should open your CD where you're going to get FDIC insurance (almost all banks carry it) and the highest rate of interest. End of story.

Things aren't so simple in the world of bonds. A higher rate of interest isn't always the best deal. When you fork over your money to buy a bond, your principal, in most cases, is guaranteed only by the issuer of the bond. That "guarantee" is only as solid as the issuer itself. (Remember my seventh-grade experience?) That's why U.S. Treasury bonds (guaranteed by the U.S. government) pay one interest rate, General Electric bonds pay another rate, Sprint

Nextel bonds pay yet another rate. Can you guess where you'll get the highest rate of interest?

You would expect the highest rate of interest to be paid by Sprint Nextel (currently a somewhat shaky company). Why? Because lending your money to Sprint involves the risk that your money may sprint off into oblivion. In other words, if the company goes belly up, you may lose a good chunk of your principal. That risk requires any shaky company to pay a relatively high rate of interest. Without being paid some kind of *risk premium,* you would be unlikely to lend your money to a company that may not be able to pay you back. Conversely, the U.S. government, which has the power to levy taxes and print money, is not going bankrupt any time soon. Therefore, U.S. Treasury bonds, which are said to carry only an infinitely small risk of *default,* tend to pay relatively modest interest rates.

If Tommy Potts were to come to me for a loan today, needless to say, I wouldn't lend him money. Or if I did, I would require a huge risk premium, along with some kind of collateral (more than his pet turtles). Bonds issued by the likes of Tommy Potts or Sprint Nextel — bonds that carry a relatively high risk of default — are commonly called *high-yield* or *junk* bonds. Bonds issued by solid companies and governments that carry very little risk of default are commonly referred to as *investment-grade* bonds.

There are many, many shades of gray in determining the quality and nature of a bond. It's not unlike wine tasting in that regard. In Chapter 4, and again in Chapter 14, I give many specific tips for "tasting" bonds and choosing the finest vintages for your portfolio.

Recognizing the difference between bonds, stocks, and Beanie Babies

Aside from the maturity and the quality of a bond, other factors could weigh heavily in how well a bond purchase treats you. In the following chapters, I introduce you to such bond characteristics as *callability, duration,* and *correlation,* and I explain how the winds of the economy, and even the whims of the bond-buying public, can affect the returns on your bond portfolio.

For the moment, I simply wish to point out that, by and large, bonds' most salient characteristic — and the one thing that most, but not all bonds share — is a certain stability and predictability, well above and beyond that of most other investments. Because you are, in most cases, receiving a steady stream of income, and because you expect to get your principal back in one piece, bonds tend to be more conservative investments than, say, stocks, commodities, or collectibles.

The bond market is HUMONGOUS

How much is invested in bonds worldwide? Are you holding onto your seat? According to the latest figures compiled by the Securities Industry and Financial Markets Association, the total value of all bonds outstanding worldwide is now slightly over $95 *trillion*. That's equal to about six times the current gross domestic product of the United States — the dollar value of all goods and services produced in this country in an entire year. Given that the stock market gets so much more attention than the bond market, you may be surprised to know that the total value of all stocks outstanding worldwide is a mere $55 trillion.

Is conservative a good thing? Not necessarily. It's true that many people (men, more often than women) invest their money too aggressively, just as many people (of both genders) invest their money too conservatively. The appropriate portfolio formula depends on what your individual investment goals are. I help you to figure that out in Chapters 12 and 13.

By the way, my comment about men investing more aggressively is not my personal take on the subject. Some solid research shows that men do tend to invest (as they drive) much more aggressively than do women.

Why Hold Bonds? (Hint: You'll Likely Make Money!)

In the real world, plenty of people own plenty of bonds — but often the wrong bonds in the wrong amounts and for the wrong reasons. Some people have too many bonds, making their portfolios too conservative; some have too few bonds, making their stock-heavy portfolios too volatile. Some have taxable bonds where they should have tax-free bonds, and vice versa. Others are so far out on a limb with shaky bonds that they may as well be lending their money to Tommy Potts.

The first step in building a bond portfolio is to have clear investment objectives. ("I want to make money" — something I hear from clients all the time — is *not* a clear investment objective!) I'll help you to develop clear objectives in Chapter 2. In the meantime, I want you to consider some of the typical reasons — both good and bad — why people buy and hold bonds.

Identifying the best reason to buy bonds: Diversification

Most people buy bonds because they perceive a need for steady income, and they think of bonds as the best way to get income without risking principal. This is one of the most common mistakes investors make: compartmentalization. They think of principal and interest as two separate and distinct money pools. They are not.

Let me explain: Joe Typical buys a bond for $1,000. At the end of six months, he collects an interest payment (income) of, say, $25. He spends the $25, figuring that his principal (the $1,000) is left intact to continue earning money. At the same time, Joe buys a stock for $1,000. At the end of six months, the price of his stock, and therefore the value of his investment, has grown to, say, $1,025. Does he spend the $25? No way. Joe reckons that spending any part of the $1,025 is spending principal and will reduce the amount of money he has left working for him.

In truth, whether Joe spends his "interest" or his "principal," whether he spends his "income" or generates "cash flow" from the sale of stock, he is left with the *very same* $1,000 in his portfolio.

Thinking of bonds, or bond funds, as the best — or only — source of cash flow or income can be a mistake.

Bonds are a better source of steady income than stocks because bonds, in theory (and usually in practice), always pay interest; stocks may or may not pay dividends and may or may not appreciate in price. Bonds also may be a logical choice for people who may need a certain sum of money at a certain point in the future — such as college tuition or cash for a new home — and can't risk a loss.

But unless you absolutely need a steady source of income, or a certain sum on a certain date, bonds may not be such a hot investment. Over the long haul, they have tended to return much less than stocks. I revisit this issue, and talk much more about the differences between stocks and bonds, in Chapter 12.

For now, the point I wish to make is that the far better reason to own bonds, for most people, is to *diversify* a portfolio. Simply put, bonds tend to zig when stocks zag, and vice versa. The key to truly successful investing, as I outline in Chapter 11, is to have at least several different *asset classes* — different investment animals with different characteristics — all of which can be expected to yield positive long-term returns, but that do not all move up and down together.

Bond map of the world

More than half of the world's bonds created in 2009 were issued in the United States (35 percent), Japan (13 percent), or the United Kingdom (5 percent). The percentages reflected in this figure were provided by the Securities Industry and Financial Markets Association and the Bank of International Settlement.

35%   5%   13%

Illustration by Wiley, Composition Services Graphics

Going for the cash

Bonds are not very popular with the get-rich-quick crowd — for good reason. The only people who get rich off bonds are generally the insiders who trade huge amounts and can clip the little guy. Nonetheless, certain categories of bonds — high-yield corporate (junk) bonds, for example — have been known to produce impressive gains.

High-yield bonds may have a role — a limited one — in your portfolio, as I discuss in Chapter 6. But know up front that high-yield bonds do not offer the potential long-term returns of stocks, and neither do they offer the portfolio protection of investment-grade bonds. Rather than zigging when the stock market zags, many high-yield bonds zag right along with your stock portfolio. Be careful!

Some high-yield bonds are better than others — and they are held by relatively few people. I recommend those in Chapter 9.

Even high quality, investment-grade bonds are often purchased with the wrong intentions. Note: A U.S. Treasury bond, though generally thought to be the safest bond of all, *will not guarantee your return of principal unless you hold it to maturity*. If you buy a 20-year bond and you want to know for sure that you're going to get your principal back, you had better plan to hold it for 20 years. If you sell it before it matures, you may lose a bundle. Bond prices, especially on long-term bonds — yes, even Uncle Sam's bonds — can fluctuate greatly! I discuss the reasons for this fluctuation in Chapter 4.

I also discuss the very complicated and often misunderstood concept of bond returns. You may buy a 20-year U.S. Treasury bond yielding 3 percent, and you may hold it for 20 years, to full maturity. And yes, you'll get your principal back, but you may actually earn far more or far less than 3 percent interest on your money! It's complicated, but I explain this variation in a way you can understand — I promise! — in Chapter 4.

Introducing the Major Players in the Bond Market

Every year, millions — yes, literally millions — of bonds are issued by thousands of different governments, government agencies, municipalities, financial institutions, and corporations. They all pay interest. In many cases, the interest rates aren't all that much different from each other. In most cases, the risk that the issuer will *default* — fail to pay back your principal — is minute. So why, as a lender of money, would you want to choose one type of issuer over another? Glad you asked!

Following are some important considerations about each of the major kinds of bonds, categorized by who issues them. I'm just going to scratch the surface right now. For a more in-depth discussion, see the five chapters in Part II.

Supporting (enabling?) your Uncle Sam with Treasury bonds

Politicians like raising money by selling bonds, as opposed to raising taxes, because voters hate taxes. Of course, when the government issues bonds, it promises to repay the bond buyers over time. The more bonds the government issues, the greater its debt. Voters may groan about the national debt, but they generally don't see it as an immediate problem.

The current debt of the United States government is slightly more than $15 trillion: almost $50,000 for every U.S. citizen. (Yikes! The figures in the first edition of this book, written only a few years ago, were $8.6 trillion and $30,000 per citizen.)

The interest payments on that debt are an enormous burden, currently totaling more than $450 billion a year. In my mind, that's a bit too much cash, but this is not a political book, so I'm not going to tell you how to vote. (Not that you would listen to me anyway.) From here on, I address only the role that Treasury bonds may play in your portfolio.

In Chapter 5, I explain all of the many, many kinds of Treasury bonds — from EE Bonds to I Bonds to TIPS — and the unique characteristics of each. For the moment, I merely wish to point out that all of them are backed by the "full faith and credit" of the federal government. Despite its huge debt, the United States of America is not going bankrupt anytime soon. And for that reason, Treasury bonds have traditionally been referred to as "risk-free." Careful! That does *not* mean that the prices of Treasury bonds do not fluctuate.

When bond experts speak of Treasury bonds as having no risk, or almost no risk, what they mean is that the bonds have no *credit* risk. But Treasury bonds are very much subject to the other kinds of risk that beset most other bonds: interest rate risk, inflation risk, and reinvestment risk. I discuss these types of risk in Chapter 10.

Collecting corporate debt

Bonds issued by for-profit companies are riskier than government bonds but tend to compensate for that added risk by paying higher rates of interest. (If they didn't, why would you or anyone else want to take the extra risk?) For the past few decades, corporate bonds in the aggregate have tended to pay about a percentage point higher than Treasuries of similar maturity. Since 2008, this spread has broadened, with ten-year corporate bonds paying about a percentage point and a half more than their governmental counterparts.

As you'll discover, I am a big fan of diversification. It is especially important to diversify when dealing with riskier investments. For that reason, I don't like to see people plunk too great a percentage of their portfolios into any individual corporate bond. Wealthier investors — those with portfolios of $1 million or more — can diversify by buying a collection of bonds. Savvy investors can temper their risks by familiarizing themselves with bond ratings and researching the issuing companies' bottom lines. But I generally advocate bond ownership — especially when it comes to corporate bonds — in bond funds. I discuss these funds at the end of this chapter and again, in greater depth, in Chapter 16.

Oh, one more little thing about corporate bonds for the moment: They tend to get *called* a lot. That means that the corporation changes its incorporated mind about wanting your money and suddenly throws it back at you, canceling the bond. Bond calls tend to happen when rates have fallen, and that's no fun! They add a heavy dose of unpredictability to what should be a predictable investment. Read all about calls and other peculiarities of the corporate bond world in Chapter 6.

Demystifying those government and government-like agencies

Federal agencies, such as the Government National Mortgage Association (Ginnie Mae), and government-sponsored enterprises (GSEs), such as the Federal Home Loan Banks, issue a good chunk of the bonds on the market. Even though these bonds can differ quite a bit, they are collectively referred to as *agency bonds*. What we call agencies are sometimes part of the actual government, and sometimes a cross between government and private industry. In the case of the Federal National Mortgage Association (Fannie Mae) and the Federal Home Loan Mortgage Corporation (Freddie Mac), they have been, following the mortgage crisis of 2008, somewhat in limbo.

To varying degrees, Congress and the Treasury will serve as protective big brothers if one of these agencies or GSEs were to take a financial beating and couldn't pay off its debt obligations.

In general, agency bonds are considered the next-safest thing to Treasury bonds. As such, the interest paid on these bonds is typically just a smidgen higher than the interest rate you would get on Treasuries of similar maturity, although in very recent times, you can get a smidgen-plus.

I discuss agency bonds — the traditional kind of bonds these agencies offer — in Chapter 7. Some bonds issued or guaranteed by the federal agencies are distinctly nontraditional in that they represent an ownership interest in pools of mortgages. These are more complicated than traditional bonds, and I'm sorry to say that many people who invest in them haven't the foggiest idea what they're investing in — although some found out the hard way in late 2007 and 2008, when some of these mortgage bonds took a serious hit. More about these babies in Chapter 7, as well.

Going cosmopolitan with municipal bonds

The bond market, unlike the stock market, is overwhelmingly institutional. In other words, most bonds are held by insurance companies, pension funds, endowment funds, and mutual funds. The only exception is the municipal bond market.

Municipal bonds (*munis*) are issued by cities, states, and counties. They are used to raise money for either the general day-to-day needs of the citizenry (schools, roads, sewer systems) or for specific projects (a new bridge, a sports stadium).

Munis' popularity with individual investors may be due in small part to the warm and fuzzy feelings to be had by investing in local infrastructure. But my guess is that their popularity comes much more from their special tax status.

The U.S. bond market pie

The U.S. Treasury has more bonds outstanding than does corporate America, and corporate bonds in the aggregate are worth more than municipal bonds. Here are a few of the largest segments of the U.S. bond market and how they compare in total dollar value. The numbers are according to the Securities Industry and Financial Markets Association (SIFMA).

Types of Bonds Outstanding (in trillions), 2011:

- ✔ Treasury bonds: $10.0 (see Chapter 5)
- ✔ Corporate bonds: $7.7 (see Chapter 6)
- ✔ Municipal bonds: $2.9 (see Chapter 8)
- ✔ Federal agency bonds: $2.4 (see Chapter 7)

Interest on most municipal bonds is exempt from federal income tax. Traditionally, the interest rates paid have been modest, but many individual investors — especially those in the higher tax brackets — could often get a better after-tax return on municipal bonds than on comparable taxable bonds. In recent years, municipals have tended to yield more than Treasuries — even on a before-tax basis.

Like corporate bonds, but unlike Treasuries, municipal bonds are often subject to being called. You may *think* you're buying a ten-year investment, but you may be forced to relinquish the bond in two years instead. (Bond brokers often fail to advertise this fact to buyers.)

Municipal bonds tend to be less risky than corporate bonds but not as safe as Treasury and agency bonds. Just as corporate bonds are given ratings, so are municipal bonds. It's important to know before investing whether the local government issuing a bond has the wherewithal to pay back your principal. Cities don't go bankrupt often, but it does happen. And lately, some pundits have expressed fears that in the future, more municipalities than ever may declare bankruptcy. (That fear is part of what has driven up the yield on these bonds.) I reveal much, much more on munis in Chapter 8.

Buying Solo or Buying in Bulk

One of the big questions about bond investing that I help you to answer later in this book is whether to invest in individual bonds or bond funds.

I generally advocate bond funds — both bond mutual funds and exchange-traded funds. Mutual funds and exchange-traded funds represent baskets of securities (usually stocks or bonds, or sometimes both) and allow for instant and easy portfolio diversification. You do, however, need to be careful about which funds you choose. Not all are created equal — far, far from it.

I outline the pros and cons of owning individual bonds versus bond funds in Chapter 14. Here, I give you a very quick sneak preview of that discussion.

Picking and choosing individual bonds

Individual bonds offer investors the opportunity to really fine-tune a fixed-income portfolio. With individual bonds, you can choose exactly what you want in terms of bond quality, maturity, and taxability.

For larger investors — especially those who do their homework — investing in individual bonds may also be more economical than investing in a bond fund. That's especially true for investors who are up on the latest advances in bond buying and selling.

Once upon a time, any buyers or sellers of individual bonds had to take a giant leap of faith that their bond broker wasn't trimming too much meat off the bone. No more. In Chapter 15, I show you how to find out exactly how much your bond broker is making off you — or trying to make off you. I show you how to compare comparable bonds to get the best deals. And I discuss some popular bond strategies, including the most popular and potent one, *laddering* your bonds, which means staggering the maturities of the bonds that you buy.

Going with a bond fund or funds

Investors now have a choice of well over 5,000 bond mutual funds or exchange-traded funds. All have the same basic drawbacks: management expenses and a certain degree of unpredictability above and beyond individual bonds. But even so, some make for very good potential investments, particularly for people with modest portfolios.

Where to begin your fund search? I promise to help you weed out the losers and pick the very best. As you'll discover (or as you know already if you have read my *Exchange-Traded Funds For Dummies*), I'm a strong proponent of buying index funds — mutual funds or exchange-traded funds that seek to provide exposure to an entire asset class (such as bonds or stocks) with very little trading and very low expenses. I believe that such funds are the way to go for most investors to get the bond exposure they need. I suggest some good bond index funds, as well as other bond funds, in Chapter 16.

If you would like to know more about funds in general, I would advise you to pick up copies of the latest editions of *Exchange-Traded Funds For Dummies* and Eric Tyson's *Mutual Funds For Dummies,* both published by Wiley.

Chapter 2

Developing Your Investment Game Plan

. . . .

In This Chapter

▶ Forecasting your future financial needs

▶ Figuring out your personal investment style

▶ Estimating how big your nest egg needs to be

▶ Doing nothing with your money — *not* an option!

▶ Selecting appropriate investment vehicles

▶ Understanding the basics of financial markets

. . . .

*T*here's a scene I like in the 1995 film *Get Shorty,* where mobster Chili Palmer (played by John Travolta) picks up a rental car in L.A.

"What is that?" asks Chili, pointing to the curb.

"It's an Oldsmobile Silhouette," says the attendant.

Chili Palmer is not happy. "I ordered a Cadillac," he says with obvious displeasure.

"Oh, well," says the attendant, "you got the Cadillac of minivans."

And off drives the pistol-packing gangster, out to collect mob debt money, driving the streets of L.A. in a boxy vehicle with built-in child seats and a rooftop luggage carrier. It's as incongruous as, well, a pistol-packing gangster aiming to make the big score by investing in Ginnie Mae bonds.

Portfolios, like Cadillacs and minivans, suit certain kinds of personalities. In order to choose the most appropriate investments — be they bonds, stocks, or pork-belly futures — it helps to know yourself fairly well. I'm not suggesting in a grand, metaphysical, Freudian or Socratic sense, but at least to the point where you — and perhaps your spouse — can formulate some reasonable household financial goals.

Unlike all the other chapters in this book, I don't focus squarely on bonds here. First, I help you discover who you are as an investor (are you a Chili Palmer, Warren Buffett, or Nervous Nelly?). Once your "inner investor" is identified, you'll be more confident in deciding whether a bond portfolio may suit you better than, say, dropping your savings into casino stocks, uranium futures, or hush money.

I also discuss some very fundamental principles in this chapter, such as reversion to the mean and the cold-clay link between risk and return. These pertain not only to bonds, but also to all financial investments. If you're already a seasoned player, these essential market truths could be part of your current game plan. But a quick review certainly couldn't hurt.

Focusing on Your Objectives

Investing in a portfolio of Ginnie Mae bonds is a conservative way to go. (See Chapter 7 for more on Ginnie Maes, Freddie Macs, and various other federal agency bonds.) It's unlikely you'll get rich investing in these — or most conservative bond portfolios. But you won't be waking up at 2 a.m. in a cold-sweat panic, worried about the whereabouts of your money.

Investing your savings in the stock of a single, small technology company can, indeed, make you rich. (Think Microsoft back when a nerdy, young Bill Gates was working out of his garage.) Beware, however: Taking a financial risk on a start-up "Big Idea" with world-changing potential may deprive you of that solid eight-hour sleep your bond-holding buddy is enjoying. Wednesday's investment may be worth a fraction of what you were expecting when you finally crawl out of bed, bleary-eyed, Thursday morning.

For most people, some kind of in-between portfolio — perhaps with Ginnie Mae bonds *and* tech stocks — would make the most sense. Deciding if you want to be smack in the middle of the continuum, or prefer to hang your hat toward the mild side or the wild side, will have a great bearing on just how much you wind up stocking up on bonds or bonding with stocks.

Deciding what you want to be when you grow up

The kind of portfolio you want to build depends on why you're investing. Ask yourself whether you're looking for immediate income, slow and steady appreciation, or pop-goes-the-weasel kind of growth.

Do you dream of quitting your day job as soon as possible to start a new career writing haiku poetry? Or do you want to pay for your kids' college tuition and expenses, and then finish building your retirement portfolio after that point? Do you want to drop out of society after the kids are grown, buy a 52-foot sailboat, and travel the Caribbean from island to island (just like in the retirement ads from the brokerage houses)? These are the kinds of questions you need to ask yourself.

Fortunately, you don't need to be all that specific in your future goals to formulate a fairly good financial plan. You merely need to be somewhat clear about how much you and your partner will likely be earning (if anything) and how much you will likely be spending over a certain period of time.

Our society has changed much in the last generation, and very many Boomers either nearing or already having entered traditional retirement age aren't looking for anything even closely resembling a traditional retirement. Me, I love what I do and hope to continue doing it for as long as I'm capable. (However, I wouldn't mind clocking fewer hours and, after my children have flown the coop, perhaps visiting a few places I've yet to see, like Malta and Chile.)

Picturing your future nest egg

In Chapter 12, I provide you with the tools to help you fine-tune your retirement goals and figure out what lump sum you will likely need — given the kind of lifestyle you envision — to replace your weekly paycheck. But for now, I'm just going to share some very loose guidelines.

It doesn't much matter whether you are like me and intend to keep working past traditional retirement age or whether you want a more old-fashioned retirement (complete with checkered pants, green golf shirts, blue hair, and mah-jongg games). Most financial planners suggest that your ultimate savings goal be something in the order of 20 times, or even better, 25 times, your annual anticipated expenses, minus any income from Social Security, pension, or part-time employment.

In other words, if you think you'll need $50,000 a year to live comfortably at age 65 or so, and you anticipate yearly income of $20,000 from a combination of Social Security payments and, say, hobby income, your goal should be to grow a nest egg worth at the very least $600,000. Simple arithmetic: $50,000 (your desired yearly income) minus the $20,000 you're anticipating from other sources = $30,000. You'll need to have, at a minimum, $30,000 in portfolio income to cover your years of retirement . . . meaning you'll need a nest egg of $600,000.

Understanding the Rule of 20

Before I explain the (rough . . . very rough) Rule of 20, let me first say I know that the number 20 may scare the heck out of you if you haven't put much away so far, but try to remember that compound interest is a very, very powerful force.

If you are still the young age of 30, investing wisely in a diversified portfolio, you would likely have to put aside only about $250 a month to have a darned good chance of building a $600,000 nest egg by age 65. If you have a job where the employer matches your 401(k) contributions by kicking in 50 percent on top of whatever you put in, $167 a month would likely do the trick. Many readers of this book will be well over 30, but, still, you get the idea: Start saving today, and you can likely make great headway.

Okay, so where does the multiplier of 20 come from? It simply gives an approximation of how much you should have by age 65 to cover your yearly expenses, based on the current average lifespan (mid 80s). With 20 times your annual withdrawal needs, the chances are good that you won't run out of money before you make your final exit. Obviously, if you can save more, so much the better.

If you think that you are likely to live longer than the average lifespan, or if you're planning to quit work before age 65, you should plan to save more than 20 times your annual living expenses. The longer you plan to live a life of ease, the more money you'll need to tap.

Here's another very rough rule: If you plan to live in retirement for 30 years, have 30 times your annual anticipated portfolio withdrawals; 40 years, 40 times, and so on.

For those of us who would like to keep working as long as we can, there's still nothing whatsoever wrong with financial independence, so I would advocate the same goal: Try to amass at least 20 times what you might need to live for a year (minus non-earned income). Again, I'm talking rough estimates here, and I can't emphasize that enough. I believe it's important, though, to illustrate how the nest egg goals you establish now have everything to do with how heavily you invest in bonds.

Choosing your investment style

Okay, what does the Rule of 20 have to do with your choice of investments and the wisdom of holding bonds? Simple: The further away you are from achieving that financial goal, the higher the rate of savings you need or the higher the rate of return you require from your portfolio — or both.

In Chapter 12, I try to answer the very difficult question, "What percent of your portfolio should be in bonds?" For now, I simply want to point out that people who need a higher rate of return generally don't want too bond-laden a portfolio. A heavy position in bonds is more appropriate for investors who don't need a lot of immediate growth but, rather, can sit back and enjoy the steady, slow growth their portfolio will offer.

Say, for example, you are 55 or 60 years old and, thanks to your good savings habits, you are now on the cusp of having your "20x" portfolio. If much of that portfolio is now in stocks or stock mutual funds, it may be time for you to start shifting a good chunk of your portfolio into bonds. Why take much risk with things like stocks or commodities if you don't need to?

You should know, however, that simple portfolio-construction formulas (that typically use age as a main determinant) often don't work! These are some very rough rules just to get you thinking about how I think in terms of investment allocation. As I explain in Chapter 12, a 55- or 60-year-old investor who may be considering adding more bonds to his or her portfolio may do better by shifting back to stocks 20 years later — if the portfolio is worth millions. (Yes, it would be great to find yourself in a position where this is an option.)

Making Your Savings and Investment Selections

True, you can shove your money under the mattress, but with inflation currently running about 3 percent a year, $1,000 in today's dollars will have only about $940 in purchasing power two years from now and $860 in purchasing power five years from now. Economists call that loss in purchasing power *inflation risk,* and it is indeed a very real kind of risk. Moral of the story: Don't keep money under the mattress. You have to do *something* with it.

In my mind, *savings* refers to money socked away that has at very best a chance of keeping even with inflation. *Investments* refers to money socked away that is projected to grow at least at the rate of inflation (over the long haul) and likely greater than the rate of inflation.

The whole point of investing is to earn a *real return,* which is to say the rate of return after inflation. If your nominal return is 8 percent but inflation is 5 percent, your real return is approximately 3 percent (8% – 5% = 3%). Getting a nominal return of 2 percent when there is no inflation is much better than getting a 15 percent return when the inflation rate is 20!

Different types of bonds can fall into either category: savings or investments. Some bonds — like U.S. savings bonds — generally keep about even with inflation (although they haven't quite done that in the past few years). Other bonds, such as high-yield corporate bonds, will usually keep you ahead of the game if you hold them for a long while.

In general, money that may be needed in the upcoming months, or even a few years down the pike, should be kept in safe savings; you can't risk a loss of principal. (Yes, loss of principal is possible with most bonds, especially long-term bonds. You discover why in Chapter 4.) Money that you most likely won't need for many years to come should be invested for growth; even if there is a loss of principal, you will likely earn that back, and then some, before you require any withdrawals.

Following are some of the most popular options for saving and investing, which I briefly compare and contrast with bond investing.

Saving your money in safety

With the following savings options, the principal is guaranteed (or close to guaranteed), but the rate of return may not keep you even with inflation:

- **Your local savings bank:** There's something to be said for keeping at least a small balance at the neighborhood bank. I do. Need a loan someday? It may be easier if you are a regular customer. Local businesses are also more likely to accept a check drawn on a local bank. Then there's the "bank experience," which may be especially important if you're a parent. Each of my two children has a saving account at the corner bank, and they love going there for the plate of free cookies.

    At all savings banks in the United States, deposits are insured up to $250,000 by the Federal Deposit Insurance Corporation (FDIC). Even if the bank goes under, you're covered. The interest rates paid by local banks tend to be very modest — especially in the low interest rate environment of recent years — more modest than those paid by most bonds.

- **Certificates of Deposit (CDs):** The longer you're willing to commit your money to the bank, the higher the interest rate. Generally a 6-month CD may pay an interest point more than passbook savings, a 12-month CD may pay a bit more, and an 18-month CD, still yet, a wee bit more. If you have one to several thousand dollars sitting around, perhaps you might put one-third into each. That way, you're not tying up all your money for the entire time, and if interest rates go higher in six months, you'll be free to take part of your money and upgrade to a higher-yielding CD.

Shop for the best rates at www.bankrate.com or www.money-rates.com. Especially if you're dealing with a local bank, ask to talk to the manager and see if you can negotiate something higher than the advertised rate. CD rates are usually comparable to very short-term bonds but are not on a par with longer-term bonds.

✔ **Internet banking:** Consider opening an account with a web-based, FDIC-insured savings bank, such as www.ally.com, www.emigrantdirect.com, or www.ingdirect.com. The rates on savings accounts are often comparable to one-year CDs, and you don't need to tie up your money at all.

✔ **Money market funds:** Money market mutual funds are not insured by the FDIC so they aren't quite, yet are almost as safe as bank accounts or U.S. savings bonds. They tend to offer returns similar to what you get in bank accounts but not as much as a bond portfolio. If you hold one of these funds outside of your retirement account, you may want to choose a tax-free money market fund, especially if you are in a higher tax bracket.

Note that with money market funds, your principal is secure but the interest rate is not; it can, and often does, vary from day to day. That's just the opposite of a bond, by the way: With a bond, your interest rate is fixed, but the value of your principal can vary day to day. (I explain this in Chapter 4.)

✔ **Short-term, high quality bonds:** Short-term bond mutual funds and exchange-traded funds, both taxable and tax-free, government and corporate, are similar to money market funds and often pay slightly higher earnings, but they also subject you to very modest volatility. Read all about them, and how to choose the best one for your portfolio, in Chapters 13 and 16.

Home sweet home

Yes, of course, home equity represents a form of savings. It is also your most *illiquid* savings. (*Liquidity* refers to the ease with which you can cash out on an investment, if you need to.) You need a place to live . . . and you always will. So for your home to ever do you much good as a store of value, you'll need to downsize. At that point, you can sell the more expensive home, pick up a cheaper abode (or rent one), and pocket the difference.

Home values in the United States rose steadily for many years — until 2006. Since then, as we've seen all too clearly, the housing market has become extremely volatile, with prices dropping in many areas of the country by 50 percent or more. That kind of broad-market drop is unlikely to happen again anytime soon. But the lesson should stand.

You never want all of your net worth tied up in any one asset, particularly the asset you call "Home, Sweet Home." Even if housing prices remain stable, or trend upward, it isn't like you can carve off a piece of your living room if you ever need a dose of cash.

What about whole life insurance, variable annuities, and such?

I've seen insurance salespeople so good that they could sell sand to a Saudi. I've been pitched all kinds of insurance products, and they sound great — absolutely wonderful — until I actually get back to my office, start punching numbers, and look for cracks in the salesperson's pitch. Those cracks are always there. I'm not saying that insurance people are bad or insurance companies are bad — not at all. Insurance is a necessary part of modern life. As a general rule, however — and a very *good* general rule — insurance products and investment products should remain separate and distinct. Is a variable annuity or a whole life insurance policy ever a good investment? Sometimes, perhaps, but rarely. More often, purchasers of such hybrid investment/insurance products wind up angry and upset with their purchases — especially when they find out that there's no going back without forfeiting a good chunk of their original investment in exorbitant *surrender fees*.

Investing your money with an eye toward growth

By sinking your savings into investments such as the ones I list here — carefully! — your payoff can be handsome. But remember, of course, you can also lose money.

- ✓ **Company stocks:** Whereas bonds represent a loan you are making to a company or government, stocks represent partial ownership in a company. Over the long run, few investments pay off as well as stocks, which have an 80-year track record of returning nearly10 percent a year — about twice the return of bonds.

 The problem with stocks is that they can be extremely volatile, perhaps going up 20 or 30 percent one year and tumbling 37 percent the next (remember 2008?). You can somewhat reduce that volatility by holding a wide variety of different kinds of stocks, most easily done with stock mutual funds or *exchange-traded funds* (which, like mutual funds, represent baskets of securities but, unlike mutual funds, trade like stocks). You can also temper the volatility of a stock portfolio by blending into that portfolio certain other kinds of investments — such as bonds — that tend to hold their own, or may even head north, when stocks head south.

- ✓ **Gold and other commodities:** In the past, commodities — gold, silver, oil, wheat, coffee — have been very difficult to invest in and extremely volatile. The volatility remains. However, investing in commodities has recently become very easy. A bevy of exchange-traded funds introduced in the past several years allow you to plunk your money into just about any commodity imaginable.

Like bonds, certain commodities may hold their own, or even go up, when stocks go down. Over the past 40 years, commodity investors overall have seen slightly higher returns than have stock investors. Commodities tend to increase value over time because the world is becoming an awfully crowded place, with more and more people consuming limited resources. But in the short run, commodity prices are very much subject to the whims of weather, politics, and investor enthusiasm.

✔ **Investment real estate:** Whether you invest in apartments to rent, shopping centers, or office space, there's money to be made in investment real estate. (Like commodities, real estate is a limited resource.) However, tending to real estate, as any landlord knows, can be a lot of work. And some tenants tend to be real pains in the butt — calling you at midnight to fix a leaky faucet! *Real estate investment trusts* (REITs) operate much like stocks and let you enjoy the fruits of others' labors, profiting merely by depositing your money. (No leaky faucets!) Of course, as with stocks, there's risk involved — more so than there is with most bond offerings. REITs, like stocks, are best purchased in the form of a mutual fund or exchange-traded fund. Most brokerage houses offer dozens of REIT funds. See Chapter 17 for more info.

✔ **Entrepreneurial ventures:** Open a restaurant . . . a dry-cleaning shop . . . a dance studio . . . a gas station. Several million Americans have the bulk of their savings invested in small businesses. You're in control that way, and there's a chance that your small business could go big. Running a business does require tons of work, and there's always a risk that profits won't materialize. When small business people come into my office, I certainly try not to discourage them from growing their businesses, but I also advise funneling some money toward other investments, such as bonds and stocks. Yes, diversification is good for the entrepreneur as well as the employee.

Understanding Five Major Investment Principles

When I first became a serious student of investments, I was amazed at how much hard academic research existed. Most of it contradicts anything and everything you've ever been told about investments by the magazines and books that shout "Get Rich Now!" or "Five Hot Stocks for the New Year!" If you know nothing else about investing, know the following five eternal, essential investment truths — all real-world tested — and you'll be way, way ahead of the game.

1. Risk and return are two sides of the same coin

If you see an investment that has gained 50 percent in the last year, sure, at least consider taking a position. But know this: Any investment that goes up 50 percent in a year can just as easily go down 50 percent in a year. That's the nature of the investment world.

Risk and return go together like fire and oxygen. Short-term, high quality bonds bring modest returns but bear little risk. Long-term, low quality bonds bring more handsome returns but bear considerable risk. Lower quality bonds *must* offer greater potential for return or no one but maybe a few loonies would invest in them. Higher quality bonds *must* offer lower rates of return or so many investors would flock to them that the price would be bid up (which would effectively lower the rate of return).

2. Financial markets are largely efficient

If someone says to you that a particular investment is "guaranteed" to return 15 percent a year with no risk, take that with a big, big, big grain of salt. Financial markets are *efficient,* which means that thousands upon thousands of buyers, sellers, fund managers, and market analysts are constantly out there looking for the best deals. If a truly safe investment were to offer a guaranteed return of 15 percent, so many people would make offers to buy that investment that the price would surely be bid up . . . and the return would then drop.

The efficiency of the markets is why even so few professional investors can beat the indexes. In numerous studies — each supporting the findings of the others — actively managed mutual funds (funds whose managers try to pick stocks or bonds that will outperform all others) very rarely manage to beat the indexes. Over the course of a decade or more, the number is infinitesimally small, and even those chosen few fail to beat the indexes by very much.

In Chapter 16, I tell you where to find the best bond *index funds* — funds that try to capture the returns of the entire market rather than attempting, usually in vain, to beat the market.

3. Diversification is just about the only free lunch you'll ever get

So if you can't pick certain securities that will outperform, how can you become a better investor than the next guy? Not that hard, really. Keep your costs low. Keep your taxes minimal. Don't trade often. Most importantly, diversify your portfolio across several *asset classes* — various kinds of investments, such as bonds, stocks, and commodities — so that all the components can contribute to your returns. Because the components move up and down at different times, the volatility of your entire portfolio is kept to a minimum.

In Chapter 11, I discuss something called *Modern Portfolio Theory (MPT)*. The essence of MPT is this: You can add a highly volatile (high risk, high return) investment to a portfolio, and — if that investment tends to zig while other investments in your portfolio zag — you may actually lower the volatility (and risk) of the entire portfolio. So who says there's no such thing as a free lunch?

4. Reversion to the mean — it means something

Sometimes called *reversion to the mean,* sometimes called *regression to the mean,* what it means is that most things in this world — from batting averages to inches of rainfall to investment returns — tend over time to revert back to their historical averages.

Suppose, for example, that a certain kind of investment (say, intermediate-term Ginnie Mae bonds) showed extraordinary returns for the last two to three years (perhaps 18 percent a year). That kind of return on a bond would be rare, but it does happen. (I explain how in Chapter 4.) We know from the past several decades that intermediate-term, high quality bonds such as Ginnie Maes typically return about one-third as much. Would you be well advised to assume that Ginnie Mae bonds will continue to earn 18 percent for the next two years?

In fact, most investors assume just that. They look at recent returns of a certain asset class and assume that those recent returns will continue. In other words, most fresh investment money pours into "hot" investment sectors. And this often spells tragedy for those who don't understand the concept of reversion to the mean. In reality, hot sectors often turn cold — and they are generally to be avoided.

In fact, if anything, you might expect an asset class that overperforms for several years to underperform in the upcoming years. Why? Because all investments (like batting averages and inches of rainfall) have a tendency to return to their historical average return.

To look at it another way, investments tend to move in and out of favor in cycles. It is hard, if not impossible, to imagine that any one investment that has historically yielded modest returns would suddenly, for any extended period of time, become a major moneymaker. That would be akin to Chili Palmer's rented Oldsmobile minivan suddenly becoming the favored vehicle of pistol-packing mobsters.

5. Investment costs matter — and they matter a lot!

Oh, sure, 1 percent doesn't sound like a prodigious sum, but the difference between investing in a bond mutual fund that charges 1.50 percent annually in management fees and one that charges 0.50 percent is enormous. Over the course of the next ten years, assuming gross returns of 5 percent, compounded annually, a $20,000 investment in the more expensive fund would leave you, after paying the fund company, with $28,212. That same investment in the less expensive fund would leave you with $31,059 — a difference of $2,847.

Of course, fund companies that charge more tend to have a lot of money to spend on advertising, and they do a great job conning the public into thinking that their funds are somehow worth the extra money. That is very rarely true. In Chapter 16, I include a sidebar on mutual bond-fund advertising, explaining how mediocre funds are often dolled up to look much better than they are.

Studies galore show that the investors who keep their costs to a minimum do best. That's especially true with bonds where the returns tend to be more modest than with stocks. Whether you are buying bond funds or purchasing individual bonds, transaction costs and operating expenses need to be minimized. That's largely what Chapters 14 through 16 of this book are all about.

Chapter 3

The (Often, But Not Always) Heroic History of Bonds

*F*or some people, success in life means owning a Rolls Royce. For others, it means having someone to love. And for still others it could mean leaving a legacy. Winston Churchill once quipped that success in life is the ability to move from one mistake to the next without losing enthusiasm. Perhaps he was right.

You can't deny that "success in life" means different things to different people. But what about "success in investing"? That, too, is a somewhat subjective term. Consider investment returns over the past century or so. By some counts, bonds, at least from the investor's vantage point, have been a lamentable failure — the veritable Edsel of investments. By other counts, bonds have been a reigning success — a Rolls Royce with a full tank and a fresh wax job.

In this chapter, I explain that puzzling contradiction. I take you back in time, way back to the Middle Ages, to explore the role of bonds before there was even a printing press. I give you some perspective on how bond markets evolved — and continue to evolve. And, as I escort you into the present era, I describe how the bond market has changed for the better, making bonds easier to invest in and potentially more profitable.

Reviewing the Triumphs and Failures of Fixed-Income Investing

Picture yourself in the year 1926. Calvin Coolidge occupies the White House. Ford's Model T can be bought for $200. Charles Lindbergh is gearing up to fly across the Atlantic. And you, having just arrived from your journey back in time, brush the time-travel dust off your shoulders and reach into your pocket. You figure that if you invest $100, you can then return to the present, cash in on your investment, and live like a corrupt king. So you plunk down the $100 into some long-term government bonds.

Fast-forward to the present, and you discover that your original investment of $100 is now worth $9,400. It grew at an average annual compound rate of return of 5.5 percent. (In fact, that's just what happened in the real world.) Even though you aren't rich, $9,400 doesn't sound too shabby. But you need to look at the whole picture.

Beating inflation, but not by very much

Yes, you enjoyed a return of 5.5 percent a year, but while your bonds were making money, inflation was eating it away . . . at a rate of about 3.3 percent a year. What that means is that your $9,400 is really worth only about $765 in 1926 dollars. Your investment, in *real* dollars (inflation-adjusted dollars), actually grew 7.65 times.

To put that another way, your real (after-inflation) yearly rate of return for long-term government bonds was 2.4 percent. In about half of the 86 years, your bond investment either didn't grow at all in real dollar terms, or actually lost money.

Compare that scenario to an investment in stocks. Had you invested the very same $100 in 1926 in the S&P 500 (500 of the largest U.S. company stocks), your investment would have grown to $298,000 in *nominal* (pre-inflation) dollars. In 1926 dollars, that would be $24,300. The average nominal return was 9.9 percent, and the average real annual rate of return for the bundle of stocks was 6.7 percent. (Those rates ignore both income taxes and the fact that you can't invest directly in an index, but they are still valid for comparison purposes.)

So? Which would you rather have invested in: stocks or bonds? Obviously, stocks were the way to go. In comparison, bonds seem to have failed to provide adequate return.

Saving the day when the day needed saving

But hold on! There's another side to the story! Yes, stocks clobbered bonds over the course of the last eight or nine decades. But who makes an investment and leaves it untouched for that long? Rip Van Winkle, maybe? But outside of fairy tale characters, no one! Real people in the real world usually invest for much shorter periods. And there have been some shorter periods over the past eight or nine decades when stocks have taken some stomach-wrenching falls.

The worst of all falls, of course, was during the Great Depression that began with the stock market crash of 1929. Any money that your grandparents may have had in the stock market in 1929 was worth not even half as much four years later. Over the next decade, stock prices would go up and down, but Grandma and Grandpa wouldn't see their $100 back until about 1943. Had they planned to retire in that period, well . . . they may have had to sell a few apples on the street just to make ends meet.

A bond portfolio, however, would have helped enormously. Had Grandma and Grandpa had a diversified portfolio of, say, 70 percent stocks and 30 percent long-term government bonds, they would have been pinched by the Great Depression but not destroyed. While $70 of stock in 1929 was worth only $33 four years later, $30 in long-term government bonds would have been worth $47. All told, instead of having a $100 all-stock portfolio fall to $46, their 70/30 diversified portfolio would have fallen only to $80. Big difference!

Closer to our present time, a $10,000 investment in the S&P 500 at the beginning of 2000 was worth only $5,800 after three years of a growly bear market. But during those same three years, long-term U.S. government bonds soared. A $10,000 70/30 (stock/bond) portfolio during those three years would have been worth $8,210 at the end. Another big difference!

In 2008, as you're well aware, stocks took a big nosedive. The S&P 500 tumbled 37 percent in that dismal calendar year. And long-term U.S. government bonds? Once again, our fixed-income friends came to the rescue, rising nearly 26 percent. In fact, nearly every investment imaginable, including all the traditional stock-market hedges, from real estate to commodities to foreign equities, fell hard that year. Treasury bonds, however, continued to stand tall.

Clearly, long-term government bonds can, and often do, rise to the challenge during times of economic turmoil. Why are bad times often good for many bonds? I explain the reasons for this phenomenon in Chapters 4 and 5. For now, know that bonds have historically been a best friend to investors at those times when investors have most needed a friend. Given that bonds have saved numerous stock investors from impoverishment, bond investing in the past eight to nine decades may be seen not as a miserable failure but as a huge success.

Whatever happened to Grandpa's bearer bonds?

For years, bonds were issued as certificates — many of them genuine works of art — called *bearer bonds*. Quite simply, if you had the certificate in your hands, the bond was yours, and the attached coupons (generally good for six months' interest) could be turned in for cold cash. Your name appeared nowhere on the bond, nor in the company's records. If you earned any interest, the IRS expected you to voluntarily report it and pay the appropriate tax.

The 25-year bearer bond shown here was issued by The New York Central Railroad Company in 1955, carried a face value of $1,000, and bore coupons redeemable every six months for $30.00 each.

Photograph courtesy of Susee Kilbanks

Needless to say, the IRS was not a big fan of bearer bonds, and in 1982, it became illegal for any corporation or municipality to issue them. With the sole exception of U.S. savings bonds, bonds have been issued electronically since that time, and anonymity is no longer possible.

You own the bond. The brokerage house has your name. You pay the tax.

On the up side, today's bonds, unlike bearer bonds, cannot be stolen or lost in a fire. Today, your ownership of a bond is registered in cyberspace and protected from thievery or flames.

Looking Back Over a Long and (Mostly) Distinguished Past

Whether or not we deem bonds a success in the 20th century, if we go back in time to the 19th century, the track record seems more clear. Not only were bonds a source of stability during most of the 1800s, but the difference in returns between stocks and bonds wasn't nearly so great as it became in later years.

Although the data from over 100 years ago isn't quite as solid as it is today, most economists believe that bonds in the United States returned to investors an average of about 5 percent a year throughout the 1800s, versus roughly 6.5 percent a year for stocks. Inflation was quite low prior to 1900, so nominal and real returns were largely one and the same.

If you consider the inherently large volatility of stocks (today's market compared to the market a century ago would probably look much the same) it would seem that bonds were perhaps the better investment during the early industrial age.

In trying to predict future returns of bonds and stocks, most investors today look at data only from the 20th century and assume that moving forward the returns for stocks and bonds will be similar to what they've been historically. However, when making predictions, it may be helpful to note that financial markets were quite active prior to 1900 . . . even prior to 1800! In fact, bonds have been issued in Europe for hundreds of years (looking rather similar to the way they look today).

Yielding returns to generations of your ancestors

Notre Dame, the Leaning Tower of Pisa, the Palace at Versailles, the Tower of London — our medieval European ancestors knew how to create things with lasting power. When the Venetian government of the 13th century issued bonds, it didn't issue the 10- or 20-year bonds that are popular today. It didn't issue 50- or 100-year bonds that were popular in the 1800s, either. No, the Venetian *prestiti* was a bond designed to pay interest *forever*, without ever paying off the principal.

The prestiti paid 5 percent interest a year, payable — like most bonds today — in two annual installments. Also like virtually all bonds today, it was not issued in certificate form. Rather, the bondholders had their claims registered in a central location: the city's loan office. Prestiti could be bought and sold on the open market and, depending on prevailing interest rates of the day, might sell at a discount or a premium of the face value of the loan — just as bonds trade today.

Confidence in the prestiti led to its use as a medium of exchange throughout medieval Europe and helped Venice grow into the most prosperous city of the era. In later years, as England and France became dominant powers, they, too, issued bonds that never matured. The Brits called theirs *consols,* and the French (who, appropriately enough, backed their bonds with a tax on wine) called theirs *rentes.*

Venice continued to pay off the interest on its prestiti until the early 1500s and stopped only when Venice was pretty much destroyed in a series of wars with the Turks. Britain and France, although no longer issuing consols and rentes, are still paying interest after hundreds of years. Of course, they are also issuing new bonds, as do most other nations today do when they need more cash to pay the bills. Throughout history, governments have needed the most cash in times of war. The United States became a major issuer of bonds during World War II, with the sale of war bonds. Most historians agree the success of war bonds helped finance the Allied victory.

Gleaning some important lessons

Bonds have been a bulwark of portfolios throughout much of modern history, but that's not to say that money — some serious money — hasn't been lost. In this section, I offer examples of some bonds that haven't fared well so you're aware that even these relatively safe investment vehicles carry some risk.

Corporate bonds

Corporate bonds — generally considered the most risky kind of bonds — did not become popular in the United States until after the Civil War, when many railroads, experiencing a major building boom, had a sudden need for capital. During a depression in the early to mid 1890s, a good number of those railroads went bankrupt, taking many bondholders down with them. Estimates indicate that more than one out of every three dollars invested in the U.S. bond market was lost. Thank goodness we haven't seen anything like that since (although during the Great Depression of the 1930s, plenty of companies of all sorts went under, and many corporate bondholders again took it on the chin).

In more recent years, the global bond default rate has been less than 1 percent a year. Still, that equates to several dozen companies a year. In recent years, a number of airlines (Delta, Northwest), energy companies (Enron), and one auto parts company (Delphi) defaulted on their bonds. Both General Motors and Ford experienced big downgrades (from *investment-grade* to *speculative-grade,* terms I explain in Chapter 4), costing bondholders (especially those who needed to cash out holdings) many millions.

Buy war bonds!

Even before the United States entered World War II, a massive effort was underway to raise money to build the military and support our allies in war-torn Europe and Asia. At the heart of the fundraising effort was the creation of war bonds. In April 1941, with great fanfare, President Franklin D. Roosevelt purchased the very first such bond from Secretary of the Treasury Henry Morgenthau, Jr. Posters (such as the ones shown here), radio commercials, newspaper advertisements, and newsreels in theaters spread the word that purchasing a bond was the patriotic thing to do. The government made it easy to invest by issuing cards with slots for quarters. When a person collected 75 quarters — $18.75 — he or she could bring the card into any post office and receive a $25 bond redeemable in ten years (with no actual interest payments in the interim). That worked out to 2.9 percent annual compound interest — considerably lower than prevailing rates at the time. More than six out of ten U.S. citizens bought war bonds, raising nearly $200 billion (worth about 13 times as much in today's dollars), and Hitler and Hirohito got what was coming to them.

Photographs courtesy of the U.S. Treasury

Closer to the present, Lehman Brothers, the fourth largest investment bank in the United States, went belly up in the financial crisis of 2008. Billions were lost by those in possession of Lehman Brothers bonds. (Many more billions were also lost in mortgage-backed securities and collateralized debt obligations. These investments are debt instruments issued by financial corporations, but they are very different animals than typical corporate bonds and rarely spoken of in the same breath. I'll get to those in Chapters 6 and 7.) Most recently, we've witnessed the collapse of once very healthy corporations, from Borders to Sharper Image to Kodak. Even Hostess recently became little more than crumbs. (It's tough to imagine that with our insatiable appetite for sugary snacks, a company could lose money on Ding Dongs and Twinkies!) As we've seen time and time again, corporations sometimes go under. None are too big to fail.

Municipal bonds

Municipal bonds, although much safer overall than typical corporate bonds, have also seen a few defaults. In 1978, Cleveland became the first major U.S. city to default on its bonds since the Great Depression. Three years prior, New York City likely would have defaulted on its bonds had the federal government not come to the rescue.

The largest default in the history of the municipal bond market was that of the Washington Public Power Supply System (WPPSS, known informally as "Whoops"). In 1982, bond investors lost $2.25 billion following the municipal corporation's failed program to build five nuclear power plants in Washington to supply electricity to the Pacific Northwest. Only one of the five planned nuclear plants was ever completed. Investors got seriously nuked.

Despite lots of talk about the prospect of massive municipal bankruptcies, not many have occurred. In recent years, we've seen record numbers, but those numbers are not huge, by any means. In fact, ten U.S. municipalities filed for bankruptcy in 2011, following six in 2010. The largest of the 2011 lot was Jefferson County, Alabama, the most populous county in the state. Bondholders have not been getting interest on their Jefferson County bonds, and, as of this writing in 2012, it is unclear whether their principal will eventually be returned in full.

Several budget-challenged cities and counties have had to make the difficult choice between paying off bondholders or making good on pension obligations for retired police, firefighters, and teachers. Thus far, the retired workers have suffered more financial pain than the bondholders, perhaps because they have less political clout — and no one wants to alienate bondholders, who may provide much-needed cash in the future.

Sovereign bonds

Nations worldwide also issue government bonds. These are often called *sovereign* bonds. The largest default of all time occurred in 1917 as revolutionaries in Russia were attempting to free the people by breaking the bonds, so to speak, of imperialist oppression. Bonds were broken, for sure; with the collapse of the czarist regime, billions and billions of rubles-worth of Russian bonds were suddenly worth less than non-alcoholic vodka. Most had been sold to Western Europeans. In France, the Parisian government urged people to reject the new Bolshevik regime and show their support of the monarch in Moscow by purchasing Russian bonds. About half of all French households held at least some Russian debt.

Sometimes history can repeat itself or, at least, create echoes of the past. In 1998, one of the largest bond defaults of the modern era occurred once again in Moscow. The Russian government, facing a collapse of its currency, stopped payment on about $40 billion of bonds. And in 2002, Argentina's financial decline forced bondholders to accept 25 cents on the dollar for its outstanding debt of $90 billion.

As I discuss in Chapter 9, bonds of *emerging-market* nations, such as Russia, Argentina, Mexico, and Turkmenistan, have been one of the hottest investment sectors in the past several years. The returns of late have been phenomenal, but how quickly people forget the past! Those bonds can be very volatile, and investing in them means risking your principal.

Indeed, the recent global awareness of serious debt problems in several European nations has resulted in fears that even these developed nations (which presumably have already emerged) could default on their bond obligations. This fear has caused their bond prices to drop dramatically and yields to rise sharply. At the time of this writing, while ten-year U.S. Treasury bonds are yielding about 2 percent, a ten-year bond issued by the Greek government is yielding 28 percent! Clearly, the collective wisdom of the bond market sees the government of Greece as very likely to default.

Realizing How Crucial Bonds Are Today

I could talk about the importance of corporate debt to the growth of the economy, the way in which municipal bonds help to repair roads and build bridges, and how Ginnie Mae and Fannie Mae bonds help to provide housing to the masses, but I think I'll just let this one sentence suffice. This is, after all, not a book on macroeconomics and social policy but a book on personal investing. So allow me to address the crucial role that bonds play in the lives of individual investors — people like you and me.

With approximately $15 trillion invested in bonds, U.S. households' economic welfare is closely tied to the fortunes of the bond market.

I would argue that with the demise of the traditional pension, bond investing is more important than ever. Back when you knew your company would take care of you in old age, you may have played footloose and fancy free with your portfolio without having to worry that a scrambled nest egg might mean you couldn't afford to buy eggs. Today, a well-tuned portfolio — that almost certainly includes a good helping of bonds — can make the difference between living on Easy Street and living *on* the street.

Keep in mind that most of the money in the bond market today is institutional money. Should you have a life insurance policy, chances are that your life insurance company has most of your future payoff invested in bonds. Should you have money in your state's prepaid college tuition program, chances are that your money is similarly indirectly invested in bonds. Should you be one of the fortunate persons whose company still offers a pension, chances are that your company has your future pension payout invested in bonds.

In total, nearly $95 trillion is invested in bonds worldwide, and the amount is growing year by year. Data reflecting this growth over a decade, provided by Standard and Poor's, are reflected in Figure 3-1. Many economists speculate that as the Boomer generation continues to move into retirement, the demand for income-generating investments like bonds will only grow. If you live and work in a developed nation, your economic well-being is much more closely tied to the bond markets than you think.

Viewing Recent Developments, Largely for the Better

As the price of everything from groceries and gas to college tuition and medical care continues to climb, it's nice to know that at least two things on this planet have gotten cheaper in the past few years: computers and bond trades. And, as any seasoned bond investor will tell you, saving money on trades isn't the only exciting development of late. Here are some others worth noting:

- ✔ **New and better bond funds:** According to Morningstar, you have almost 2,000 bond funds in which to invest. (If I were to include various "classes" of these funds, such as many mutual-fund companies offer, basically for small investors and large investors, the number would be well over 5,000.) Of these, at least 180 are bond *index funds* — funds that

seek to capture the returns of an entire swatch of the bond market —
which, from my vantage point, tend to be the best options for most bond
investors. These funds carry an average yearly expense ratio of 32 basis
points (32/100 of 1 percent), which is way, way less than most bond
funds (the overall average is 1 percent).

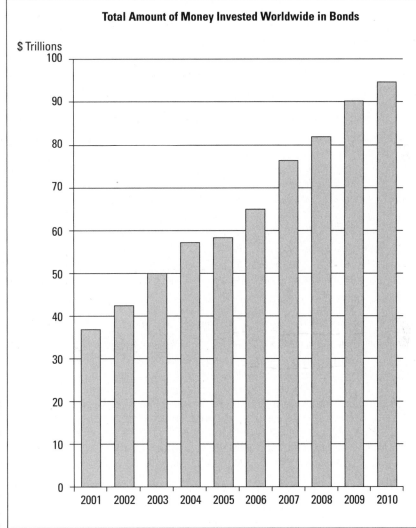

Total Amount of Money Invested Worldwide in Bonds

Figure 3-1:
Ten years of
impressive
growth in
the fixed-
income
market.

Illustration by Wiley, Composition Services Graphics

The newest kid on the block, *exchange-traded funds* (ETFs) — index funds similar to mutual funds — are the greatest thing to happen to bond investing in a very long time. ETFs allow small investors to invest like the Big Boys, with extremely low expenses and no minimum investment requirements. As of this printing, approximately 150 bond ETFs exist. Some of them, such as several offerings from Vanguard and PIMCO, carry annual expense ratios of a mere 9 basis points (9/100 of 1 percent).

I discuss both ETFs and mutual funds in Chapter 16.

✔ **Greater access to information:** One of the advantages of all index funds, but especially exchange-traded funds over traditional actively managed mutual funds, is their relative *transparency*. That means that when you invest in an ETF, you know exactly what you're buying. Traditional mutual funds are not required to reveal their specific investments; you may think you're buying one thing and end up with another.

When it comes to buying and selling individual bonds, it's as if a muddy pond has been transformed into a glass aquarium. Not long ago, a bond broker would give you a price for a bond, and you'd have absolutely no idea how fair a deal you were getting. Nowadays, you can search online and usually get a very good idea of how fair a deal you're getting, how much the broker is making, and whether better deals can be had. I give you a complete tour of the aquarium in Chapter 15.

✔ **The expansion of Uncle Sam's treasury chest:** If you are going to invest in individual bonds, U.S. Treasury bonds may make the most sense. The Treasury now has a website, www.treasurydirect.gov, where you can buy its bonds directly and not have to deal with any brokers whatsoever, nor will you need to fork over any kind of markup. I walk you through the process in Chapter 5.

One special kind of Treasury bond — Treasury Inflation-Protected Securities, or TIPS — has been in existence since the mid-1990s. It is a very exciting development in the world of bonds. TIPS offer only very modest interest rates, but the principal is readjusted twice annually to keep up with inflation. TIPS represent an entirely new *asset class* (kind of investment), and I advocate that most of my clients hold at least one-quarter of their bond allocation in TIPS. They can be important portfolio diversifiers. Read all about them in Chapter 5.

✔ **Internationalization of the bond market:** The U.S. government isn't the only government to issue bonds. U.S. corporations aren't the only corporations to issue bonds, either. For added portfolio diversification, and possibly a higher yield, you may want to look abroad. Until recently, international diversification in fixed income was very difficult. Now, it's as easy as (but not as American as) apple pie. As with U.S. bonds, you have your pick of short-term or long-term bonds, safe-and-simple or risky-with-high-return potential. You can invest in the relatively calm waters of Canada, Japan, or Germany. Or you can travel to countries such as Russia and Brazil where the bond markets are choppy and exciting. Join me on the voyage abroad in Chapter 9.

Need a hobby? Try scripophily

The term *scripophily* (pronounced *scrip awful lee*) derives from a contest held by the *Financial Times* newspaper in 1978 to come up with an appropriate name for collecting antique stocks and bonds. Bob Kerstein, CEO of Scripophily. com, estimates that the hobby boasts 20,000 to 30,000 enthusiasts in the United States alone.

Kerstein's website (www.scripophily. com) features more than 17,000 old certificates from various nations, industries, and eras. Many of them are works of art, some even featuring paintings from famous artists of their day. But the vast majority of the old stocks and bonds have one thing in common, says Kerstein: "They may be valuable as collector items, but they are worthless as redeemable securities." He says he has seen scams whereby con artists try to sell old corporate bonds (both domestic and international) as redeemable securities, even though they have no market value, other than as a collectible. "Those old bonds may look like they're still redeemable, but they are not," he warns.

Liberty Bonds, sold during World War I, are *very* popular among collectors — much more popular than when they were first issued. (The lack of consumer enthusiasm for them proved to be a bit of an embarrassment to the U.S. Treasury; unlike World War II, which rallied tremendous public support, World War I wasn't very popular among Americans.) Kerstein advises, "If you happen to have a Liberty Bond, don't cash it in with the government — a collector might pay you many times as much as the government."

Chapter 4

Sweet Interest Is the Name of the Game

. . . .

. . . .

1n the city of Uruk, in the month of Ululu, on the 11th day of the 9th year of Nebuchadnezzar (that would be 595 b.c.), a man named Nabu-usabsi lent a half mina (about half a pound) of silver to Nabu-sar-ashesu. They signed an agreement witnessed by a holy priest and four countrymen. The agreement stated that within one year, Nabu-sar-ashesu would return to Nabu-usabsi his half mina of silver plus another ten shekels, each shekel equal to about 1⁄60 of a pound of silver. If you do the math, that equates to a yearly rate of interest of 16⅔ percent.

That story from an ancient Babylonian text was retold, nearly 2,600 years later, in *A History of Interest Rates,* a 700-page textbook by Sidney Homer and Richard Sylla, first published in 1963. (A fourth edition was published by Wiley in 2005.) The book is an amazing collection of research into credit and interest rates going back not only to the 9th year of Nebuchadnezzar, but even offering some speculation that interest payments of one sort or another existed in prehistoric times.

And why, pray tell, am I bringing this up in a book on bond investing in the computer age? Because most of today's credit is tied up in bonds, and the most salient feature of any bond is the interest rate paid. Interestingly (pardon the pun), many of the same forces that drove interest rates 2,600 years ago are *still* driving interest rates today, as you find out in this chapter.

On the following pages, I examine what forces affect interest rates and the demand for credit. I introduce the many (and often confusing, sometimes *purposely* confusing) ways in which bond returns are measured and reported. And I give you the tools you need to determine whether Mr. Nabu-usabsi was getting a fair return on his investment, as well as what you, as a thoroughly modern bond investor, should expect in return for *your* bond investments.

Calculating Rates of Return Can Be Like Deciphering Ancient Babylonian

Bond investing can be tricky business indeed — way trickier than stock investing. To help me explain why, I'm going to call upon our Babylonian friends, Nabu-usabsi and Nabu-sar-ashesu. And I'm going to introduce two new characters, Lila-Ir-lender and Kudur-Broker. The two Nabus are real characters from a bygone era. Lila-Ir-lender (said to be a distant cousin of Hammurabi) is fictional. Kudur-Broker is also fictional.

(Note to any Hollywood types: These are *my* characters; if you decide to turn *Bond Investing For Dummies* into a blockbuster movie, I demand a cut!)

Lila-Ir-lender, like Nabu-sar-ashesu, is a moneylender. Kudur-Broker is, appropriately enough, a broker. Instead of dealing only in minas and shekels and agreements written on parchment, let's assume the existence of bonds. With lenders, borrowers, and a broker, we have a complete bond market!

Figure 4-1 shows our four players in the fictional Babylonian bond market, illustrated by Addie Wild, my daughter, and polished for publication by the Wiley graphics team.

Figure 4-1:
Nabu-sar-ashesu, bond issuer; Nabu-usabsi, bond buyer; Lila-Ir-lender, bond buyer; and Kudur-Broker, bond broker.

Illustration courtesy of Addie Wild

Okay, are you ready now to see why this bond business can be so tricky? Good. Let's return to ancient Babylonia!

Cutting deals

Instead of merely signing an agreement, suppose that Nabu-usabsi, in return for lending his half mina of silver to Nabu-sar-ashesu, gets a bond. Nabu-sar-ashesu's bond clearly states that Nabu-usabsi will get his investment back in one year, plus 16⅔ percent interest. In the parlance of the bond world, the bond is issued with a *face value* of a half mina of silver, a *coupon rate* (or *interest rate*) of 16⅔ percent, and a *maturity* (or *expiration date*) of one year. I talk about these terms in more detail later.

For now, I want to impress upon you that measuring bond returns is not always an easy matter. Why not? After all, the agreement calls for 16⅔ percent interest. Simple enough, eh? Not really.

Suppose that Nabu-usabsi wants to get his 16⅔ percent interest not as a lump sum at the end of the year but in two installments (as most bonds work): 8⅓ percent after six months, and another 8⅓ percent after another six months. That is obviously a better deal for Nabu-usabsi because he gets the 8⅓ percent sooner and can, if he wishes, reinvest that money for another six months. Let's suppose that, in fact, he is able to reinvest that money for a very high interest rate. By the end of the year, Nabu-usabsi will actually earn more than 16⅔ percent on his original investment. But how is his *real* rate of return calculated?

Changing hands

To complicate matters further, suppose that Nabu-sar-ashesu, our bond issuer, has agreed that his bond can be sold, and that he will continue to pay 16⅔ percent interest to whomever buys the bond. In walks Lila-Ir-lender, who wants to buy the bond from Nabu-usabsi but uses Kudur-Broker, the bond broker, to make the deal. Kudur-Broker pays Nabu-usabsi one-half pound of silver to obtain the bond. He turns around and sells it to Lila-Ir-lender for ⁹⁄₁₀ pound of silver and pockets the difference for himself.

Lila-Ir-lender is now the proud owner of a bond that is paying 16⅔ percent on the *original face value* (one-half pound of silver). She, however, paid more for the bond, thanks to the bond broker's markup. So even though she is holding a bond that is paying 16⅔ percent, she isn't really getting 16⅔ percent on her money; she's getting less.

Now how much is the true rate of return on the bond? Is it 16⅔ percent, or is it 13.88 percent, which is the actual percentage return that Lila-Ir-lender would be getting on the money she laid out?

Embracing the complications

You see why this bond business can be so confusing? (Yes, it would be just as confusing if the names were "Mike" and "Sue" instead of Nabu-usabsi and Nabu-sar-ashesu!)

I need to warn you that this chapter is the most technical one in the book. You are about to read some things that confuse even many financial professionals. I do my best to present the information clearly, and I promise to give you an intermission halfway through the chapter so you can catch your breath! But you are probably right now wondering the following: Do you really need to know all this? Can you skim this chapter, or should you really know how to calculate yield-to-maturity, yield-to-call, and things like that? It depends.

If you are okay investing in bond mutual funds, especially the bond index funds that I recommend later in this book (see Chapter 16), and you're going to buy and hold your investment, then a cursory knowledge of what makes bonds tick is probably just fine. (Knowing how they fit into a well-diversified portfolio, as outlined in Chapters 11 and 12, is probably more important.) If you are intent, however, on dealing in individual bonds or trying to flip bonds to make a profit (good luck!), you'd better either know this stuff or find a bond broker you can really trust.

Understanding what follows is easier than finding a bond broker you can really trust. Trust me.

Conducting Three Levels of Research to Measure the Desirability of a Bond

Determining the true value of a bond investment, and how much you're really going to get out of it in the end, requires three levels of research. I could compare it to buying a home. Shopping for a home, here are the three levels of research you conduct:

✔ **Level one:** You notice the curb appeal. You take note of the size of the home and whether or not you find it attractive. You also, of course, note the offering price.

✔ **Level two:** You look at the property taxes, the age of the plumbing, the cost of utilities, and the condition of the roof.

✔ **Level three:** You expand your view to look critically at the surroundings. How are the schools? Are area homes appreciating? Do the neighbors park their pick-up trucks on the front lawn?

With a bond, you need to go through similar levels of research:

- ✓ **Level one:** You notice the curb appeal of the bond: What is the face value, coupon rate, and sales price?

- ✓ **Level two:** You dig deeper into the qualities of the bond: What are its ratings and maturity, and is it callable?

- ✓ **Level three:** You look at broader economic factors (the bond's "neighborhood"), which can greatly influence the value of your bond investment: the prevailing interest rates, inflation rate, state of the economy, and forces of supply and demand in the fixed-income market.

I know that you may not be familiar with all the terms I'm using here, such as *ratings* and *callable.* You soon will be! I introduce them all in this chapter.

Level one: Getting the basic information

Here are the first things you want to know about a bond:

- ✓ What is its face value?

- ✓ What is the coupon rate?

- ✓ How much are you being asked to pay for the bond?

These can all be ascertained quite readily, either by looking at the bond offer itself or by having a conversation with the broker.

Face value

Also known as *par value* or the *principal,* the *face value* is the original dollar amount of the bond. This is the amount that the bond issuer promises to pay the bond buyer at maturity. The face value of the vast majority of bonds in today's market is $1,000. But note that a $1,000 par value bond doesn't necessarily have to sell for $1,000. After the bond is on the open market, it may sell for an amount above or below par. If it sells above par, it's known as a *premium* bond. If it sells below par, it's known as a *discount* bond.

Know this: Discount bonds are discounted for a reason . . . or, perhaps, two or three reasons. Most commonly, the discounted bond isn't paying a very high rate of interest compared to other similar bonds. Or the issuer of the bond is showing some signs of financial weakness that could potentially lead to a default. Don't think you are necessarily getting a bargain by paying less than face value for a bond. Chances are, you aren't.

Coupon rate

The *coupon rate* is the interest rate the bond issuer (the debtor) has agreed to pay the bondholder (the creditor), given as a percent of the face value. The term *coupon rate* refers to the fact that in the old days, bonds had actual coupons attached that you would rip off at regular intervals to redeem for cash. Bonds no longer have such coupons; in fact, they aren't printed on paper anymore. Bonds are all electronic, but the term remains.

The coupon rate never changes. That's the reason that bonds, like CDs, are called *fixed-income* investments, even though (as you see shortly) the term is a bit of a misnomer. A 5 percent bond always pays 5 percent of the face value (which is usually $50 a year, typically paid as $25 every six months). As I mention in the previous section, the bond doesn't have to be bought or sold at par. But the selling price of a bond doesn't affect the coupon rate.

Know this: The coupon rate, set in stone, tells you how much cash you'll get from your bond each year. Simply take the coupon rate and multiply it by the face value of the bond. Divide that amount in half. That's how much cash you'll typically receive twice a year. A $1,000 bond paying 8 percent gives you $40 cash twice a year.

Sale price

In general, a bond sells at a *premium* (above face value) when prevailing interest rates have dropped since the time that bond was issued. If you think about it, that makes sense. Say your bond is paying 6 percent, and interest rates across the board have dropped to 4 percent. The bond in your hand, which is paying considerably more than new bonds being issued, becomes a valuable commodity. On the other hand, when general interest rates rise, existing bonds tend to move to *discount* status (selling below face value). Who wants them when new bonds are paying higher rates?

Don't ask why, but bond people quote the price of a bond on a scale of 100. If a bond is selling at *par* (face value), it will be quoted as selling at 100. But that doesn't mean that you can buy the bond for $100. It means you can buy it at par. On a $1,000 par bond, that means you can buy the bond for $1,000. If the same bond is selling at 95, that means you're looking at a discount bond, selling for $950. And if that bond is selling for 105, it's a premium bond; you need to fork over $1,050.

Know this: Most investors put too much weight on whether a bond is a discount bond or a premium bond. Although it matters somewhat, especially with regard to a bond's volatility (see the final section of this chapter), it doesn't necessarily affect a bond's total return. *Total return* refers to the sum of your principal and income, capital gains on your original investment, *plus* any income or capital gains on money you've earned on your original investment and have been able to reinvest. Total return is, very simply, the entire amount of money you end up with after a certain investment period, minus what you began with. More on that later in this chapter.

Level two: Finding out intimate details

After you know the face value, coupon rate, and sale price (discount or premium), you are ready to start a little digging. Here's what you want to know next about the bond:

- ✔ Is the bond issuer capable of repaying you your money? Or could the issuer go belly-up and *default* on (fail to repay) all or part of your loan?
- ✔ When will you see your principal returned?
- ✔ Is there a chance that the bond will be called?

Ratings: Separating quality from junk

Not all bonds pay the same coupon rates. In fact, some bonds pay way more than others. One of the major determinants of a bond's coupon rate is the financial standing of the issuer.

The U.S. Treasury, a major issuer of bonds, pays modest rates of return on its bonds (generally a full percentage point less than similar bonds issued by corporations). The reason? Uncle Sam doesn't have to pay more. People assume that the U.S. government isn't going to welsh on its debts, so they are willing to lend the government money without demanding a high return. Shakier entities, such as a new company, a city in financial trouble, or the Russian government (which has a history of defaulting) would have to offer higher rates of return to find any creditors. So they must, and so they do.

An entire industry of bond-rating companies, such as Moody's, Standard and Poor's (S&P), and Fitch Ratings, exists to help bond investors figure their odds of getting paid back from a company or municipality to which they lend money. These firms dig into a bond issuer's financial books to see how solvent the entity is. Theoretically, the higher the rating, the safer your investment; the lower the rating, the more risk you take. In addition, other resources can tell you how much extra interest you should expect for taking on the added risk of lending to a shaky company. Much more on the ratings in Chapter 6.

Know this: Ratings are very helpful — it's hard to imagine markets working without them — but neither the ratings nor the raters are infallible. In the case of Enron, the major ratings firms — S&P and Moody's — had the company's bonds rated as *investment-grade* until four days prior to the company declaring bankruptcy. Investment-grade means that the risk of loss is very low and the odds of getting repaid very high. Weren't Enron bondholders surprised!

That was 2002. Six years later came the subprime mortgage crisis, in which investors in certain mortgage bonds lost a bundle. Just about the time that everyone thought the ratings agencies had learned something since the Enron debacle and reestablished the public's trust, they once again failed investors quite miserably. They apparently failed to see — or perhaps they did see but failed to report — the impending collapse of these mortgage bonds. As Michael Lewis writes in his 2010 book *The Big Short* (W. W. Norton & Company), a colorful exposé of the subprime scandal, "The rating agencies, who were paid fat fees by Goldman Sachs and other Wall Street firms for each deal they rated, pronounced 80 percent of the new tower of debt triple-A."

Insurance

Some bonds come insured and are advertised as such. This is most common in the municipal bond market, although less common than it was years ago. Even though default rates are very low among municipalities, cities know that people buy their bonds expecting safety. So they sometimes insure. If a municipality goes to the trouble of having an insurance company back its bonds, you know that you are getting a safer investment, but you shouldn't expect an especially high rate of interest. (No, you can't decline the insurance on an insured bond. It doesn't work like auto-rental insurance.)

Know this: Some proponents of holding individual bonds say that you should delve not only into the financial health of the bond issuer but also, in the case of an insured bond, the financial health of the insurance company standing behind the issuer. That's a fair amount of work, which is one reason I tend to favor bond funds for most middle-class family portfolios.

Maturity

Generally, the longer the maturity of the bond, the higher the interest rate paid. The reason is simple enough: Borrowers generally want your money for longer periods of time and are willing to pay accordingly. Lenders generally don't want their money tied up for long periods and require extra incentive to make such a commitment. And finally, the longer you invest your money in a bond, the greater the risk you are taking — both that the issuer could default and that interest rates could pop, lessening the value of your bond.

Know this: I don't care who the issuer is, when you buy a 20-year bond, you are taking a risk. Anything can happen in 20 years. Who would have thought 20 years ago that General Motors could find itself on the verge of bankruptcy (as it was when I wrote the first edition of this book)? Or that Eastman Kodak would be in bankruptcy, its bonds selling for pennies to the dollar (as is true while I'm typing these words for the second edition)?

Callability

A bond that is *callable* is a bond that can be retired by the company or municipality on a certain date prior to the bond's maturity. Because bonds tend to be retired when interest rates fall, you don't want your bond to be retired; you generally aren't going to be able to replace it with anything paying as much. Because of the added risk, callable bonds tend to carry higher coupon rates to compensate bond buyers.

Know this: Please be careful when buying any individual callable bond. Much of the real pain I've seen in the bond market has occurred over calls. I've seen cases where a bond buyer will pay a broker a hefty sum to buy a bond callable in, say, six months. The bond, sure enough, gets called, and the bondholder suddenly realizes that he paid the broker a fat fee and made nothing — perhaps got a *negative* return — on his investment. Of course, the broker never bothered to point out this potentially ugly scenario. (Reading this book, especially Chapter 15, will ensure that *you* never meet with a similar fate!)

Taxes

Back in the early days of the bond market in the United States, the federal government made a deal with the cities and states: You don't tax our bonds, and we won't tax yours. And, so far, all parties have kept their word. When you invest in Treasury bonds, you pay no state or local tax on the interest. And when you invest in municipal bonds, you pay no federal tax on the interest. Accordingly, muni bonds pay a lower rate of interest than equivalent corporate bonds. But you may still wind up ahead on an after-tax basis.

Know this: Whether or not the tax-free status of municipal bonds makes them appropriate for your portfolio is the subject of Chapter 8. I'll warn you in advance that the simple taxable versus tax-free calculators you find online don't always steer you in the best direction.

Okay, I promised earlier that I'd give you a break about halfway through this chapter. Now's the time: INTERMISSION! Feel free to step away, get a snack, and come back when the glaze has cleared from your eyes.

All right . . . Ready to move onto that third level now? Remember, this chapter is all about estimating the value of a bond investment. As I show next, getting that estimate requires the use of a wide-angle lens.

Level three: Examining the neighborhood

Your home, no matter how well you maintain it or whether you renovate the kitchen, tends to rise or fall in value along with the value of all other houses in your neighborhood. Many things outside of your control — the quality of the schools, employment opportunities, crime rates, and earthquake tremors — can greatly influence the value of homes in your area, including yours. Similarly, a bond, no matter its quality or maturity, tends to rise and fall in value with the general conditions of the markets and of the economy.

Prevailing interest rates

Nothing affects the value of bonds (at least in the short to intermediate run) like prevailing interest rates. When interest rates go up, bond prices go down, usually in lockstep. When interest rates fall, bond prices climb. The relationship is straightforward and logical enough. If you're holding a bond paying yesterday's interest rate, and today's interest rate is lower, then you are holding something that is going to be in hot demand, and people will pay you dearly for it. If you're holding a bond paying yesterday's interest rate, and today's rate is higher, then you are holding mud.

Okay, that part is simple. Interest rates drive bond prices. But what drives interest rates?

Interest rates come in many different flavors. At any point in time, there are prevailing interest rates for home mortgages, credit card payments, bank loans, short-term bonds, and long-term bonds, but to a great extent they all move up and down together. The forces that drive interest rates are numerous, entwined, and largely unpredictable (even though many people claim they can predict).

In the short run — from hour to hour, day to day — the Federal Reserve, which controls monetary policy in the United States, has great power to manipulate interest rates across the board. The Federal Reserve's job is to help smooth the economy by tinkering with interest rates to help curb inflation and boost growth. Low interest rates make borrowing easy, both for businesses and consumers. That helps to heat up the economy, but it can also result in inflation. High interest rates discourage borrowing and so tend to slow economic growth, but they also help to rein in inflation. So when inflation is running too high, in the eyes of the Fed, it moves to raise interest rates. And when the economy is growing too slowly, the Fed tends to lower interest rates. Obviously, it's a balancing act, and perfect balance is hard to achieve.

In the longer run — month to month, year to year — interest rates tend to rise and fall with inflation and with the anticipated rate of future inflation.

Know this: Rising interest rates are, in the short run, a bondholder's worst enemy. The possibility that interest rates will rise — and bond prices will therefore fall — is what makes long-term bonds somewhat risky. If you wish to avoid the risk of price volatility, go with short-term bonds, but be willing to accept less cash flow from your bond holdings.

The rate of inflation

The *inflation rate* signals the degree to which you have to cough up more money to buy the same basket of goods; it indicates your loss of purchasing power. In the long run, the inflation rate has great bearing on returns enjoyed by bondholders. The ties between the inflation rate and the bond market are numerous.

In economic theory, bondholders are rational beings with rational desires and motivations. (In reality, individual investors often act irrationally, but as a group, the markets seem to work rather rationally.) A rational buyer of bonds demands a certain *inflation-risk premium*. That is, the higher the rate of inflation or the expected rate of inflation, the higher an interest rate bondholders demand. If inflation is running at 3 percent, which it has, more or less, for the past several years, bond buyers know that they need returns of at least 3 percent just to break even. If the inflation rate jumps to 6 percent, the inflation-risk premium doubles; bond buyers won't invest their money (or won't invest it happily) unless they get double what they were getting before.

Inflation is also a pretty good indicator of how hot the economy is. When prices are rising, it usually reflects full employment and companies expanding. When companies are expanding, they need capital. The need for capital raises the demand for borrowing. An increased demand for borrowing raises prevailing interest rates, which lowers the price of bonds.

Know this: As a bondholder, you can get stung by inflation. Badly. That's why I recommend that a certain portion of your bonds (around one-quarter, or more if you are shunning stocks) be held in inflation-adjusted bonds, such as Treasury Inflation-Protected Securities (TIPS). It's also why a 100-percent bond portfolio rarely, if ever, makes sense. Stocks have a much better track record at keeping ahead of inflation. Real estate and commodities can do a pretty good job, too.

How exactly does the Federal Reserve move interest rates?

The U.S. Federal Reserve has three "magic" powers with which to expand or contract the money supply, or move interest rates: open market operations, the discount rate, and reserve requirements:

✔ **Open market operations:** This term means nothing more than the buying and selling of Treasury and federal agency bonds. When bonds are sold (and the public's money is funneled into government hands), the money supply is tightened, inflation tends to slow, and interest rates tend to rise. When bonds are purchased back (and the public's money is returned), the economy is given a boost, and interest rates tend to fall.

✔ **The discount rate:** This term refers to the interest rate that commercial banks must pay for government loans. The more the banks have to pay, the more they tend to charge their customers, and interest rates tend to rise.

✔ **Reserve requirements:** The *reserve* is the amount of money that banks must hold on hand as a percentage of their outstanding loans. The higher the reserve requirements, the tougher it is for banks to lend money, and interest rates tend to rise as a result.

Forces of supply and demand

The public is fickle, and that fickleness is perhaps nowhere better seen than in the stock market. Although the bond market tends to be less affected by the public's whims, it does happen. At times, the public feels pessimistic, and when the public feels pessimistic, it usually favors the stability of government bonds. When the public is feeling optimistic, it tends to favor the higher return potential of corporate bonds. When the public feels that taxes are going to rise, it tends to favor tax-free municipal bonds. As in any other market — shoes, automobiles, lettuce — high consumer demand can raise prices, and low demand tends to lower prices.

Understanding (and Misunderstanding) the Concept of Yield

Okay, time to hold onto your hat. Now that you know something about researching the particulars of a bond offering, and the climate of the bond market, it's time to talk *yield.* Yield is what you want in a bond. Yield is income. Yield contributes to return. Yield is confusion! People (including overly eager bond salespeople) often misuse the term or use it inappropriately to gain an advantage in the bond market.

Don't be a yield sucker! Understand what kind of yield is being promised on a bond or bond fund, and know what it really means.

Coupon yield

This one is easy. The coupon yield, or the coupon rate, is part of the bond offering. A $1,000 bond with a coupon yield of 4 percent is going to pay $40 a year. A $1,000 bond with a coupon yield of 6 percent is going to pay $60 a year. Usually, the $40 or $60 or whatever is split in half and paid out twice a year on an individual bond.

Bond funds don't really have coupon yields, although they have an average coupon yield for all the bonds in the pool. That average tells you something, for sure, but you need to remember that a bond fund may start the year and end the year with a completely different set of bonds — and a completely different average coupon yield.

Current yield

Like coupon yield, current yield is easy to understand, at least on a superficial level. But a deeper level exists, and because of that, current yield is the most often misused kind of yield. In short, *current yield* is derived by taking the bond's coupon yield and dividing it by the bond's price.

Suppose you had a $1,000 face value bond with a coupon rate of 5 percent, which would equate to $50 a year in your pocket. If the bond sells today for 98 (in other words, it is selling at a discount for $980), the current yield is $50 divided by $980 = 5.10 percent. If that same bond rises in price to a premium of 103 (selling for $1,030), the current yield is $50 divided by $1,030 = 4.85 percent.

The current yield is a sort of snapshot that gives you a very rough (and possibly entirely inaccurate) estimate of the return you can expect on that bond over the coming months. If you take the current yield for just one day (translated into nickels and dimes) and multiply that amount by 30, you'd think that would give you a good estimate of how much income your bond will generate in the next month, but that's not the case. The current yield changes too quickly for that kind of prediction to hold true. The equivalent would be taking a measure of today's rainfall, multiplying it by 30, and using that number to estimate rainfall for the month. (Well, the current yield would be *a bit* more accurate, but you get my point.)

Yield-to-maturity

A much more accurate measure of return, although still far from perfect, is the *yield-to-maturity*. It's a considerably more complicated deal than figuring out current yield. Yield-to-maturity factors in not only the coupon rate and the price you paid for the bond, but also how far you have to go to get your principal back, and how much that principal will be.

Yield-to-maturity calculations make a big assumption that may or may not prove true: They assume that as you collect your interest payments every six months, you reinvest them at the same interest rate you're getting on the bond. With this (often faulty) assumption in mind, here's the formula for calculating yield-to-maturity:

Um, I don't know.

I can't remember it. Like most other financial planners, I would have to look it up. It's a terribly long formula with all kinds of horrible Greek symbols and lots of multiplication and division and I think there's a muffler and an ice tray thrown in. But (thank goodness) I don't need to know the formula!

Thanks to the miracle of modern technology, I can punch a few numbers into my financial calculator, or I can go to any number of online calculators. (Try putting "yield-to-maturity calculator" in your favorite search engine.) I like the calculator on www.moneychimp.com (a great financial website that features all sorts of cool calculators).

After you find a yield-to-maturity calculator, you'll be asked to put in the par (face) value of the bond (almost always $1,000), the price you are considering paying for the bond, the number of years to maturity, and the coupon rate. Then you simply punch the "calculate" icon. If, for example, I were to purchase a $1,000 par bond for $980, and that bond was paying 5 percent, and it matured in ten years, the yield-to-maturity would be 5.262 percent.

A few paragraphs ago, I calculated the current yield for such a bond to be 5.10 percent. The yield-to-maturity on a discounted bond (a bond selling for below par) is always higher than the current yield. Why? Because when you eventually get your principal back at maturity, you'll be, in essence, making a profit. You paid only $980, but you'll see a check for $1,000. That extra $20 adds to your yield-to-maturity. The reverse is true of bonds purchased at a premium (a price higher than par value). In those cases, the yield-to-maturity is lower than the current yield.

Unscrupulous bond brokers have been known to tout current yield, and only current yield, when selling especially premium-priced bonds. The current yield may look great, but you take a hit when the bond matures by collecting less in principal than you paid for the bond. Your yield-to-maturity, which matters more than current yield, may, in fact, stink.

Yield-to-call

If you buy a *callable* bond, the company or municipality that issues your bond can ask for it back, at a specific price, long before the bond matures. Premium bonds, because they carry higher-than-average coupon yields, are often called. What that means is that your yield-to-maturity is pretty much a moot point. What you're likely to see in the way of yield is yield-to-call. This amount is figured out the same way that you figure out yield-to-maturity (use www.moneychimp.com if you don't have a financial calculator), but the end result — your actual return — may be considerably lower.

Keep in mind that bonds are generally called when market interest rates have fallen. In that case, not only is your yield on the bond you're holding diminished, but your opportunity to invest your money in anything paying as high an interest rate has passed. From a bondholder's perspective, calls are not pretty, which is why callable bonds must pay higher rates of interest to find any buyers. (From the issuing company's or municipality's perspective, callable bonds are just peachy; after the call, the company or municipality can, if it wishes, issue a new bond that pays a lower interest rate.)

Certain hungry bond brokers may "forget" to mention yield-to-call and instead quote you only current yield or yield-to-maturity numbers. In such cases, you may pay the broker a big cut to get the bond, hold it for a short period, and then have to render it to the bond issuer, actually earning yourself a *negative* total return. Ouch. Fortunately, regulatory authorities have gotten somewhat tougher, and such forgetfulness on the part of brokers is less common, but it still happens.

Worst-case basis yield

Usually a callable bond has not just one possible call date, but several. *Worst-case basis yield* (or *yield-to-worst-call*) looks at all possible yields and tells you what your yield would be if the company or municipality decides to call your bond at the worst possible time.

Callable bonds involve considerably more risk than noncallable bonds. If interest rates drop, your bond will likely be called. Your yield on the existing bond just dropped from what you expected, and you won't be able to reinvest your money for a like rate of return. If interest rates have risen, the company probably won't call your bond, but you are stuck with an asset, if you should try to sell it, that has lost principal value. (Bond prices always drop when interest rates rise.)

The 30-day SEC yield

Because you have so many ways of measuring yield, and because bond mutual funds were once notorious for manipulating yield figures, the U.S. Securities and Exchange Commission (SEC) requires that all bond funds report yield in the same manner. The 30-day SEC yield, which attempts to consolidate the yield-to-maturity of all the bonds in the portfolio, exists so the mutual fund bond shopper can have some measure with which to comparison shop. This measure isn't perfect, in large part because the bonds in your bond fund today may not be the same bonds in your bond fund three weeks from now. Nonetheless, the 30-day SEC yield can be helpful in choosing the right funds. (More on fund shopping in Chapter 16.)

Recognizing Total Return (This Is What Matters Most!)

Even though bonds are called *fixed-income* investments, and even though bond returns are easier to predict than stock returns, ultimately you can't know the exact total return of any bond investment until after the investment period has come and gone. That's true for bond funds, and it's also true for most individual bonds (although many die-hard investors in individual bonds refuse to admit it). *Total return* is the entire pot of money you wind up with after the investment period has come and gone. In the case of bonds or bond funds, that amount involves not only your original principal and your interest, but also any changes in the value of your original principal. Ignoring for the moment the risk of default (and potentially losing all your principal), here are other ways in which your principal can shrink or grow.

Figuring in capital gains and losses

In the case of a bond fund, your principal is represented by a certain number of shares in the fund multiplied by the share price of the fund. As bond prices go up and down (usually due to a number of factors, but primarily in response to prevailing interest rates), so too does the share price of the bond fund go up and down. As I discuss in a couple of pages when I get to bond volatility, the share price of a bond fund may go up and down quite a bit, especially if the bond fund is holding long-term bonds, and doubly especially if those long-term bonds are of questionable quality (junk bonds).

In the case of individual bonds, unless you buy a bond selling at a premium, your principal comes back to you whole — but only if you hold the bond to maturity or if the bond is called. If, on the other hand, you choose to sell the bond before maturity, you wind up with whatever market price you can get for the bond at that point. If the market price has appreciated (the bond sells at a premium), you can count your capital gains as part of your total return. If the market price has fallen (the bond sells at a discount), the capital losses offset any interest you've made on the bond.

Factoring in reinvestment rates of return

Total return of a bond can come from three sources:

- ✔ Interest on the bond

- ✔ Any possible capital gains (or losses)

- ✔ Whatever rate of return you get, if you get any, when you reinvest the money coming to you every six months.

Believe it or not, on a very long-term bond, the last factor — your so-called *reinvestment rate* — is probably the most important of the three! That's because of the amazing power of compound interest.

The only kind of bond where the reinvestment rate is not a factor is a bond where your only interest payment comes at the very end when the bond matures. These kinds of bonds are called *zero-coupon* bonds. In the case of zero-coupon bonds, no compounding occurs. The coupon rate of the bond is your actual rate of return, not accounting for inflation or taxes.

Example: Suppose you buy a 30-year, $1,000 bond that pays 6 percent on a semiannual basis. If you spend the $30 you collect twice a year, you get $1,000 back for your bond at the end of 30 years, and your total annual rate of return (ignoring taxes and inflation) is 6 percent simple interest. But now suppose that on each and every day that you collect those $30 checks, you immediately reinvest them at the same coupon rate. Over the course of 30 years, that pile of reinvested money grows at an annual rate of 6 percent *compounded*.

In this scenario, at the end of six months, your investment is worth $1,030. At the end of one year, your investment is worth $1,060.90. (The extra 90 cents represents a half year's interest on the $30.) The following six months, you earn 6 percent on the new amount, and so on, for 30 more years. Instead of winding up with $1,000 after 30 years, as you would if you spent the semiannual bond payments, you instead wind up with $5,891.60 — almost six times as much!

Allowing for inflation adjustments

Of course, that $5,891.60 due to 6 percent compound interest probably won't be worth $5,891.60 in 30 years. Your truest total rate of return needs to account for inflation. If *inflation* — the rise in the general level of prices — were 3 percent a year for the next 30 years (roughly what it has been in the past decade), your $5,891.60 will be worth only $2,366.24 in today's dollars — a real compound return of 2.91 percent.

To account for inflation when determining the real rate of return on an investment, you can simply take the nominal rate of return (6 percent in our example) and subtract the annual rate of inflation (3 percent in our example). That gives you a very rough estimate of your total real return.

But if you want a more exact figure, here's the formula to use:

1 + nominal rate of return / 1 + inflation rate – 1 × 100 = Real rate of return

Assuming a 6 percent nominal rate of return and 3 percent inflation:

1.06 / 1.03 – 1 × 100 = 2.91

Why the more complicated calculation? You can't just subtract 3 from 6 because inflation is eating away at both your principal *and* your gains throughout the year.

Weighing pre-tax versus post-tax

Of course, we can't finish up this discussion without mentioning taxes. Taxes almost always eat into your bond returns. Here are two exceptions:

- ✔ Tax-free municipal bonds where you experience neither a capital gain nor a capital loss, nor is the bondholder subject to any alternative minimum tax. (More on taxes and munis in Chapter 8.)

- ✔ Bonds held in a tax-advantaged account, such as a Roth IRA or a 529 college savings plan.

For most bonds, the interest payments are taxed as regular income, and any rise in the value of the principal, if the bond is sold (and sometimes even if the bond is not sold), is taxed as capital gain.

For most people these days, long-term capital gains (more than one year) on bond principal are taxed at 15 percent. Any appreciated fixed-income asset bought and sold within a year is taxed at your normal income-tax rate, whatever that is. (Most middle-income Americans today are paying somewhere around 30 percent in income tax.)

Measuring the Volatility of Your Bond Holdings

When investment pros talk of *volatility,* they are talking about risk. When they talk about risk, they are talking about volatility. Volatility in an investment means that what is worth $1,000 today may be worth $900 . . . or $800 . . . tomorrow. Bonds are typically way less risky than stocks (that's why we love bonds so much), but bonds can fall in value. Some bonds are much more volatile than others, and before you invest in any bond, you should have a good idea what kind of volatility (risk) you are looking at.

Time frame matters most

The more time until the bond matures, the greater the bond's volatility. In other words, with long-term bonds, there's a greater chance that the principal value of the bond can rise or fall dramatically. Short-term bonds sway much less. On the other hand — and here's a somewhat funny contradiction — the further off your need to tap into the bond's principal, the less that volatility should matter to you.

As I explain earlier in this chapter, nothing affects the value of your bond holdings as much as prevailing interest rates. If you're holding a bond that pays 5 percent, and prevailing interest rates are 6 percent, your bond isn't worth nearly as much as it would be if prevailing interest rates were 5 percent (or, better yet, 4 percent). But just how sensitive is the price of a bond to the ups and downs of interest rates? It depends, mostly on the maturity of the bond.

Suppose you are holding a fresh 30-year bond with a coupon rate of 5 percent, and suddenly prevailing interest rates move from 5 percent to 6 percent. You are now looking at potentially 30 years of holding a bond that is paying less than the prevailing interest rate. So how attractive does that bond look to you, or anyone else? Answer: It looks like used oil dripping from the bottom of an old car.

But suppose you are holding either a very short-term bond or an old 30-year bond that matures next month. In either case, you will see your principal very soon. Does it matter much that prevailing interest rates have risen? No, not really. The price of your bond isn't going to be much affected.

Quality counts

High quality, investment-grade bonds, issued by solid governments or corporations, tend to be less volatile than junk bonds. This has nothing to do with interest rates but, rather, with the risk of default. When the economy is looking shaky and investor optimism fades, few people want to be holding the debt of entities that may fail. In times of recession and depression, high quality bonds may rise in value and junk bonds may fall, as people clamor for safety. Overall, the junk bonds bounce in price much more than the investment-grade bonds.

The coupon rate matters, too

Returning to the effect of interest rates on bond prices, not all bonds of like maturity have the same sensitivity to changes in prevailing rates. Aside from the maturity, you also need to consider the coupon rate. Bonds with the highest coupon rates on the market (bonds currently selling at a premium) tend to have the least volatility. Can you guess why that might be?

Imagine that you are considering the purchase of two $1,000 bonds: One matures in three years and is paying a 10 percent interest rate ($100 a year). The other also matures in three years and is paying a 5 percent rate of interest ($50 a year). Obviously, the market price of the 10 percent bond will be much higher. (It will sell at a premium vis-à-vis the 5 percent bond.) It will also be less sensitive to interest rates because you are, in effect, getting your money back sooner.

With the 5 percent bond, your investment won't pay off until the bond matures and you get your $1,000 face value (probably much more than you paid for the bond). And who knows where interest rates will be then? With the 10 percent bond, you get your investment paid back much sooner, and you are free to reinvest that money. You have much less *reinvestment* risk — the risk that you will be able to reinvest your money only at pitifully low rates.

The most volatile of bonds — those most sensitive to fluxes in interest rates — are zero-coupon bonds that pay all their interest at maturity.

Fortunately, a mathematical whiz named Frederick Macaulay gave us a formula back in the 1930s for calculating the sensitivity of a bond to prevailing interest rates. The formula works regardless of whether the bond is a zero-coupon bond or is paying regular coupons. The formula allows us to compare and contrast various bonds of various kinds to estimate their future volatility.

The wickedly complex formula measures something called *duration*. Duration tells you how much a bond will move in price if interest rates change by 1 percent.

Figuring out the duration of a bond is pretty much impossible without either a PhD in mathematics from M.I.T. or a computer. If you don't have the PhD, use the computer (just search "bond duration calculator"), or ask the broker who wants to sell you the bond to do it for you. If you're considering purchasing a bond mutual fund, you'll find the fund's average duration (sometimes called *average effective duration*) in the prospectus or other fund literature. You'll also find it on www.morningstar.com, your brokerage firm's website, or a number of sources where bond funds are contrasted and compared.

The duration formula takes into account a bond's or bonds' par value, coupon rate, yield-to-maturity, and the number of years until the bond or bonds mature. It then spits out a single number. Here is what that number means: The principal value of a bond or bond fund with a duration of, say, 6, can be expected to change 6 percent with every 1 percent change in interest rates. If prevailing interest rates go up 1 percent, the bond or bond fund should drop in value 6 percent. If interest rates fall by 1 percent, the bond or bond fund should rise 6 percent.

Of course, if you're holding an individual bond to maturity, or if you have no intention of selling off your bond fund any time in the near future, such fluctuations in price are less important than if you plan to collect your money and run any time soon.

Foreign bonds, added risk

In Chapter 9, I talk of bonds issued outside the borders of the United States. Many of these bonds are denominated not in dollars, but in yen, pounds, euros, or other currencies. When a bond is denominated in another currency, you can make out like a bandit if that currency appreciates against the dollar during the time you are holding the bond. Ah, but that gate can swing both ways: If you are holding a bond denominated in a currency that depreciates against the dollar, you may walk away from your investment with much less than you'd planned.

The coupon rate on international bonds can sometimes be very attractive — but beware. Currency exchange rates are highly unpredictable. Many international bond funds also charge way too much, but that's another story that I cover in Chapter 9 as well.

Returning to the Bonds of Babylonia

Before moving along to Part II, I'd like to return for a moment to the beginning of this chapter and to ancient Babylonia. Here's my question: Was Mr. Nabu-usabsi's 16⅔ percent return a good or bad investment?

Part of the answer lies in the ability of Mr. Nabu-sar-ashesu (the guy who got the silver) to repay the loan. History doesn't tell us if he was a good credit risk or if, in fact, the loan was ever repaid. The other part of the answer is whether that interest rate was fair for the time. Was it in line with other similar loans? We don't quite know that, either.

Interest short run, interest long run

What we do know is that lending money at a certain fixed interest rate (such as you do when you buy a bond) is often a good idea if prevailing interest rates are falling and a bad idea if interest rates are rising. At least that's true in the short run, such as a one-year period. Mr. Nabu-usabsi was probably gleeful if interest rates fell throughout the 9th year of Nebuchadnezzar.

In the longer run, it isn't clear that falling interest rates are a bond buyer's best friend. Buying bonds at a time of rising interest rates is not necessarily a mistake. I explain in Part IV how to strategize your bond buys and sells to make money in just about any kind of economy, any interest-rate environment.

Interest rates as a barometer of society's strength

A History of Interest Rates, the tome I reference at the start of this chapter, tracks the great ups and downs of interest rates over the centuries. It covers *everything*. Starting with ancient Babylonia, then onward to medieval Europe, it moves along to America's colonial days and leads you to the present. The one conclusion that can be drawn, say the authors, is that interest rates generally show a progressive decline as each society develops and thrives, and then they rise sharply as each society declines and falls.

In Ancient Rome, for example, prevailing short-term interest rates were above 8 percent until about 250 b.c. They then fell and continued to fall until, at the height of the Roman Empire

(100 b.c.–100 a.d.), loans could be had for about 4 percent. As the empire fell apart over the ensuing centuries, interest rates rose to over 12 percent by the fourth century. Similar patterns can be seen in Ancient Greece and Babylonia, and in most societies since.

The tie between interest rates and society's fortunes is easily explained. When the times are uncertain, lenders demand more in compensation for tying up their money. After all, anything could happen in the interim. When the barbarians are knocking at the gate, you aren't going to buy any low-interest bonds in the hopes of a comfortable retirement watching gladiator games in the Coliseum.

Interest past, interest future

Historical records make it clear that interest rates have fluctuated all across the board over the millennia. But lending your money (as you do when you buy a bond), if done wisely, is a time-honored way of making your money work for you. Throughout the rest of this book, I show you exactly how to do that.

Part II
Numerous and Varied Ways to Make Money in Bonds

The 5th Wave   By Rich Tennant

"I'm not sure – I like the global bonds with rotating dollar signs, but the dancing municipal bonds look good too."

In this part . . .

In the next five chapters, you get a good picture of the major categories of bonds, including Treasuries (Chapter 5), corporate bonds (Chapter 6), agencies (Chapter 7), and municipal bonds (Chapter 8). Should none of the major categories suit you, I provide in Chapter 9 a thumbnail sketch of some of the more unusual, sometimes quirky kinds of bond offerings available, such as church bonds and catastrophe bonds.

In each chapter, you discover the nuances that make each bond category unique. I show you why certain kinds of bonds pay higher rates of interest than others and, at the same time, may carry more risk. You can start to zero in on the kinds of bonds that make the most sense for you — the kinds of bonds that will make your portfolio shine.

Chapter 5

"Risk-Free" Investing:
U.S. Treasury Bonds

- -

In This Chapter

▶ Sizing up the government bond market

▶ Trusting that U.S. debt is still a pretty safe bet

▶ Deciding whether Treasuries belong in your portfolio

▶ Understanding the mechanics of buying and selling

- -

Although not from a terribly religious family, I did have a bar mitzvah. As Jewish boys have done for several millennia, I stood before the congregation and recited from the teachings of the Torah, whereupon the rabbi blessed me and told me that I had become a man.

Who was I to argue?

Soon following the rabbi's pronouncement, I found myself in a large, Long Island catering hall where I was smiled upon by the masses, told *mazel tov!* ("way to go!" in Hebrew), and handed many crisp white envelopes. Much later that memorable night, I went home, sat on my bed, and opened those envelopes. Out poured U.S. savings bond after U.S. savings bond. I was rich!

Or so I thought.

Little did I know at the time that a freshly minted U.S. savings bond with $100 emblazoned all over it isn't worth $100 at all. Adults like giving savings bonds as gifts to young people because, well, I guess they figure that young people are gullible. Even smart 13-year-olds who read the Torah can get fooled. The ancient teachings may help us to know right from wrong, but, alas, they say nothing whatsoever about U.S. government debt securities.

Some things a young boy-turned-man just has to figure out for himself. And I eventually figured out that all those savings bonds strewn across my bed were worth only half as much as whatever denominations were printed on them. (I'm not complaining, mind you. I'm grateful for that money, but discovering that I had only half as much as I thought came as a bit of a blow.) Over the years, I've learned a number of other things about savings bonds and other Treasury debt securities, and in this chapter, I share that knowledge.

Please join me. You don't have to be Jewish.

Exploring the Many Ways of Investing with Uncle Sam

Umpteen different kinds of debt securities are issued by the U.S. Treasury. *Savings bonds,* which can be purchased for small amounts and, until recently, came in certificate form (making for nice, if not slightly deceptive, bar mitzvah and birthday gifts), are but one kind. In fact, when investment people speak of *Treasuries,* they usually are not talking about savings bonds but about larger-denomination bonds known formally as *Treasury bills, Treasury notes,* and *Treasury bonds.* (I explain the differences among bills, notes, and bonds very shortly.) All of these are now issued only in electronic (sometimes called *book-entry*) form.

That's right. As of the start of 2012, those glorious U.S. savings bonds — which bar mitzvah boys and other youngsters had received as gifts since 1935 — are available in electronic form only. Aside from their cyber commonality, all U.S. Treasury debt securities, whether a $50 savings bond or a $1,000 Treasury note, have four other important things in common:

- ✔ Every bond, an IOU of sorts from Uncle Sam, is backed by the "full faith and credit" of the U.S. government and, therefore, is considered by many investors — Americans and Chinese alike — to be one of the safest bets around.

- ✔ Because it's assumed that any principal you invest is safe from default, Treasury bonds, of whatever kind, tend to pay relatively modest rates of interest — lower than other comparable bonds, such as corporate bonds, that may put your principal at some risk.

- ✔ True, the U.S. government is very unlikely to go bankrupt anytime soon, but Treasury bonds are nonetheless still subject to other risks inherent in the bond market. Prices on Treasury bonds, especially those with long-term maturities, can swoop up and down like hungry hawks in response to such things as prevailing interest rates and investor confidence in the economy.

✔ All interest on U.S. government bonds is off-limits to state and local tax authorities (just as the interest on most municipal bonds is off-limits to the Internal Revenue Service). However, except in rare cases, you are required to pay federal tax.

Beyond these similarities, the differences among U.S. government debt securities are many and, in some cases, like night and day. Only because I started this chapter talking about savings bonds, I address those first.

Savings bonds as gifts or small investments

Until recently, U.S. savings bonds had been popular as gifts in part because they were sold as nicely designed certificates. On January 1, 2012, however, they became electronic entities, just like other Treasury securities. It remains to be seen if they will still be desirable as gifts in this less attractive, less personal format. You may now buy your electronic savings bonds straight from the official Treasury website: www.treasurydirect.gov.

If your purchase is intended as a gift, the website allows you to print a gift certificate, which may be presented in lieu of the once keepsake-quality, elaborately designed bond. If I have another bar mitzvah (not likely, but you never know), and a certain Mr. Homer Simpson wants to present me with a $100 U.S. savings bond, he can log onto the Treasury website, pay by credit card, and hand me a certificate he was able to print on his home computer.

Of course, savings bonds can be more than just gifts: You can buy one for yourself. People do so, despite their awfully low interest rates of late. Savings bonds start as low as $25. Beyond that, you don't need to pick a specific denomination. If you wish to invest, say, $43.45, go for it, or if you want to invest $312.56, that's fine too. Any amount over $25 but under $10,000 (per individual, per year) is accepted.

Note that these "denomination-free" bonds are available only through the Treasury website and available only for savings bonds. The other Treasury securities (bills, notes, or bonds) can also be purchased through the website, and elsewhere, but only in specific increments.

Aside from the ability to invest a small amount, savings bonds are also unique among Treasury debt securities in that they are strictly non-marketable. When you buy a U.S. savings bond, you either put your own name and Social Security number on the bond or the name and Social Security number of the giftee. The only person entitled to receive interest is the one whose name appears on the bond. The bond itself (just like an airline ticket) cannot be sold to another buyer — in stark contrast to Treasury bills and bonds that can, and often do, pass hands more often than poker chips.

Through history, there have been various kinds of savings bonds. At present, the Treasury produces only two: EE Series bonds and I bonds. Some others you may have stored away in your dresser drawers may include E Series bonds and HH bonds. Each has its own characteristics.

EE bonds

EE bonds (from 2001 to 2011, many were called "Patriot Bonds") are the most traditional kind of savings bond — the kind I received on my bar mitzvah (although they were called something different back then). Series EE bonds carry a face value of twice their purchase price. They are *accrual bonds,* which means they earn interest as the years roll on even though you aren't seeing any cash. You can pay taxes on that interest as it accrues, but in most cases it makes more sense to defer paying the taxes until you decide to redeem the bond. Uncle Sam allows you to do that.

Series EE bonds issued prior to May 2005 pay various rates of interest depending on the date of the bond. Most of these rates are based on fairly complicated formulas and fluctuate over time. If you own a pre-May 2005 savings bond and you aren't sure what kind of interest the bond is paying, the best thing to do is to look it up on the Treasury website, www.treasurydirect.gov. EE bonds issued during May 2005 or afterward pay a fixed interest rate. At the time I'm typing this paragraph, that rate is a rather unimpressive 0.60 percent. I don't know what it will be when you are reading this chapter, but I can guarantee that it will be modest.

EE bonds are nonredeemable for the first year you own them, and if you hold them for fewer than five years, you surrender three months of interest. Any individual can buy up to $10,000 in EE savings bonds a year. Interest compounds twice a year for 30 years.

If you use your savings bonds to fund an education, the interest may be tax-free.

Russell's recommendation: Historically, savings bonds have paid a rate of interest that has barely kept up with inflation. Therefore, you don't want to make them a major part of your investment scheme. If you already have savings bonds, you may want to consider swapping them for a higher yielding investment. If you wish to keep them, consider opening an account at www.treasurydirect.gov and turning your paper bonds into electronic securities. That way, you won't need to worry about them getting lost or destroyed.

I bonds

These babies are built to buttress inflation. The I Series bonds offer a fixed rate of return plus an adjustment for rising prices. Every May 1 and November 1, the Treasury announces both the fixed rate for all new I bonds and the inflation adjustment for all new and existing I bonds. While I'm writing this, the fixed rate is 0 percent, and the inflation adjustment is an annual 3.06 percent.

After you buy an I bond, the fixed rate is yours for the life of the bond (since the current rate is zero, you probably aren't breaking out the champagne right now). The inflation rate adjusts every six months. You collect all your interest only after cashing in the bond. (That is called *accrual* interest.)

The rules and parameters for I bonds are pretty much the same as they are for EEs: You have to hold them a year, and if you sell within five years, you pay a penalty. There's a limit to how many I bonds you can invest in — $10,000 a year, per person. And in certain circumstances, the proceeds may become tax-free if used for education expenses.

Russell's recommendation: Because the rate of inflation can vary dramatically from one six-month period to another, at times I bonds make for fabulous short-term investments. In November 2005, for example, following a spike in the price of oil after Hurricane Katrina, the official inflation rate shot up, and I bonds were paying a very impressive 6.73 percent. At that point, I was recommending that anyone who had cash to invest might want to consider them very seriously. But, by the following May, with inflation having cooled, the yield on I bonds dropped rather precipitously to 2.43 percent. They were no longer such a hot investment — you could have done much better with a bank CD.

If you plan to hold I bonds as a long-term investment — longer than a year or two — you should be more concerned with the fixed rate (which will be in effect throughout the life of the bond) than the inflation adjustment (which will vary). Remember that if you cash out before five years, you'll pay a penalty of three months' interest. You can purchase I Bonds at the Treasury website, `www.treasurydirect.gov`.

Savings bonds for education

The interest on savings bonds — both EE and I bonds — may be tax-free if you use the proceeds to pay for higher education expenses. The guidelines are fairly complex, and you're eligible only if your income falls below a certain limit. Currently, for single taxpayers, the tax exclusion begins to be reduced at a $70,100 modified adjusted gross income and is eliminated for adjusted gross incomes of $85,100 and above. For married taxpayers filing jointly, the tax exclusion begins to be reduced with a $105,100 modified adjusted gross income and is eliminated at $135,100. If you're uncertain whether you qualify, speak to your tax adviser.

Check your savings bond stash for dead wood

According to www.treasurydirect.gov, the following savings bonds no longer earn any interest. Cash them in!

Series	Issue Date
E	All issues
H	All issues
HH	January 1980–January 1992
Savings Notes	All issues
A, B, C, D, F, G, J, K	All issues

The dinosaurs

Other kinds of savings bonds pre-date today's EE and I bonds. Each series of the past has its own peculiarities, but because you won't be buying any of them, I don't need to get into detail. Suffice to say that some of the older bonds are still paying interest, and others are not. (See the sidebars "Check your savings bond stash for dead wood" and "Savings bonds don't pay interest forever!" for more info.) If you have any questions on the status of a savings bond you have tucked away in the back of your sock drawer, you can simply type the serial number into the Savings Bond Calculator at www.treasurydirect.gov or jot down the serial number and write a letter to:

> Bureau of the Public Debt
> P.O. Box 7012
> Parkersburg, WV 26106-7012

The Bureau of the Public Debt needs a written and signed request from the owner of the bond, at which point it will tell you whether the bond is still earning interest, when it will stop paying interest, and how much you could redeem it for today.

Treasury bills, notes, and bonds for more serious investing

About 99 percent of the approximately $15 trillion in outstanding Treasury debt is made up not of savings bonds but of *marketable* (tradable) securities known as bills, notes, and bonds. This "bills, notes, and bonds" stuff can be a little confusing because technically they are all bonds. They are all backed by the full faith and credit of the U.S. government. They are all issued electronically (you don't get a fancy piece of paper). They can all be purchased either directly from the Treasury, through a broker, or in fund form. They can all trade like hotcakes. The major difference among them is the time you need to wait to collect your principal:

- Treasury bills have maturities of a year or less.
- Treasury notes are issued with maturities from two to ten years.
- Treasury bonds are long-term investments that have maturities of 10 to 30 years from their issue date.

The bills carry denominations of $100 but are sold on the open market at a discount from their face value. You get the full amount when the bill matures. The notes and bonds, on the other hand, are sold at their face value, have a fixed interest rate, and kick off interest payments once every six months. The minimum denomination for notes and bonds is $1,000.

Russell's suggestion: The main difference among various Treasury offerings is the maturity. Generally, but not always, the longer the term, the higher the rate of interest. Therefore, the longer you can tie up your money, the greater your investment returns are likely to be. So one of the first questions you need to ask yourself before investing in Treasuries (or most other bonds, for that matter) is the following: *When might I need to cash this baby out?*

Keep in mind that you don't have to hold any of these securities (bills, notes, or bonds) until maturity. You can, in fact, cash out at any point. The more time remaining before your bond is fully matured, the more its price can fluctuate and the more you risk losing money. (It's because of this risk, primarily, that I put the quotation marks around "Risk-Free" in the heading of this chapter — just in case you were wondering.)

Savings bonds don't pay interest forever!

Here's how long savings bonds earn interest based on their series and issue date:

Series	Issue Date	Number of Years Bonds Earn Interest
E	May 1941–November 1965	40 years
	December 1965–June 1980	30 years
EE	All issues	30 years
H	June 1952–January 1957	29 years, 8 months
	February 1957–December 1979	30 years
HH	All issues	20 years
I	All issues	30 years
Savings Notes	All issues	30 years

Treasury Inflation-Protected Securities (TIPS)

Like the I bonds, Treasury Inflation-Protected Securities (TIPS), introduced in 1997, receive both interest and a twice-yearly kick up of principal for inflation. As with interest on other Treasury securities, interest on TIPS is free from state and local income taxes. Federal income tax, however, must be coughed up each year on both the interest payments and the growth in principal.

TIPS, unlike I bonds, are transferable. You can buy TIPS directly from the Treasury or through a broker. (More detailed purchasing instructions are coming later in this chapter.) They are currently being issued with terms of 5, 10, and 30 years, although plenty of 20-year term TIPS are in circulation. The minimum investment is $100.

One of the sweet things about TIPS is that if inflation goes on a rampage, your principal moves north right along with it. If *deflation,* a lowering of prices, occurs — though it hasn't since the 1930s — you won't get any inflation adjustment, but you won't get a deflation adjustment, either. You'll get back at least the face value of the bond.

TIPS sound great, and in many ways they are. Be aware though, that the coupon rate on TIPS varies with market conditions and tends to be minimal — perhaps a couple of percentage points . . . or less. If inflation is calmer than expected moving into the future, you will almost certainly do better with traditional Treasuries. If inflation turns out to be higher than expected, your TIPS will be the stars of your fixed-income portfolio.

Also remember that TIPS with longer maturities can be quite volatile, even more so than other bonds. Steven Pollock, a Certified Financial Planner and a fellow National Association of Personal Financial Advisors–registered financial planner, has been carefully tracking the ups and downs of TIPS as compared to nominal Treasury bonds. His take is this: "The market for TIPS is more driven by investor sentiment than is the large Treasury market. TIPS returns have been over 70 percent more volatile than nominal bonds." But, he adds, the returns for TIPs in past years have been higher than for nominal bonds, as well.

Keep in mind what Pollock's words mean: TIPS are designed to keep you even with inflation, and they may do just that, but there is no guarantee. We may, for example, experience an inflation rate of 5 percent over the course of the next year. In that case, your $1,000 invested in TIPS will get you $50 from Uncle Sam. On that score, you have your guarantee. But if investor sentiment turns away from TIPS, your principal may potentially drop by $50 or even more. So as you can see, TIPS are not manna from heaven.

U.S. Treasuries are the Mickey Mice of the international investment world

Never mind Mickey Mouse T-shirts and McDonald's hamburgers — the U.S. product that foreigners are hottest for these days is the U.S. Treasury bond. The percentage of all U.S. government bonds held by non-U.S. citizens increased from about one-quarter a decade ago to something approaching half today (roughly $5 trillion out of $10 trillion). Some economists are very thankful for this foreign investment because it arguably fills a desperately needed role. The American people, strapped by their medical and college bills, aren't saving, and without saving, there can't be economic growth. But other pundits argue that all that U.S. debt in foreign hands is creating a potential debt bomb. They argue that the United States is becoming terribly vulnerable, its economy resting in the hands of foreigners who could at any moment turn evil (as foreigners often do in movies) and crush us by suddenly dumping all their Treasury bonds.

I'm not losing any sleep over this one. It's not as if all those bonds are in the hands of one rogue nation, led by a crazed colonel in fatigues. They are in the hands of many nations that by and large embrace capitalism (yes, that includes China), and besides, they can't stand each other. Heck, if the Chinese, who own about a quarter of all foreign-owned Treasury bonds, tried to dump them, the Japanese, who own almost as much as the Chinese, would buy those bonds up just to spite the Chinese. If the Japanese were to start dumping, the Koreans would buy them up just to anger the Japanese. And if the Canadians were to start dumping, eh? Canadians are way too polite and would never do such a thing. We should worry more about other economic issues, such as why those medical and college bills are so astronomical, than we should the exportation of our national debt.

Russell's suggestion: Over the very long haul, I would fully expect the return on TIPS to be roughly the same as that on other similar-maturity Treasuries. But on a year-to-year basis, the two kinds of bonds will flip-flop. Flip-flopping — another word for diversification — is a good thing! I generally recommend to clients that about one-quarter of their bond portfolio be devoted to inflation-protected securities. I would recommend less than that to anyone who has a portfolio with lots of stocks (and, perhaps, commodities and real estate), as these have a good track record of keeping up with inflation. I might recommend something slightly more than one-quarter of the fixed-income allocation for someone with an all-bond or close to an all-bond portfolio.

Easing Your Fears of Default

The U.S. government, despite carrying a mountainous load of debt, is not going under anytime soon. That's because there's a lot of money in the United States (the gross domestic product of California alone is larger than that of all but six countries), and the federal government can always raise taxes. So why, in August 2011, did Standard & Poor's — in a move that received more publicity than a royal wedding or an Elvis sighting — lower the rating on U.S. Treasuries from AAA (the highest rating) to AA?

More than anything, it was the raters' fear of possible political gridlock in Washington. If push ever comes to shove, and the U.S. government can't pay off its debt obligations without raising taxes, and Congress won't allow taxes to be raised because certain congressional members prove to be more dogmatic than the craziest of cultists . . . maybe then it is theoretically possible that holders of Treasury bonds could get stiffed. But S&P realizes that that scenario is very unlikely (cultists don't need to be concerned with votes; members of Congress do). And that is why the federal government still has an S&P AA rating, while other agencies still rate Treasuries the safest investment in the land.

I think it's fair to say that you don't need to concern yourself nearly as much with the prospect of default when you shop for Treasuries as you do when shopping for corporate or municipal bonds. (I cover corporates and munis in Chapters 6 and 8.) Far from it. At least for the time being, and for the foreseeable future, don't worry about default on Treasuries other than to consider it a remote — very remote — possibility.

Deciding Whether, When, and How to Invest in Treasuries

I'm not a big fan of trying to pick stocks; I happen to think that doing so has little value and looks a lot like gambling. (If you've read any of my other books, you already know I'm a much bigger fan of investing in index funds.) And picking Treasury bonds? It makes about as much sense as flapping your arms and expecting to go into orbit. That's because the markets for Treasuries are extremely *efficient:* So many buyers and sellers are involved, and any information worth having is so public, that any true "deal" is very hard to find.

The only really important questions you should ask yourself about Treasuries are the following:

- ✔ Do I want Treasuries in my portfolio and, if so, how much?
- ✔ Do I want short-term, intermediate-term, or long-term Treasuries?
- ✔ Do I want inflation protection with my Treasuries?
- ✔ How do I go about buying a Treasury?

In this section, I help you consider the first three questions. The fourth gets answered in the final section of this chapter.

Figuring out whether you want Treasuries

Here, I focus on why Treasuries likely belong in your portfolio and what kind of returns you can realistically expect.

Turning to Treasuries in times of turmoil

When you buy Treasury bonds, not only do you get the full faith and credit of the U.S. government assuring you your money back, but you get other perks as well. For example, there's no chance of an early call should interest rates fall. And the *liquidity* — the ability to sell your bond on the open market — is downright oceanic. As far as another agency, such as Moody's or Fitch, downgrading the rating on Treasuries, or S&P downgrading again, simply look at what happened after the S&P downgrade in 2011: Treasury prices soared for months afterward. The problems of downgrading (and the often resulting price tumbles), callability, and lack of liquidity are alien to investors in Treasuries (but all too common to investors in corporate bonds and municipal bonds, which I discuss in Chapters 6 and 8 respectively).

Perhaps the most succulent thing about Treasuries, however, is their delightfully low correlation to the stock market. When the world is in turmoil and the economy starts to quiver, stocks tend to tumble. But Treasuries — as money pours in from investors looking for a safe place to hide — start to shine. History has seen this scenario over and over.

According to data from Ibbotson Associates, a Morningstar company, during the darkest economic days of September 1929 through June 1932, long-term Treasuries showed a total annualized return of 4.84 percent. Not bad for a time when the general price level was dropping. During the bear market of September 2000 through September 2002, Treasuries returned an annual 12.81 percent as people flocked to safety and prevailing interest rates fell. In 2008, when the stock market plunged by nearly 40 percent and junk bonds took a very serious beating, long-term Treasury bonds returned nearly 26 percent. And in 2011, the very year that the S&P downgraded Treasuries from AAA to AA, the government bonds again jumped 28 percent.

Keeping expectations realistic

The downside to Treasuries is this: modest returns over the very long run, and modest returns (almost certainly) looking forward. Since 1926, the U.S. stock market has seen an average annual return of 9.9 percent. Long-term government bonds have seen an average annual return of 5.5 percent. These numbers are before inflation. After inflation, the numbers move quite far apart: 6.7 percent annual return for the stock market and 2.4 percent for Treasuries — a considerable real-return advantage for stocks. (Inflation eats away at your investment every day of the year, while interest is paid semiannually, so the formula for figuring post-inflation returns is a bit complicated. Trust me, the numbers above are correct.)

In recent decades, Treasuries have done spectacularly well, and the performance of stocks has been especially poor. In the 30 years from 1981 to 2011, long-term Treasuries have seen an annual return of 11.03 percent, which is 0.05 percent above the S&P 500.

The reasons for this historical anomaly are several:

- ✔ People flock to safety in times of turmoil, and there has been quite a bit of turmoil lately. Not since the Great Depression has the stock market seen the volatility of the past several years.

- ✔ While the U.S. government lost its S&P AAA rating, so have other countries, such as France and Austria. Several European nations, including Spain and Italy, saw their ratings drop not by one, but by several notches. So where could investors go for safety if not the United States?

- ✔ Perhaps the largest contributor to high Treasury returns has been the steady drop in general interest rates over the past years. Do you remember how, in the early 1980s, you could get double-digit returns on a mere CD? When interest rates fall, bond yields go up (see Chapter 4). Ten-year Treasuries are now yielding roughly 2 percent; in 1981, they were yielding about 14 percent.

Can the Treasury rally continue? No, not really. The rally has most likely run out of steam. Long-term Treasuries, as a result of their sharp price increases in past years, are (as of 2012) yielding lower interest rates than ever. Regardless of what happens in the stock markets (and no one can *really* know, can they?), the future of Treasuries — not in the next year, but in the next decade or so — is at least somewhat predictable. Yes, world turmoil may continue, but interest rates cannot keep dropping as they have in the past. The return you get on Treasuries in the next decade will very, very likely return to its historical norm — that is, modest.

The yield curve and what it means

Every amateur weathercaster knows that black clouds above mean a stormy day ahead. For economists, an *inverted yield curve* serves as a black cloud indicating stormy economic times ahead.

An inverted yield curve simply means that short-term Treasuries are paying higher yields than long-term Treasuries. In normal times, longer-term bonds pay higher interest rates than short-term bonds. That's because investors demand higher returns for agreeing to tie up their money for longer and to take the inherent risks that doing so involves.

Why might things occasionally turn on their head? The common belief is that inverted yield curves result when bond buyers collectively get nervous about the economic future. To alleviate their anxiety, they commit their money to long-term bonds. That way, they figure, when things tank and interest rates drop (as they often do in times of recession), their existing bonds will be worth more.

Are bond buyers right? Can they foretell a recession coming? Historically, the answer is sometimes yes and sometimes no. While an inverted yield curve has preceded a number of recessions, there have also been times, such as in 1995 and again in 1998, when yield-curve inversions were followed by a decidedly robust year. Like all other economic indicators, the bond yield curve, although better than tea leaves at predicting the future, is far from perfect.

Here is what a normal bond yield curve looks like and what an inverted one looks like. Note that what you're looking at, unlike a stock chart, does not show price movements over time. Rather, it shows the current interest being paid on short-term bonds versus long-term bonds.

A Normal Yield Curve

An Inverted Yield Curve

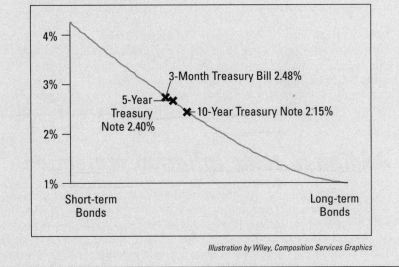

Illustration by Wiley, Composition Services Graphics

Russell's suggestion: Yes, you want Treasuries in your portfolio. Given their modest expected returns, you don't want overkill, however. Some Treasuries, some higher-yielding corporate or other bonds, some stock, some commodities, and maybe some real estate make the most sense for most people. As for the fixed-income side of your portfolio, depending on your risk profile, you may want to put somewhere between one-quarter and one-half of your total bond allocation into Treasuries (see Chapter 13).

Picking your own maturity

Just like the question of bonds versus stocks, and government bonds versus corporate bonds, the question of maturity is largely a question of how much risk you care to stomach. In general, the more years till a bond's maturity, the more volatile the price swings.

Not only are price swings an issue when buying a long-term bond (granted, less of an issue if you plan to hold the bond till maturity), but long-term bonds carry a much greater *reinvestment* risk. In other words, if you're holding a 20-year Treasury bond and the coupon rate is 3 percent, you have no guarantee that you'll be able to reinvest your twice-yearly interest payments at 3 percent — at least not in anything as safe as Treasuries. If prevailing interest rates drop, you stand to lose.

Of course, the longer the term of the bond, generally the higher the coupon rate. At this particular point in history, with interest rates so low, reinvestment risk is definitely lower than it has been in the past. So choosing a maturity can be a very tricky decision. Many financial professionals suggest a compromise and going primarily with intermediate-term Treasuries (seven- to ten-year maturities).

Russell's suggestion: For the individual investor, short-term Treasuries generally make sense only when the rate those bonds are paying is higher than that of money market funds and bank CDs. Sometimes that will be the case, other times not. Long-term Treasuries can be wickedly volatile, and in times of extremely low interest rates, that volatility could potentially lose you a lot of money. Shoot for the middle ground, with mostly intermediate Treasuries.

Adding in some inflation protection

As I'm writing this chapter, the current yield on a traditional ten-year Treasury is about 2 percent. The yield on ten-year TIPS is about zero, but the principal on TIPS will be inflation-adjusted as the years go by. I look at each. I compare. All things being equal, if inflation runs at 2 percent or greater, I'll do better with TIPS. If inflation falls beneath that point — the *break-even point* — conventional Treasury bonds will do better.

Treasury strips

One kind of Treasury issue is available only through brokers, and that is called a *strip*. A Treasury strip is something of a strange duck. It is, in essence, a single interest payment of a bond that has been "stripped" from the rest of the bond.

For example, a $1,000, 20-year Treasury bond paying 3 percent offers 40 semiannual payments of $15 and one final principal payment of $1,000. If you want to invest in such a bond but have no need for immediate income, you may purchase a strip, which would offer you, say, only the final interest payment and the principal.

Strips are sold, like Treasury bills, at a deep discount. And that, to the individual investor, is

their main advantage. You don't need to invest very much to assure yourself a specific sum in the future. You may, for example, pay $300 for a strip that will pay you back $1,000 in 30 years, representing an annual interest rate of 4.095 percent. Debt securities that work this way are called *zero-coupon* securities. Zero-coupons can be very volatile. If you need to cash out early, you may not get nearly what you'd anticipated. They are also not very tax friendly. You're taxed on the interest as if you are paid annually, even though you get no cash. You may want to consider a strip only for your retirement account.

What's my best investment? Who the heck knows.

Russell's suggestion: Unless you can tell the future and predict interest rates and inflation (um, you can't), you want both traditional bonds *and* inflation-protected bonds in your portfolio.

Entering the Treasury Marketplace

Buying a Treasury bill, note, bond, or inflation-protected security is a heck of a lot easier than buying most other bonds. With Treasuries, you needn't worry about such things as credit rating, callability, liquidity, and getting socked with high broker markups. (I talk about all these delightful aspects of bond-buying in the next several chapters.)

Uncle Sam's bonds can be purchased directly from, and sold to, the old man himself. Or not. It's your call.

Buying direct or through a broker

Buying directly from, or selling to, the federal government is simply a matter of logging onto the website www.treasurydirect.gov. Or, if you prefer to do it the old fashioned way, you can contact Treasury Direct at 1-800-722-2678, from 8 a.m. to 6 p.m. Eastern time. (For savings bonds, call 1-800-245-2804.)

Buying and selling direct is certainly the most economical way to go. In fact, you pay no charge for any transactions. You can keep all your Treasuries with Treasury Direct, and you incur no fee.

The only reason to go through a broker, really, would be if you have a compulsion to house all your assets under one roof. Most brokers charge a minimal amount for dealing in Treasuries.

The market for Treasuries is extremely *efficient,* which means that it involves so many buyers and sellers and bonds that the chance of finding a deal (as you may — or may not — in the corporate bond market) is rather remote. What you pay for a ten-year Treasury is pretty much what the next guy is going to pay. Your yield is pretty much what the next guy is going to get.

Before you deal with any bond broker, whether for Treasuries or any other bond, please read Chapter 15. For Treasuries, I'd rather see you buy direct.

Choosing a new or used bond

Does it make much difference whether you buy new (*on-the-run*) or old (*off-the-run*) Treasuries? In other words, if you want to make a 10-year investment in Treasuries, does it matter whether you buy a new 10-year note or an old 20-year bond that has 10 years till maturity? No, not much. The yields should be very, very similar. The only difference, really, is that when buying the old bond, you'll have to go through a broker, and the broker will likely charge you a nominal fee.

No repose for investors in repos

Repos, short for *repurchase agreements,* are contracts for the sale and future repurchase of a financial asset, most usually Treasury securities. The repo market is huge and complex, and most of the players are professional investment types. For the average person with a mortgage to pay and mouths to feed, plunking money into repos is potentially dangerous business. But if risk is your middle name, you can enter the repo market through most large brokerage houses.

In essence, you buy a barrelful of Treasuries for little money. That's known as *leveraging.* If you're familiar with buying stocks on margin, it's somewhat similar to that. But instead of banking on a company stock's rise or fall, you'll be banking on a rise or fall in interest rates, which in turn affects the price of Treasuries. If interest rates fall and bond prices go up, you can make out like a bandit. If you're wrong, however, you pay the piper. The broker will be lending you money to finance this speculation; make sure you ask for the repo rate of interest, which is generally less than the interest on other kinds of borrowing (as it should be, because the broker has your leveraged bonds as collateral).

Tapping Treasuries through mutual funds and exchange-traded funds

U.S. investors have hundreds of federal government bond mutual funds and exchange-traded funds from which to choose. You can also buy your government bonds packed in something called a *unit investment trust*. Whichever of these three options you choose, you could, in a flash, own a bevy of Treasuries, either with similar or different maturities, conventional or inflation-adjusted. If you choose your fund well, your instant diversification comes at very little cost.

Diversification of Treasury bonds isn't as important as it is with, say, corporate high-yield bonds, but still . . . for the minimal cost of some bond funds (as little as 10 *basis points*, or 10/100 percent a year in operating expenses), they make a darned good option for most investors. I share my pick of favorite Treasury funds in Chapter 16.

Chapter 6

Industrial Returns: Corporate Bonds

. . . .

In This Chapter

▶ Understanding the pros and cons of lending money to men in fancy suits

▶ Knowing what credit ratings are all about

▶ Weighing the issues of callability and convertability

▶ Junking your preconceptions of junk bonds

. . . .

*O*h sure, the strength of our economy and the vigor of our industry rely much on the progress of science, the foundations of democracy, and the labors of a motivated and educated workforce. I don't mean to belittle any of that, but what *really* moves our economy and bolsters our industry, the single most driving force in capitalism, without which we'd all be living in huts and eating cold gruel, is *OPM:* Other People's Money.

New businesses start every day, with the initial funding typically coming from the savings of an intrepid entrepreneur or the good graces of a supportive mom and dad. But to move a seedling of a business from the garage (where Bill Gates started) to the storefront on Main Street to the malls or industrial parks of America requires OPM. And OPM comes to a business mainly from two sources: selling shares of the business to stockholders, or borrowing money from bondholders.

In this chapter, I ask you to consider becoming a corporate bondholder. By so doing, you can help drive our economy and our society to new heights and spare the masses from having to eat gruel. Well, maybe. That's perhaps an overstatement. And possibly, it's beside the point. Let's forget about society and gruel for the moment and just talk about what corporate bonds can do for your personal wealth, shall we?

Why Invest in These Sometimes Pains-in-the-Butt?

To put it bluntly, corporate bonds can be something of a pain in the pants, especially when compared to Treasury bonds (see Chapter 5). Here's what you need to worry about when investing in corporate bonds:

- ✔ **The solidity of the company issuing the bond:** If the company goes down, you may lose some or all of your money. Even if the company doesn't go down but merely limps, you can lose money.

- ✔ **Callability:** There's a chance that the issuing company may call in your bond and spit your money back in your face at some terribly inopportune moment (such as when prevailing interest rates have just taken a tumble).

- ✔ **Liquidity:** Will someone be there to offer you a fair price if and when you need to sell? Will selling the bond require paying some broker a big, fat markup?

- ✔ **Economic upheaval:** In tough economic times, when many companies are closing their doors (and the stocks in your portfolio are plummeting), your bonds may decide to join in the unhappy nosedive, *en masse*. There go your hopes for an easy, sleep-in-late retirement.

So why even mess with corporate bonds?

Ah . . . that is a question that some of the world's most prominent investment experts have also asked, and they don't all come up with the same answer. Some argue that corporate bonds are indeed worth all the hassle and doubt because the higher rates of interest they pay make them preferable to Treasuries. Others argue that the difference in interest rates between corporate bonds and Treasuries (known as *the spread*) isn't worth the potential trouble of holding corporates.

Comparing corporate bonds to Treasuries

You may ask yourself why I start a chapter on corporate bonds by comparing them to Treasuries. There are, of course, other kinds of bonds. Municipals (which I cover in Chapter 8) are often appropriate for people in higher income brackets, but they are generally not a good choice for tax-advantaged accounts such as IRAs and 401(k) plans, where the vast majority of Americans have most of their savings. Agency bonds (Chapter 7) can sometimes substitute for

Treasuries, but their inordinate complexities make them inappropriate for many individual investors. High-yield bonds, otherwise known as *junk bonds* (which I discuss later in this chapter), don't add much stability to a portfolio. And international bonds (Chapter 9) are good for added diversification but, largely because of currency flux, should probably play a limited role in your investment strategies.

No, when it comes to adding stability to a portfolio — the number one reason that bonds belong in your portfolio, if you ask me — Treasuries and investment-grade (high quality) corporate bonds are your two best choices. They may have saved your grandparents from destitution during the Great Depression. They may have spared your 401(k) when most stocks hit the skids in 2000–2002 or when your savings again took a nosedive in 2008.

But which is preferable: bonds issued by the government, or bonds issued by the for-profit sector of our economy?

Hearing it from the naysayers

Some people, including David Swensen, chief investment officer of Yale University, see little virtue in corporate debt. Swensen argues in *Unconventional Success: A Fundamental Approach to Personal Investment* (Free Press) that corporations have a primary duty to their shareholders to make as much money as possible — and that means the financial officers have a duty to make sure that their bondholders never get a fair shake. Those who buy corporate bonds, thinking they are getting something for nothing with the higher yields than they would get on Treasuries, are deluding themselves. Swensen writes:

> At the end of the day, excess returns prove illusory as credit risk, illiquidity, and optionality work against the holder of corporate obligations, providing less than nothing to the corporate bond investor.

"In general, I'd say that Swensen is right, and the modestly excess yield you're going to get in corporates is not worth it," says Don Taylor, PhD, CFP, who teaches finance at The University of Pennsylvania. "With Treasuries, you're getting the full faith and credit of the U.S. government, and you're buying an asset class that is not correlated to the stock market," he says. "You're going to get better diversification — and you're especially going to get better protection in a worst-case market scenario."

But then there's the other side of the argument.

Taking a cue from the corporate fan club

"Those people who make unequivocal statements about never buying corporate bonds because the excess return over Treasuries is so paltry are generally not the same people who have to live on a limited fixed income," says Marilyn

Cohen, president of Envision Capital Management, an investment advisory firm in southern California specializing in fixed income. "The experts are generally pretty well-heeled people, and it's hard for them to relate to the small investor, especially the retired small investor, who is seeing his grocery prices go up every week and desperately needs a few extra *basis points* just to pay the bills." (One basis point equals 1/100 of a percentage point.)

Dan Fuss, vice chairman of Loomis, Sayles & Company, a highly regarded investment management company, says there's nothing wrong with Treasuries, for sure, but despite the credit risk and the frequent callability features, corporate bonds often offer real economic opportunity — "especially for those willing to do some work, and uncover value in the marketplace." The veteran fund manager isn't just blowing smoke. His flagship Loomis Sayles Bond Fund (LSBRX), which taps mostly higher quality corporate bonds, has a 20-year annualized return of more than 10 percent, placing it far, far ahead of most similar funds. (I talk more about Loomis Sayles and other bond funds in Chapter 16. In Chapter 21, I feature a Q&A with Dan Fuss.)

So there you have it. What, you may wonder, do I expect you to do with this contradictory advice?

Well, not to cop a line from old King Solomon or anything, but you could split the baby and include both Treasuries *and* corporate bonds in your portfolio. That's what I do with my own money and for most of my clients. That way, you get the best of both worlds.

Considering historical returns

It's hard to argue with Professor Don Taylor's logic: During worst-case scenarios, people do flock to safety. However, if we look at some of the worst economic times in our nation's history, corporate investment-grade (high quality) bonds have held up remarkably well. According to data from Ibbotson Associates, a Morningstar company, during the gloomiest economic days of September 1929 through June 1932, long-term corporate bonds showed a total annualized return of 2.99 percent a year, versus 4.84 percent for long-term Treasuries. During the more recent bear market of September 2000 through September 2002, long-term corporates surprisingly outperformed Treasuries, 15.08 percent versus 12.81 percent.

In the big market swoon of 2008, however, Treasuries reigned supreme — although corporate bonds, or at least most corporate bonds, did okay. Long-term Treasury bonds that year returned nearly 26 percent, while corporate bonds overall returned 9 percent. High-yield (junk) corporate bonds, however, got pretty seriously hammered (although they didn't take quite the same hit as stocks).

Generally, corporate bonds tend to outperform Treasuries when the economy is good and underperform when the economy lags.

Over the long run, corporate bonds outdistance Treasuries by a solid margin. According to Barclays Capital data, corporate investment-grade bonds of all maturities and durations have collectively outperformed their counterpart Treasury issues in 20 of the past 30 years (see Figure 6-1).

Figure 6-1:
Treasury versus corporate investment-grade bond returns: 1982–2011.

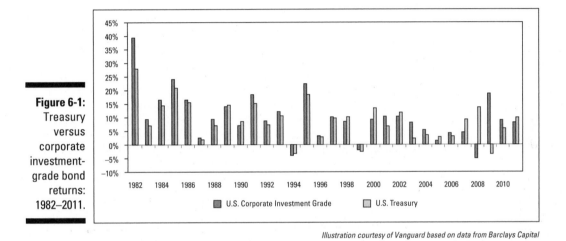

U.S. Corporate Investment Grade   U.S. Treasury

Illustration courtesy of Vanguard based on data from Barclays Capital

Since 1982, the overall annualized real return on Treasuries has been about 8.6 percent. The overall annualized return on corporate investment-grade bonds has been roughly 9.7 percent. A basket of corporate bonds invested over the past 30 years would now be worth roughly one-third more than a basket of Treasury bonds.

Getting Moody: The Crucial Credit Ratings

Appropriately weighing potential risk and return is what good investing is all about, really. As for the risk and return on corporate bonds, the potential return (always something of a guessing game) is quoted in terms of yield, and there are many kinds of yield. If you haven't yet read Chapter 4, now may be a good time to do so; I detail the various kinds of yield there. One of the most oft-quoted kinds of yield, used for example by *The Wall Street Journal* and most other business papers, is the yield-to-maturity.

The spread between corporate bonds and government bonds is quoted daily in the financial press. Investment-grade corporate bonds, as a whole, typically offer a yield-to-maturity a percentage point or so higher than that of Treasury bonds of similar maturity. So, for example, if a 10-year Treasury bond were currently yielding 2 percent to maturity (which is the case at the time of this writing), you would expect 10-year corporate bonds to offer a yield-to-maturity of about 3 percent — although the actual yield will vary to a large degree depending on the financial health and ratings of the company offering the bond, and on market sentiment.

Spreads between corporate bonds and Treasuries can widen and narrow greatly, and sometimes with great rapidity, depending on that market sentiment.

"Corporate bond spreads are like an accordion," says David Lambert, a fixed-income expert with Artisan Wealth Management of Lebanon, New Jersey. "The accordion widens when the 'air' is being sucked out of the market by a weakening economy. It generally tightens when the economy is expanding." In other words, when people feel good about the economy, they are more likely to trust in corporations, and the corporations don't need to offer the higher interest rates that they do when people are feeling pessimistic.

Regardless of market sentiment, or which way the accordion presses and the air is flowing, corporate bonds almost always produce higher yield of some sort. Is the extra juice worth the added risk of owning a corporate bond? Only you can decide what suits you best. Whether you decide to invest your money with corporate bond purveyors, and to what degree, will depend on your individual risk tolerance, your need for return, and your trust in the economy. I help you make determinations like these throughout this book, especially in Chapter 10.

Just as risk-return tradeoff exists between corporate bonds and Treasuries, there is also a big risk-return tradeoff among corporate bonds. The largest determinant of the risk and return you take on a bond is the fiscal muscle of the company behind the bond. That fiscal muscle is measured in theory, and often but not always in practice, by a company's credit ratings.

Revisiting your ABCs

An entire industry is devoted to rating companies by their financial strength. The most common ratings come from Moody's and Standard & Poor's, but other rating services exist, such as Fitch Ratings, Dominion, and A.M. Best. (See the sidebar "Growing discomfort with the credit-rating business.") Your broker, I assure you, subscribes to at least two of these services and will be happy to share the ratings with you.

The highest ratings — Moody's Aaa and Standard & Poor's AAA — are the safest of the safe among corporate bonds, and those ratings are given to few corporations. If you lend money to one of these stellar companies, you should expect in return a rate of interest only modestly higher than Treasuries (even though S&P in 2011 downgraded Treasuries to a "mere" AA rating). As you progress from these five-star companies down the ladder, you can expect higher rates of interest to compensate you for your added risk.

Table 6-1 shows how Moody's, Standard and Poor's, and Fitch define bond credit quality ratings.

Table 6-1	Bond Credit Quality Ratings		
Credit Risk	*Moody's*	*Standard & Poor's*	*Fitch*
Investment grade			
Tip-top quality	Aaa	AAA	AAA
Premium quality	Aa	AA	AA
Near-premium quality	A	A	A
Take-home-to-Mom quality	Baa	BBB	BBB
Not investment grade			
Borderline ugly	Ba	BB	BB
Ugly	B	B	B
Definitely don't-take-home-to-Mom quality	Caa	CCC	CCC
You'll be extremely lucky to get your money back	Ca	CC	CC
Interest payments have halted or bankruptcy is in process	C	D	C
Already in default	C	D	D

If you are going to invest in individual bonds, diversification through owning multiple bonds becomes more important as you go lower on the quality ladder. The risk of default is much greater down there, so you'd be awfully foolish to have all your eggs in a basket rated Caa or CCC. (*Default* in bond-talk means that you bid adieu to your principal — or at least a good chunk of it.)

Keep in mind that one risk inherent to corporate bonds is that they may be downgraded, even if they never default. Say a bond is rated A by Moody's. If Moody's gets moody and later rates that bond a Baa, the market will respond unfavorably. Chances are, in such a case, that the value of your bond will drop. Of course, the opposite is true, as well. If you buy a Baa bond and it suddenly becomes an A bond, you'll be sitting pretty. If you wish to hold your bond to maturity, such downgrades and upgrades are not going to matter much. But should you decide to sell your bond, they can matter very much.

Diversifying your bonds not only by company but also by industry is a very good idea. If, say, the utility industry experiences a major upheaval, the rate of both downgrades and defaults is sure to rise. In such a case, you would be better off not having all utility bonds.

One of the latest crazes in the world of funds, especially exchange-traded funds, is to compartmentalize bonds the way stocks have been compartmentalized into various industry sectors. You can now, for the first time, buy a fund that allows you to invest in bonds issued by only certain kinds of companies, be they financial companies, utility companies, or the industrial sector of the corporate economy. Bad idea. Steer clear.

Gauging the risk of default

How often do defaults occur?

According to data from Standard & Poor's covering the years 1981 to 2010, the odds of a corporate bond rated AAA or AA defaulting were rather minor: less than 1 percent over a period of 20 years. Of all corporate bonds, only a select few are given those gloriously high ratings.

Moving down the ladder, as you would expect, the default numbers jump. Bonds rated A defaulted at a rate of about 5 percent over 20 years. Among BBB bonds, more than 20 percent went belly up within two decades.

By the time you get down to CCC bonds, the rate of default was over half within two decades. Of course, these rates can vary greatly with economic conditions.

In fact, the rates of default over the past decade or two have been much higher than previous decades, to a great extent the result of the housing market crash and the subsequent credit bust, which led to 265 corporate defaults in 2009 — the largest number since the Great Depression. The outcome represented a single year default rate of 0.32 percent for investment-grade bonds (higher quality bonds, as deemed by the ratings agencies) and 9.45 percent for speculative-grade bonds. Among the defaulters in that tough year for corporate bonds were Ford Motor Co., General Motors, Reader's Digest, Red Roof Inns, and The Great Atlantic & Pacific Tea Co.

Growing discomfort with the credit-rating business

Two of the bond-rating service companies, Moody's and Standard & Poor's, together control some 80 percent of the very lucrative credit-rating market. Add Fitch to the short list, and you're looking at over 95 percent. The U.S. government was willing to look the other way until these companies failed to notice some rather serious problems at both Enron and WorldCom shortly before they went bankrupt in 2001 and 2002.

After years of investigation, a law was signed in September 2006 called The Credit Agency Reform Act. The act gave birth to specific guidelines required for credit agencies to qualify for NRSRO (Nationally Recognized Statistical Rating Organization) status. This designation is currently held by Moody's, Standard & Poor's, Fitch, and a handful of other firms. Agency insiders seemed to agree with the new rules of behavior imposed upon them and collectively agreed that things would get better.

But in 2008, the credit agencies blew it once again. Many subprime mortgage bonds wound up clearly overrated and subsequently failed to return all or some principal to bondholders. And if that situation wasn't bad enough, the failure of The Credit Agency Reform Act became totally apparent when Lehman Brothers — awarded by all the major credit agencies with the highest ratings — defaulted on its bonds in 2008, leaving investors in a terrible lurch.

The year prior to the mess of 2009 wasn't pretty either. Some 126 corporations went under in 2008, including Lehman Brothers, the fourth largest investment banking house in America, with more than $600 billion in assets. Thought to be "too big to fail," Lehman collapsed in a matter of weeks — the largest bankruptcy in history. Lehman's bondholders lost more than 80 percent of their savings.

Special Considerations for Investing in Corporate Debt

Just as maturity is a major consideration when choosing a Treasury (see Chapter 5), it should also be a big consideration when choosing corporate bonds. In general (but certainly not always), the longer the bond's maturity, the higher its interest rate will be because your money will potentially be tied up longer. And the longer the maturity, the greater the volatility of the price of the bond should you wish to cash out at any point.

One consideration that pertains to corporate bonds but not to Treasuries is the nasty issue of callability. Treasuries aren't called. (Once upon a time they were, but no longer.) Corporate bonds (as well as municipal bonds) often are. And that can make a huge difference in the profitability of your investment.

Calculating callability

Few things in life are as frustrating as a computer crashing. It seems to catch all of us at the least opportune moment, such as right smack in the middle of a huge work project. If you own a callable bond, chances are that it will be called at the worst moment — just as interest rates are falling and the value of your bond is on the rise. At that moment, the company that issued the bond, if it has the right to issue a call, no doubt will. And why not? Interest rates have fallen. The firm can pay you off and find someone else to borrow money from at a lower rate.

Because calls aren't fun, callable bonds must pay higher rates of interest.

If you're inclined to go for the extra juice that comes with a callable bond, I say fine. *But* you should always do so with the assumption that your callable bond will be called. With that in mind, ask the broker to tell you how much (after taking his markup into consideration) your yield will be between today and the call date. Consider that a worst-case-yield. (It's often referred to as *yield-to-worst-call,* sometimes abbreviated YTW.) Consider it the yield you'll get, and compare it to the yield you'll be getting on other comparable bonds. If you choose the callable bond and it winds up not being called, hey, that's gravy.

I speak more of comparing yields in Chapter 15, where I discuss the mechanics of buying and selling individual bonds. For now, I'll just say that some squir-relly bond brokers, to encourage you to place your order to buy, will assure you that a certain callable bond is unlikely to be called. They may be right in some cases, but you should never bank on such promises.

That being said, interest rates are likely to be climbing rather than falling in the coming years, so callability probably won't be as big an issue as it has been in the past.

Coveting convertibility

Another wrinkle in corporate bonds is a particular kind of issue called a *convertible* bond. Some corporate bond issuers sell bonds that can be converted into a fixed number of shares of common stock. With a convertible bond, a lender (bondholder) can become a part owner (stockholder) of the company by converting the bond into company stock. Having this option is a desirable thing (options are always desirable, no?), and so convertible bonds generally pay lower interest rates than do similar bonds that are not convertible.

If the stock performs poorly, no conversion happens; you are stuck with your bond's lower return (lower than what a nonconvertible corporate bond would get). If the stock performs well, a conversion happens, so you win — so to speak.

Know this: Convertible bonds, which are fairly common among corporate bonds, introduce a certain measure of unpredictability into a portfolio. As I explain in Chapter 12, perhaps the most important investment decision you can make is how to divide your portfolio between stocks and bonds. With convertibles, whatever careful allotment you come up with can be changed overnight. Your bonds suddenly become stocks. You are rewarded for making a good investment, but just as soon as you receive that reward, your portfolio becomes riskier. It's the old trade-off in action.

While I'm not saying that convertible bonds are horrible investments, I'm not sure they deserve a very sizeable allotment in most individuals' portfolios.

Reversing convertibility . . . imagine that

One relative newcomer to the world of corporate bonds is the *reverse convertible* security, sometimes referred to as *a revertible* or *a revertible note*. I've gotten a lot of calls lately from hungry and pushy salespeople trying to get me to buy one, but I'm really not too thrilled with this product.

A reverse convertible converts to a stock automatically if a certain company stock tumbles below a certain point by a certain date. Why would anyone want such a thing? You guessed it: The bond pays a thrillingly high interest rate (perhaps 2 or 3 or more percentage points above and beyond even the high rates paid on junk bonds), but only for a year or so. That's the hook. The catch is that the company paying the high interest rate is often in dire trouble. If it goes under, you could lose a bundle. Is that really the kind of risk you want to take with a fixed-income investment?

Dealing in "death puts"

Many new corporate bonds today are being issued with a *death put* — not a sweet term, but the feature can make sweet sense for certain investors, particularly the elderly. The death put, if it exists on a bond, allows a deceased bondholder's heirs to cash in the inherited bond at face value, no matter what the market price. The death put, in essence, makes a 20-year bond little more sensitive to interest-rate risk than a 5-year bond. If you are in your 80s or above, and you want a position in corporate bonds, talk death puts with a knowledgeable broker. In these days of super low interest rates, getting higher yield without taking on undue risk is tricky business; this is one rabbit you may be able to pull from the hat.

Appreciating High-Yield for What It Is

No definitive line exists between investment-grade and high-yield bonds, sometimes known as *junk* bonds. But generally, if a bond receives a rating less than a Baa from Moody's or a BBB from Standard & Poor's, the market considers it high-yield.

High-yield bonds offer greater excitement for the masses. The old adage that risk equals return is clear as day in the world of bonds. High-yield bonds offer greater yield than investment-grade bonds, and they are more volatile. But they are also one other thing: much more correlated to the stock market. In fact, Treasuries and investment-grade corporate bonds generally aren't correlated to the stock market at all. So if bonds are going to serve as ballast for our portfolios, which is what they do best, why would anyone want high-yield bonds?

I think that many people misunderstand them, and if they understood them better, they probably wouldn't invest. They certainly would not opt to give high-yield bonds a major allocation on the fixed-income side of the portfolio.

Anticipating good times ahead

If the economy is strong, then companies are making money, the public is optimistic, and stocks are going to sail. So may high-yield bonds, but stocks historically return much more than high-yield bonds.

In general, a basket of high-yield bonds may return a percentage point or two or three more than high quality corporate bonds but very rarely more than that. Stocks have a century-old track record of returning about five percentage points more than high quality bonds. And, unless you have those bonds in a retirement account, you're going to pay income tax on the interest. Most of the gain in your stocks won't be taxed at all until you sell the stock. Even then, it will most likely be taxed as long-term capital gains — 15 percent — which is probably lower than your income tax.

If good times are coming, stocks are very likely going to do better than any kind of fixed income.

Preparing for the bad times

If the economy starts to sour and companies start closing their doors, then stocks will fall and high-yield bonds very likely will too. In 2000, for example, when the stock market started to crumble, a basket of high-yield bonds would have lost between 3 and 4 percent. And in 2008, when stocks took an even more precipitous drop . . . yup, high-yield bonds went right down with them, harder than ever. Most junk bonds lost 20 to 25 percent of their value. In my mind, the last thing you want is for your bonds to turn south right along with your stocks.

Investing in high-yields judiciously

You can see that I'm not a big fan of high-yield bonds. For most people, I don't suggest a very large allocation, if any at all.

For people who really want junk bonds in their portfolios, I often suggest a serious look at foreign high-yield bonds, especially the bonds of emerging-market nations, which can make a lot of sense. That's because they don't have much, if any, correlation to the ups and downs on Wall Street. I discuss emerging-market bonds in Chapter 9.

In some cases, I may add domestic high-yield bonds to a portfolio as a means of reducing risk. But rather than substituting high-yield bonds for investment-grade bonds, I substitute the high-yield bonds for stocks. Less potential return. Less potential loss. High-yield bonds are a sort of hybrid equity/fixed income. But I generally suggest this strategy only if you can place the high-yields in a tax-advantaged account, such as an IRA.

Whenever you invest in riskier securities, the importance of diversification becomes magnified. Investing in individual junk bonds, unless you're very wealthy and can spread the risk among many junk bonds, is not something I would ever recommend. Some very good high-yield bond funds are available, and I would suggest you choose one of those. I list some of my favorites in Chapter 16.

If you're wealthy (or not-so-wealthy but you choose to ignore my advice and invest in individual high-yields anyway), know that the broker markups can sometimes kill you. I discuss how to buy individual corporate bonds and not get killed in Chapter 15.

Chapter 7

Lots of Protection (and Just a Touch of Confusion): Agency Bonds

....

....

*Y*ou've no doubt heard the story of the three blind, er, sight-impaired men and the elephant . . . how the first man touches the tail and assumes the elephant is like a snake; the second touches the tusk and assumes the elephant is like a spear; and the third touches the side of the animal and assumes the elephant is like a wall. Welcome to the touch-me, feel-me, open-to-wide-interpretation world of agency bonds!

Don't get me wrong — there are some good investments to be had here. All you have to do is figure out the tusk from the tail.

Some agency bonds are, like Treasury bonds (see Chapter 5), backed by the so-called full faith and credit of the U.S. government. You're going to get your principal back even if Congress has to do the unthinkable and tax the rich.

Most agency bonds, however, are not backed by the full faith and credit, but perhaps by half the faith and credit, of the U.S. government. The language used is that the federal government has assumed a "moral obligation" or "an implied guarantee" to stand behind these bonds. We investment experts nod when we hear this, try to look smart, and say that we know what that means. Truth be told, we're all a bit cloudy on the concept. No one I've ever met seems to know what "an implied guarantee" really means. I can tell you, however, that no one ever lost his principal investing in agency bonds due to a default.

Some agency bonds are traditional in the sense that they pay a steady rate of interest and usually, like most bonds, issue payments twice a year. Others are more free-floating. But the majority of agency bonds, roughly three-quarters of them, are entirely different animals — not big elephants with tusks and tails, but maybe odd ducks with oily wings. These odd ducks are called *mortgage-backed securities*; they pay interest *and* principal, usually monthly, with the amount potentially varying greatly from payment to payment.

It would be impossible in one chapter, perhaps even in an entire book, to cover all the ins and outs, whys and wherefores of agency bonds. I do my best on the following pages to give you a good overview.

Identifying the Bond Issuers

Who or what issues agency bonds? The answer to that question is more complex than you may imagine. Stick with me through this section, and I'll help you sort it out.

Slurping up your alphabet soup

Following are just some of the many agencies that issue bonds:

- Federal Farm Credit Banks (FFCB)
- Federal Home Loan Banks (FHLB)
- Federal Home Loan Mortgage Corporation (FHLMC)
- Federal National Mortgage Association (FNMA)
- Financial Assistance Corporation (FAC)
- Financing Corporation (FICO)
- General Services Administration (GSA)
- Government National Mortgage Association (GNMA)
- Government Trust Certificates (GTC)
- Private Export Funding Corporation (PEFCO)
- Resolution Funding Corporation (REFCORP)
- Small Business Administration (SBA)
- Tennessee Valley Authority (TVA)
- U.S. Agency for International Development (USAID)

Don't get lost in this alphabetical muck!

Separating federal agency bonds from GSEs

The first thing to know about these various government agencies is that they fit under two large umbrellas . . . well, maybe three umbrellas at the moment. Some of the agencies that issue bonds really are U.S. federal agencies; they are an actual part of the government just as Congress, the jet engines on Air Force One, and the fancy silverware at the White House are. Such official agencies include the General Services Administration, the Government National Mortgage Association, and the Small Business Administration. The U.S. Post Office also once issued bonds but has not done so lately.

Most of the so-called agencies, however, aren't quite parts of the government. They are, technically speaking, *government-sponsored enterprises* (GSEs): corporations created by Congress to work for the common good but then set out more or less on their own. Many of these faux agencies are publicly held, issuing stock on the major exchanges. Such pseudo-agencies include the Federal Home Loan Mortgage Corporation (known colloquially as *Freddie Mac*), the Federal National Mortgage Association (known as *Fannie Mae*), and the Federal Home Loan Banks. You notice, of course, that these nongovernmental enterprises start with the word "Federal." Confusing, isn't it?!

What's the difference between the two groups, especially with regard to their bonds? The first group (the official-government group) issues bonds that carry the full faith and credit of the U.S. government. The second group, well, their bonds carry that mysterious implicit guarantee or moral obligation. Because this second group is much larger than the first — both in terms of the number of agencies and the value of the bonds they issue — when investment experts speak of "agency bonds," they are almost always talking about the bonds of the GSEs.

Now, if matters weren't complicated enough, you'll recall that I mention above the recent appearance of a third umbrella. Ready? After finding themselves in hot water during the subprime mortgage crisis, the two largest of the GSEs — Freddie Mac and Fannie Mae — are currently in *receivership*. In other words, they've been more or less taken over by the federal government. So for the moment, they are, in effect, more like real federal agencies than they are GSEs. At least as far as bondholders are concerned, the bonds of these two agencies now — for the time being — no longer carry the implicit government guarantee of your investments. Instead, they now carry an explicit guarantee. The future remains uncertain.

Sizing up the government's actual commitment

No GSE yet has defaulted on its bonds — either traditional bonds or mortgage-backed securities. The closest we've ever seen was the Federal Farm Credit Banks (FFCB) during the 1980s when banks were foreclosing on small farms faster than a swarm of locusts can chew up a crop. No FFCB bonds were defaulted, but nervousness in the markets caused their prices to plunge. Would the Treasury have stepped in to save the day if the crisis continued? Perhaps, in theory, yes. But because the theory has never really been put to the test, investors got sweaty palms.

Those who sold their FFCB bonds prior to maturity lost a bundle. Of course, those intrepid investors who scooped up the bonds at bargain prices made a mint.

Because of the very small risk of default inherent in agency bonds and the greater risk of price volatility due to public sentiment, and because of lesser liquidity and less certain tax considerations, agency bonds — at least those that are not mortgage-backed — tend to pay slightly higher rates of interest than Treasury bonds. The spread between Treasuries and the agency bonds is extremely small, almost never beyond half a percentage point.

The mortgage-backed securities issued by agencies tend to yield higher returns than other agency bonds — not because of the risk of default but because of their greater volatility given the ups and downs of the mortgage market (particularly of late) to which the interest payments are tied.

Introducing the agency biggies

To give you an idea of what the specific agencies are and what they do, I describe here the four largest (and most popular with retail investors): the Federal National Mortgage Association (Fannie Mae), the Federal Home Loan Mortgage Corporation (Freddie Mac), the Federal Home Loan Banks (FHLB), and the Government National Mortgage Association (GNMA or Ginnie Mae). Before I do, I offer two charts that demonstrate how dominant these four are in the agency bond market.

How big is big?

Many GSEs exist, but as Figure 7-1 shows, Fannie Mae, Freddie Mac, and FHLB issue the vast majority of non-mortgage-backed bonds (sometimes referred to as *debentures*). The percentages reflected in this figure, which are for 2010, were supplied by the Securities Industry and Financial Markets Association (SIFMA).

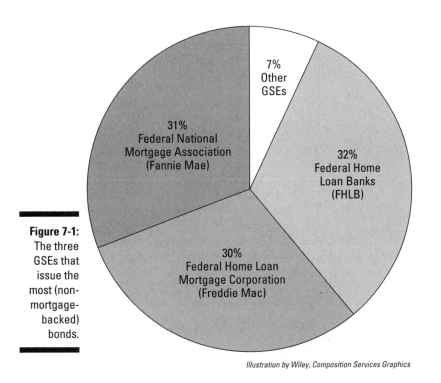

7%
Other
GSEs

31%
Federal National
Mortgage Association
(Fannie Mae)

32%
Federal Home
Loan Banks
(FHLB)

30%
Federal Home Loan
Mortgage Corporation
(Freddie Mac)

Figure 7-1:
The three
GSEs that
issue the
most (non-
mortgage-
backed)
bonds.

Illustration by Wiley, Composition Services Graphics

And as Figure 7-2 shows, more than 95 percent of all mortgage-backed securities issued in the United States are issued by Fannie Mae, Freddie Mac, and Ginnie Mae. Again, the percentages reflected in the figure, which are for 2010, were supplied by the Securities Industry and Financial Markets Association (SIFMA).

Federal National Mortgage Association (Fannie Mae)

Fannie Mae, founded in 1938 but incorporated as a publicly traded company in 1968, raises money by selling bonds. It then turns some of that money over to banks. The banks use the money to make loans, mostly to homebuyers. A sizeable chunk of all home loans in America are either owned or guaranteed by Fannie Mae or its close cousin, Freddie Mac.

Most Fannie Mae bonds (generally available in increments of $1,000) are purchased by institutions: insurance companies, other nation's central banks (especially China's), university endowments, and so on. But individual investors are certainly welcome to join in the fun, too. The agency issues bonds of varying maturities, and there's a large secondary market where you can find any maturity from several months to many years down the pike.

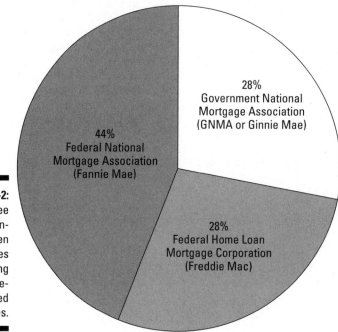

28%
Government National
Mortgage Association
(GNMA or Ginnie Mae)

44%
Federal National
Mortgage Association
(Fannie Mae)

28%
Federal Home Loan
Mortgage Corporation
(Freddie Mac)

Figure 7-2:
The three
big agen-
cies when
it comes
to issuing
mortgage-
backed
securities.

Illustration by Wiley, Composition Services Graphics

Fannie Mae sounds like a public agency, but it's really a private corporation.
That private corporation, like all GSEs, was under government oversight
until the housing-market collapse and subprime mortgage fiasco of several
years ago. Fannie Mae's losses were so great that the government placed the
company under conservatorship. For all intents and purposes, Fannie Mae
is now operating as an official arm of the government. The takeover meant
misery for those who held stock in the private company, but for Fannie Mae
bondholders, the government takeover wasn't a bad thing. In fact, it made
the bonds perhaps even safer for those investors. For more information, see
www.fanniemae.com.

If you believe that agency debt belongs in your portfolio (it certainly isn't a
necessity but is a good option for many investors), Fannie Mae bonds may
be an okay choice. You may want to see what happens with Fannie Mae in
the near future. But even if the agency moves ahead to operate as it has in
the past (presumably being more careful about taking on too many subprime
mortgages), the desirability of the bonds will still depend on the price your
broker offers you.

Note that Fannie Mae bonds may be traditional interest-bearing bonds, or
they may be mortgage-backed bonds. If you are considering the mortgage-
backed variety, please make sure to read what I write about them later in this
chapter. Mortgage-backed bonds are not for everyone!

Federal Home Loan Mortgage Corporation (Freddie Mac)

Just like Fannie Mae, this agency is technically a private corporation tied to the government. It was formed in 1970. And like Fannie Mae, Freddie Mac recently fell on hard times, too. In September 2008, the corporation was placed under the control of the Federal Housing Finance Agency. Stockholders were stung, but bondholders fared perfectly fine (as often happens in times of turmoil).

Freddie Mac offers a multitude of bond issues with many maturities, denominations of $1,000, and a choice of traditional or mortgage-backed.

Freddie Mac buys one residential mortgage every few seconds and, by doing so, helps to finance one in six homes in the United States. Most of the mortgages are purchased from primary lenders (such as your neighborhood bank). With the money these lenders get from Freddie Mac, they can go out and make more loans.

Like Fannie Maes, most Freddie Macs are bought by institutions. And as with Fannies, you may want some Freddies in your portfolio, but they aren't a necessity, and you don't want to buy them willy-nilly.

Federal Home Loan Banks

The FHLB is not a single agency but a coalition of 12 regional banks formed in 1932. Its mission is to fund low-income housing and housing projects. The money used for the funding comes from — you guessed it — selling bonds. *Lots* of bonds.

This coalition, considered a government-sponsored enterprise (GSE), is the largest issuer of so-called agency debenture bonds. These bonds are a bit more popular with individual investors than Freddies and Fannies — as well they should be, at least for those in higher tax brackets: The interest earned is exempt from state and local taxes. For more information, see www.fhlbanks.com.

Like Fannies and Freddies, FHLB bonds come in many different flavors as far as denominations and maturities.

Government National Mortgage Association (GNMA or Ginnie Mae)

Very much unlike Freddie Mac and Fannie Mae, Ginnie Mae — founded in 1968 to promote home ownership — was, and has always been, a fully owned government corporation. As such, Ginnie Mae bonds have always had the full faith and credit guarantee of Uncle Sam.

Ginnie Mae bonds also differ from Freddie Mac and Fannie Mae bonds, as well as FHLB bonds, in that all Ginnie Maes bonds to date have been mortgage-backed. A pool of mortgages is the meat behind each GNMA bond. When you buy the bond, your money is passed along to help buy someone's house. But Ginnie Mae doesn't actually create the bonds, nor does it actually sell any mortgages. Instead, certain banks are authorized to do that under Ginnie Mae's approval and guarantee.

An agency that broke its ties: Student Loan Marketing Association (Sallie Mae)

The Student Loan Marketing Association, otherwise known as Sallie Mae, owns and manages student loans for 10 million Americans. It used to be a government-sponsored enterprise (GSE), but in 2004, after some years in transition, Sallie Mae became a private corporation with no government ties whatsoever. However, the millions and millions of dollars in bonds issued by Sallie Mae under its status as a GSE are currently grandfathered as agency debt, and will be until their maturity. If anything happens to Sallie Mae, the U.S. government has taken on a moral obligation to pay back the principal on Sallie Mae bonds — at least those issued prior to 2004.

If you buy a Sallie Mae issued prior to 2004, expect a price and yield comparable to other agency bonds. If you buy a Sallie Mae issued post-2004, expect a price and yield comparable to corporate bonds of similar quality. (Sallie Mae of late hasn't had great credit ratings, bordering between investment-grade and junk.) In either case, ask yourself if agency bonds or corporate bonds truly belong in your portfolio, and do your research (as outlined in Chapter 15) to compare and contrast these with other bonds to make sure you are getting the best investment possible.

Your investment in these bonds is then passed along to potential homebuyers in the form of affordable loans. In other words, Ginnie Mae is like Good Housekeeping. Its seal of approval and guarantee (for which banks pay good money) assure you, the bondholder, that you aren't going to get stuck with the same kind of mortgage bonds — backed by a whim and a prayer — that helped to sink Lehman Brothers.

For more information, see www.ginniemae.gov.

Comparing and Contrasting Agency Bonds

All agency bonds are considered high quality with very little risk of default, but they aren't all created exactly equal. In this section, I sort through some considerations to keep in mind when researching agency bonds for your portfolio.

Eyeing default risks, yields, markups, and more

The honest-and-true federal agencies, such as the Small Business Administration (SBA), are said to have no risk of default; therefore, their bonds pay more or less what Treasuries do (see Chapter 5). You may get a smidgen more interest (maybe 5 basis points, or 5/100 of 1 percent) to compensate you for the lesser *liquidity* of such agency bonds (the lesser ability to sell them in a flash).

Other agency bonds are issued by government-sponsored enterprises (GSEs), and the risk of default, although real, is probably next to nothing. You get a higher rate of interest on these bonds than you do with Treasuries to compensate you for the fact that the risk of default does exist.

With all agency bonds, you pay a markup when you buy and sell, which you don't with Treasuries if you buy them directly from the government. (I discuss buying and selling Treasuries in Chapter 5.) If you're not careful, that markup could easily eat up your first several months of earnings. It also could make the difference between agency bonds and Treasury bonds a wash.

Most agency bonds pay a fixed rate of interest twice a year. About 25 percent of them are *callable*, meaning that the agencies issuing the bonds have the right to cancel the bond and give you back your principal. The other 75 percent are non-callable bonds (sometimes referred to as *bullet* bonds). Callable bonds tend to pay somewhat higher rates of interest, but your investment takes on a certain degree of uncertainty. (See Chapter 6 for more on callability.)

Investing in individual agency bonds, or individual bonds of any kind, for that matter, is not an activity for poor people. Although you may be able to get into the game for as little as $1,000, bond brokers typically mark up such small transactions to the point that they simply don't make sense. I wouldn't suggest even looking at individual agency bonds unless you've got at least $50,000 to invest in a pop. Otherwise, you should be looking at bond funds or at individual Treasuries that you can buy without paying any markup whatsoever.

When choosing among different agencies, you want to carefully compare yields-to-maturity (see Chapter 4) and make sure that you know full well whether you are buying a traditional bond or a mortgage-backed security. They are totally different animals.

Weighing taxation matters

The taxes you pay on agency bonds vary. Interest from bonds issued by Freddie Mac and Fannie Mae is fully taxable. The interest on most other agency bonds — including the king of agency bonds, the Federal Home Loan Banks — is exempt from state and local tax.

Treasury bonds, which most resemble agency bonds, are always exempt from state and local tax. Municipal bonds are almost always free from federal tax. Needless to say, your personal tax bracket will make some bonds look better than others. I help you to better measure the effect of taxation on your bond selections in Chapter 8.

Making like John Travolta: Discos, floaters, and step-ups

Some agencies, in addition to issuing traditional bonds that pay semiannual interest, also issue *no-coupon discount notes,* known among bond traders as *discos.* Discos are similar to Treasury bills. They usually carry short-term maturities (up to one year), sell at a discount, and pay all interest along with principal at maturity. They are used more by institutions than by individuals, which is probably a good thing: Most individuals who buy bonds tend to enjoy the more regular income. I mention discos here mostly to appease your curiosity, should you come across the interesting term. They have nothing to do with dancing.

Another type of agency bond is called a *floater.* The coupon rate of a floater is based on some benchmark, such as the three-month T-bill (Treasury bill) rate, and can change from month to month. These are complicated beasts, and I suggest steering clear. Fixed-income investments should be fixed.

Not quite as unpredictable as the floater, yet another kind of agency bond is known as a *step-up.* With a step-up, you get a coupon rate that "steps up" according to a pre-set calendar. As time rolls on, you may collect more interest. Step-ups can be good investments in that they shield you from having to eat crow with a low-interest investment when interest rates are on the rise. The problem with them is that they are typically *callable,* which means the agency can toss your principal back to you at any time, and you're left holding cold cash with perhaps nowhere to go.

Banking Your Money on Other People's Mortgages

Far more complicated even than floaters are the mortgage-backed securities issued by federal agencies such as Ginnie Mae and by some government-sponsored enterprises, such as Fannie Mae and Freddie Mac (see "Introducing the agency biggies" earlier in the chapter).

Mortgage-backed securities— the vast majority of which are issued by agencies — are very different than most other bonds. They do not offer as consistent and predictable a stream of interest income as do most bonds.

Bathing in the mortgage pool

When you purchase a mortgage-backed security from, say, Ginnie Mae (minimum investment $25,000), your money goes into a pool of mortgages. Whereas most bonds pay you a set rate of interest, usually twice a year, mortgage-backed securities pay you a certain rate of interest plus the steady or not-so-steady return of your principal. (You don't get a big lump sum when the bond matures.) Most mortgage-backed securities issue monthly payments.

The amount of principal you get back on a monthly basis is determined largely by the rate at which mortgage-holders pay off their debt. If interest rates drop and thousands of the mortgage holders decide suddenly to prepay their existing mortgages (in order to refinance), you may get back your principal much faster than you had anticipated. In a sense, a mortgage-backed security has the same *back-at-ya* risk as a callable bond.

Deciding whether to invest in the housing market

You don't need to invest the $25,000 minimum required by Ginnie Mae to invest in mortgage-back securities. You can get a Freddie Mac for as little as $1,000. But should you?

No, I don't think so.

Neither does David Lambert, a financial planning colleague of mine who is the founding partner of Artisan Wealth Management, based in Lebanon, New Jersey. Lambert was formerly the head trader at the agency-bond desk for a major Wall Street firm. This guy knows *a lot* about agency bonds. "If I were a retail investor, unless I had a really huge amount of money and felt that I really knew what I was doing, I wouldn't invest directly in mortgage-backed securities," Lambert says. "The complexity of them makes them inappropriate for the average investor."

Instead, says Lambert, if you want to invest in mortgage-backed securities, do so by investing in, say, a good mortgage-backed security fund. "There are plenty of good ones out there — both mutual funds and exchange-traded funds. I'd look to a solid company like Vanguard, Fidelity, iShares or PIMCO," he says. I discuss bond funds, and fund companies such as these (which I also tend to like), in depth in Chapter 16.

Considering Agencies for Your Portfolio

You don't *need* agency bonds. Their overall characteristics are similar enough to Treasuries that the substitution of one for the other isn't likely to make a huge difference in either the risk profile or the potential return of your overall portfolio. If, however, you are a smart bond buyer (which you certainly can be after reading this book!), substituting agency bonds for Treasuries may garner you a few extra bucks.

Mortgage-backed bonds, usually best purchased in mutual fund form, add a smidgen of diversification to a portfolio and potentially a bit more return than do most other agency bonds. Again, there's no urgency to add mortgage-backed bonds to a portfolio, but if you have a large fixed-income allocation, a position in mortgage-backed bonds may make sense. Generally, you do better with mortgage-backed securities than traditional bonds when prevailing interest rates are stable. They tend to chug along or droop when interest rates begin to bounce.

Given their overall safety, agency bonds tend to be conservative investments and produce modest rates of return. Therefore, you *must* make sure that the return isn't eaten up in transaction costs or management fees.

If you plan to invest in an agency bond fund or funds, make sure you comb through Chapter 16 to find one with reasonable expenses. And if you think you may want to invest in individual agency bonds, read Chapter 15 so you don't get clipped with a high broker markup. Can't decide which is right for you, fund or individual bond? Chapter 13 is here to help!

Chapter 8

(Almost) Tax-Free Havens: Municipal Bonds

....

In This Chapter

▶ Analyzing the advantages of tax-free bond investing (beyond the obvious!)

▶ Evaluating the economic strength of the issuers

▶ Crunching the tax numbers to figure out if munis make sense for you

▶ Realizing that you may still pay some taxes

▶ Knowing how to purchase munis

....

> *I'm proud to be paying taxes in the United States. The only thing is — I could be just as proud for half the money.*
>
> — Arthur Godfrey

*W*ould you believe that this quote from the famous dead guy actually appeared on the home page of the official Internal Revenue Service website? No kidding. Who says these guys don't have a sense of humor?

No one, probably not even the webmaster for the IRS website, likes paying taxes. That's why municipal bonds (commonly called *munis*), with their juicy exempt-from-federal-tax status, are such a darling investment, especially for those Camembert- and Evian-gulping folks in the northern tax brackets.

Perhaps you're an anti-government zealot who stockpiles guns in your linen closet for the upcoming revolution, and you'd rather die than pay taxes to Uncle Sam. In that case, munis should be your bond of choice. If you'd describe yourself in slightly more rational terms, what matters most is not the taxes you pay or don't pay, but what you take home at the end of the day. In that case, munis may make sense for you, or they may not. Munis, you see, have historically paid lower rates of interest than have taxable bonds. If you're a rational person, a municipal bond paying 4 percent, for example, would outshine a taxable bond paying 8 percent only if your tax bracket were way north of Norway.

In this chapter, I reveal the formula to figure out whether a tax-free muni will likely mean greater take-home than a comparable taxable bond. (It's a simple formula, really — no PhD in mathematics necessary.) But I also point out that the formula should be used merely as a starting point. Munis may or may not belong in your portfolio for other reasons, as well, regardless of what you keep in your linen closet.

Appreciating the Purpose and Power of Munis

If not for the fact that municipal bonds are exempt from federal income tax, their popularity over the years would have rivaled a pitcher of buttermilk at a college keg party. Historically, the returns on high-quality munis have been about 80 percent of what Treasuries have paid. But a strange thing has happened lately. In the past couple of years, munis, as a bond category, have paid out at just about the same rate as Treasuries — at times, even more. Keep in mind, of course, that Treasuries aren't exactly world-famous for their high returns — they never were, and they especially aren't these days. However, while munis are generally safe investments (despite what you may have heard on *60 Minutes,* which I'll get to shortly), they aren't as safe as Treasuries.

But of course, most munis *are* tax-exempt.

Why is that? Because in 1895, the Supremes (nine guys in black robes, not the lady singers) decided on a case involving "intergovernmental tax immunity." In essence, they ruled that the federal government had no right to mess with any local government's efforts to raise money. And the Supremes determined that taxing local bonds would, in fact, be a form of messing. From that point on, interest on municipal bonds has been largely untouched by those fun-loving Arthur Godfrey fans at the IRS.

When anyone in Washington is ever inclined to challenge that 1895 ruling (oh, yes, it does happen from time to time), he never gets very far. That's because the tax-exempt status of munis allows local governments, such as your township, to issue bonds that carry very modest interest rates. If local governments across the United States couldn't issue those bonds — couldn't get those relatively cheap loans — we'd probably start seeing potholes in the street as big as Rhode Island (which would obviously be a very serious problem in Rhode Island). A drying up of cheap loans might mean a drying up of ports; bridges and tunnels might not get built; and construction of new schools and low-income housing projects might come to a crawl.

Munis also have a lot of support among politicians because those Americans who contribute the most to political campaigns are the ones who, given their higher incomes and nominal tax brackets, are the most likely holders of municipal bonds.

Sizing up the muni market

The municipal bond market is now about $3.7 trillion, which is a little more than one-third the size of the Treasury market. But unlike Treasuries, which are held by investors all over the world — by both individuals and governments — municipal bonds are purchased primarily by U.S. households. Munis, due to their tantalizing tax advantage, are generally the only major kind of bond more popular with individual investors than with institutions.

So who or what exactly issues these tax-exempt wonders, and what other qualities distinguish them from all other bonds? I'm so glad you asked!

The issuers of municipal bonds include, of course, municipalities (duh), such as cities and towns. But they also include counties, public universities, certain private universities, airports, not-for-profit hospitals, public power plants, water and sewer administrations, various and sundry nonprofit organizations, bridge and tunnel authorities, housing authorities, and an occasional research foundation.

Any government, local agency, nonprofit, or what-have-you that is deemed to serve the public good, with a blessing from the IRS (and sometimes voters), may have the honor of issuing a municipal bond.

Comparing and contrasting with other bonds

The tax-exempt status of munis is unquestionably their most notable and easily recognizable characteristic — the equivalent of Groucho Marx's mustache or Alec Baldwin's temper.

Like most bonds, munis come with differing maturities. Some mature in a year or less, others in 20 or 30 years, and a select few have even longer maturities. Unlike most bonds, they tend to be issued in minimal denominations of $5,000 and multiples of $5,000 (not a minimum of $1,000 and multiples of $1,000, like corporate bonds and most Treasuries).

Unlike Treasuries, both corporate bonds and munis are often *callable,* meaning the issuer can kick back your money and sever your relationship before the bond matures. Like other bonds, the interest rate on munis is generally fixed, but the price of the bond can go up and down; unless you hold your bond to maturity, you may or may not get your principal returned in full. (And even if you get your principal back in full, it may have been seriously eaten away by inflation after several decades in hiding.) If the maturity of the bond is many years off, the price of the bond can go up and down considerably — usually in inverse relation to interest rates (see Chapter 4).

Delighting in the diversification of municipals

The tax-exempt status of munis isn't the only reason they may belong in your portfolio. Municipal bonds also offer a fair degree of diversification, even from other bonds.

Because they are the only kind of bond more popular with households than with institutions, the muni market may, at times, be swayed more by public demand than other bond markets. For example, when the stock market tanks and individual investors get butterflies in their stomachs, they tend to sell out of their stock holdings (often a mistake) and load up on what they see as less risky investments — bonds of all sorts, including munis.

But the butterflies may also flock in the other direction. At the end of 2010, CBS's *60 Minutes* aired a story titled "The Day of Reckoning" featuring the predictions of a highly reputable bank analyst, Meredith Whitney. Her forecast, backed by interviews with several state governors and comptrollers, proclaimed that a muni-market collapse was in our imminent future. Because of this widely seen segment, the muni market nearly did collapse. Investors panicked about the market for any securities issued by local governments. Prices on munis, especially those issued in financially troubled areas of the country, took a nosedive. Fortunately, the air cleared quickly, and the value of the muni market made a quick recovery.

When the demand for munis goes up, just as when the demand for, say, gold or oil goes up, it tends to drive prices higher. And when the demand for munis goes down, yup . . . we saw that in December 2010. Popular demand or lack of demand can have a huge effect on muni pricing — more so than individual-investor caprices influence the values of corporate bonds and Treasuries. Those taxable bonds, in contrast, tend to be more interest-rate sensitive. As I discuss in Chapter 4, when interest rates rise, bond prices generally fall; when interest rates drop, bond prices tend to move up.

Care to buy a bond that matures in 2111?

Today's low interest rate environment means cheap money for borrowers, and no borrower has jumped on this situation like the California Institute of Technology in Pasadena. In December 2011, the university sold $350 million in tax-free bonds maturing in 100 years. That's right . . . the bonds will pay 4.744 percent annually until 2111. Not many so-called *century* bonds are issued these days (they were much more popular in the Middle Ages). Even though the Cal Tech bonds, which carry an S&P rating of AA, are the lowest yielding century bonds on the market, investors gobbled them up. The timing was obviously right.

The differences among the many kinds of bonds indicate it's likely a good idea to hold at least several varieties in your portfolio. As an example of the kind of diversification I'm talking about, consider that in 2010, investment-grade (high quality) corporate bonds returned nearly 18 percent. (Interest rates were falling, which is good for bonds, and corporations were starting to look stronger after the pummeling of 2008.) But that same year, munis — partly due to the *60 Minutes* story — returned a mere 2 percent. The following year (2011), munis made a phenomenal comeback; it was their turn to shine. They earned, in the aggregate, a (tax-free) 10 percent. Meanwhile, corporate bonds began to slow, earning about 7.5 percent for the year.

Knowing That All Cities (Bridges or Ports) Are Not Created Equal

Like the corporations that issue corporate bonds, the entities (cities, hospitals, universities, and so on) that issue municipal bonds are of varying economic strength — although the degree of variance isn't quite as large as it is in the corporate world. In this section, I examine the risks you take when purchasing munis. I start with a discussion of the much feared but rarely realized municipal default.

Dealing with the rare default

Despite all the talk by Meredith Whitney and others about a collapse looming over the muni market, municipal downfalls have been few. Really. In 2011, only ten municipal defaults occurred; in 2010, that number was six. The largest wasn't New York or Los Angeles, but Jefferson County, Alabama. Bondholders there have not been receiving interest payments, and they may or may not get back their full principal — though it's likely that at least a good part of it will eventually be returned.

Whitney and the other doomsayers were correct in late 2010 in regard to the federal government suffering its own economic challenges. Aid to the states was indeed cut, forcing the states to subsequently pass these cuts down to financially strained municipalities. But Whitney and company seem to have underestimated the degree and speed to which municipalities were willing to reduce public services, cutting pension benefits to policemen and teachers, or reducing medical services for the poor, in order to continue paying interest to creditors.

One study by Moody's looked at municipal issuers of bonds (all those that warranted ratings, which would be the vast majority) for the period 1970 through 2009 and found a total of 54 defaults. Your odds of having a single investment-grade municipal bond default over a five-year period — making the big assumption that the future will be anything like the past — are about 3 in 1,000, according to the findings. This compares to nearly 1 in 100 for investment-grade corporate bonds. As for speculative-grade bonds, otherwise known as "high-yield," the odds are about 3 in 100 for munis, as compared to 21 in 100 for corporate junk bonds. Again, these numbers are based on holding the bonds over a five-year period.

Historical recovery rates for defaulted U.S. municipal bonds indicate that the chances of recovering your principal (or at least part of your principal) after a default are much greater, on average, than those for corporate bonds. Over the past 40 years, the average investor in a defaulted muni bond has received 60 cents to the dollar on his principal. That's far more than the typical investor in a defaulted corporate bond, who ended up with only 37 cents to the dollar.

Defaulted municipal bonds tend to be revenue bonds rather than general obligation bonds. *General obligation bonds* are secured by the full faith and credit of the issuer and are typically supported by that issuer's power to tax the hell out of the citizenry, if necessary. Interest and principal on *revenue bonds* are secured only from earnings derived from a specific project; if the project goes bust, so does the bond. Nearly three quarters of the defaults studied by Moody's occurred not only in revenue bonds but also in particular kinds of revenue bonds — those in the healthcare and housing project finance sectors.

Enjoying low risk

So by and large, municipal bonds are very safe animals — at least the vast majority of those given high ratings by the major agencies such as Moody's. If the mild nature of the beast weren't enough to put your investing soul at ease, some municipal bonds come insured; you can't lose your principal unless the issuer *and* its insurance company go under. Even if the insurance company were to fail, the general feeling among industry insiders is that most states would be extremely reluctant to allow one of their cities to default on a general obligation bond. In 2011, for instance, Harrisburg, Pennsylvania, dallied with the idea of going bankrupt, but the state legislators (who happen to hang out a lot in Harrisburg) refused to allow it.

Municipal bonds, like corporate and federal government bonds, are rated by the major bond-rating agencies. For many years, munis had their own rating system. Recently, however, the rating systems have been unified. If you want to see what the individual ratings are, see Table 6-1 in Chapter 6, where I discuss corporate bonds.

Choosing from a vast array of possibilities

You definitely want munis that are rated. Some municipal offerings are not rated, and these can be risky investments or very *illiquid* (you may not be able to sell them when you want, if at all). I suggest, if you are an average investor, going mostly with the top-rated munis: Moody's Aa or higher. The lower-rated munis may give you a bit extra yield but probably aren't worth the added risk, except perhaps for a limited portion of your portfolio.

Keep in mind that a lower-rated bond can be more volatile than a high-rated bond. Default isn't the only risk. If you suddenly need to cash out the muni part of your portfolio, and high-yield munis are in the tank, you may not have access to much of your cash.

As for the insurance guarantee offered on so many munis today, as long as a muni has a high rating and is a general obligation muni (not a revenue muni), consider going without the insurance for that possible drop of extra juice. General obligation bonds generally don't default. On average, we've seen only one such default each decade. That's not to say it can't happen to you tomorrow, but if you choose a top-rated general obligation bond, your odds of losing money to a default are about on a par with the odds that my dog, Norman, will run for public office.

If you're looking for even more safety in a muni than a top-rated general obligation bond, you can try to find a pre-refunded municipal bond. That means the municipality put money aside into an escrow account to ensure payment to pay bondholders. "If the money in escrow is held in U.S. Treasuries, as it often is, then your investment in the municipal bond is backed by the federal government — and you won't get safer than that," says Bill Conger, a principal and senior portfolio manager of Red Hook Management in Morristown, New Jersey. Of course, great safety means low yields. Pre-refunded bonds are not going to give you quite the same interest rate as other munis. Still, Conger points out, you're going to get a higher return than you would on Treasuries.

You also want to choose a municipal bond that carries a maturity you can live with. (Most pre-refunded bonds have short maturities.) If the bond is callable, well, is that something you can live with and still be happy? Callable bonds pay slightly higher coupon rates but are less predictable than noncallable bonds. (See Chapter 6 for further discussion of callability.)

Of great importance in choosing munis are clearly their tax benefits, which can vary. Do you want a muni that is merely free from federal income tax, or do you want a muni that is double- or triple-tax-free? (Note: Some munis, called Build America Bonds, or BABs, are entirely taxable. I get to those at the end of this chapter.)

Here's the scoop:

- ✔ *National munis* are exempt from federal tax but are not necessarily exempt from state income tax. (Some states tax bond coupon payments, and others do not.)

- ✔ *State munis,* if purchased by residents of the same state, are typically exempt from state tax, if there is one. Some, but not all, state munis are also exempt from all local taxes.

- ✔ Munis that are exempt from both federal and state tax are called *double-tax-free* bonds. Some locally issued bonds may be exempt from federal, state, *and* local tax; these are often referred to as *triple-tax-free* bonds.

- ✔ Munis issued by Puerto Rico and Guam are free from federal and state taxes, regardless of where you live.

You need to do a bit of math to determine which kind is better for you: national or state, double- or triple-tax-free. If math doesn't frighten you too much, read on! Keep in mind, however, that the formulas I'm about to give you should be used only as rough guides. Consult your tax adviser before laying out any big money on munis. The tax rules are complicated and forever changing. Some states — but not all — impose taxes if you invest in states other than your own, but others may even tax you on munis issued by your own state. Bonds issued in Puerto Rico and other U.S. territories carry their own tax peculiarities. It's a jungle out there!

Consulting the Taxman

Your personal federal tax bracket, as well as the income taxes you pay in your state or to your local government, have a great bearing on whether munis make sense for you. If you decide to invest in munis, what kind should you select: national or local?

You need to consider a great many things when choosing which munis to buy, according to bond expert Conger. Obviously, one is your personal tax bracket. You also need to take a close look at the yields of bonds issued in your home state as compared to those issued elsewhere. (This stuff is complex, so you may need a calculator. I get to that shortly.) But Conger advises that yield and taxes should never be your only considerations. "You always want to keep diversification in mind," he says.

"If you're only investing in AAA-rated bonds, then okay, you might be best off investing in all home-state bonds, and taking advantage of their double- or triple-tax-free status," Conger advises. "But if you are looking at bonds with more than negligible default risk, you'll want to spread out your risks geographically — regardless of your tax bracket."

In this section, I walk you through some basic considerations — tax-related and otherwise — to keep in mind when deciding whether to add munis to your portfolio (and which kinds to purchase).

Bringing your bracket to bear

When looking at a national muni — a bond that is exempt from federal tax only — it isn't very hard to determine whether your after-tax take-home will be greater with that bond or with a fully taxable bond. For illustration purposes, suppose you are comparing two bonds: a $5,000 Metropolis 20-year muni paying 5 percent, and a $5,000 taxable bond from the International Dummies Consolidated Corporation (IDCC) paying 6.5 percent.

 First, determine your tax bracket. You can pretty easily locate this information online from a site such as http://tax.laws.com/federal-tax-brackets. Your tax bracket shows the likely percent of tax you'll pay on any interest from a taxable bond (unless that bond is held in a tax-advantaged account, such as an IRA).

Okay, got your tax bracket? Good. Now you can compare the take-home from the IDCC taxable bond to the federally tax-exempt Metropolis municipal 20-year bond paying 5 percent a year.

Start with 100, a good round number. Subtract your tax bracket. Let's suppose you are in the 28 percent bracket: 100 – 28 = 72. That number — 72 — we'll call the *reciprocal* of your tax bracket. When you have the reciprocal, divide the municipal yield by the reciprocal and it tells you, just like magic, what you would have to earn on the taxable bond to equal the amount you would get on the tax-exempt muni.

So, in this particular case, Metropolis muni is paying 5 percent. Divide 5 by 72 (the reciprocal of your tax bracket), and you get 6.94 percent.

New York, California ... where does muni bond risk live?

Different states. Different climates. Different bonds. And different feelings among bondholders as to how likely those states, and the municipalities within those states, are to find themselves in fiscal boiling water. As a result, some states' muni bonds offer higher yields than others to compensate for what the market sees as added risk. The differences between the municipal bonds issued in various states can be quite significant. To the extent that high yields forecast fiscal earthquakes, California is a likely candidate. If you are buying California munis, I advise some caution. At the time of this writing, here is the average yield on five-year, general obligation bonds issued by municipalities in five different states:

California	1.3 percent
New York	1.1 percent
Vermont	1.0 percent
Massachusetts	0.8 percent
Maryland	0.7 percent

That number, 6.94, represents your *tax-equivalent yield,* or your break-even between taxable and tax-exempt bond investing. If you can get 5 percent on a muni versus 6.94 percent on a taxable bond, go flip a coin. It won't matter which you choose, as far as take-home pay. (Of course, other factors may matter, such as the quality or the maturity of the bond.) If the taxable bond is paying more than 6.94 percent, the taxable bond is likely your best bet. If the taxable bond is paying less than 6.94 percent, you're better off with the muni. If the IDCC taxable bond is paying only 6.5 percent, you are better off, most likely, with the Metropolis tax-free bond paying 5 percent.

So far, so good?

Singling out your home state

Life in these United States is rarely simple. Chances are that you live in a state with income tax. Most people do.

In that case, figuring out your tax-equivalent yield is no longer a simple matter. State taxes, you see, are deductible from your federal taxes. So to figure out your tax-equivalent yield requires more math than any normal person with an Internet connection should ever have to suffer.

So instead of walking you through the long and painful formula, I'm simply going to suggest that you log onto one of the 50,000 tax-equivalent yield calculators on the Internet. One of my favorites is to be found on www.dinkytown. net. Click <u>Investments</u> in the column on the left side of your screen. Then click on <u>Municipal Bond Tax Equivalent Yield</u>. You can plug in your state income tax, and the calculator shows you the tax-equivalent yields, in colorful chart form, for federally exempt munis as well as munis exempt from state and local taxes.

Don't know your state tax? You can look that up online also; Bankrate.com offers a handy tool that can help (at `www.bankrate.com/finance/taxes/check-taxes-in-your-state.aspx`).

Matching munis to the appropriate accounts

Municipal bonds, like any tax-free investment, make most sense in a taxable account. In fact, I'd say that putting a tax-free muni into any kind of tax-advantaged account, such as an IRA or Roth IRA, makes about as much sense as putting a kidney pie on a vegetarian buffet.

If you're looking to fill your IRA with fixed-income investments (which may or may not make sense; see Chapter 13), don't be looking at munis that are tax-exempt. Taxable bonds generally provide greater return, and if the taxes can be postponed (as in an IRA) or avoided (as in a Roth IRA), then taxable bonds are almost always the way to go.

Recognizing Why This Chapter is Titled "(Almost) Tax-Free Havens"

Will you *never* pay federal tax on a muni? Never say never. In some very rare instances, the tax can grab you from behind and make you not want to wake up on the morning of April 15.

Reckoning with the AMT tax

The alternative minimum tax (AMT) is complicated enough to have made Albert Einstein pull at his already wild-looking hair. The AMT is a federal tax that exists in a parallel universe (Albert proved that they exist), which you enter unwillingly when you make a fair chunk of change, claim too many exemptions, or take too many deductions. Ask your tax guru if you are likely to be smacked by AMT at any point in the near future. If so, you may want to handpick your munis (and muni funds) to include only those that are exempt from the AMT.

In general, the interest on municipal bonds sold by state and local governments to finance very specific projects, as well as bonds issued by not-for-profit organizations and other "private activity" issuers such as airports and universities, is going to be included in the AMT. So if you are liable to pay the AMT, the tax-exempt status of these bonds will no longer be so entirely exempt.

If buying up these AMT-triggering bonds is not a liability concern, investing in them may make good sense. This type of muni tends to provide a slightly higher yield than do non-AMT munis.

Capping your capital gains

If you buy a security at a certain price and then sell it at a higher price, that's a good thing! But you may be subject to pay capital gains tax to the IRS . . . even if the security you sold is a tax-exempt municipal bond. If you pay $1,000 to pick up a muni selling at par, and you later sell it for $1,100, you very likely owe the government capital gains tax on your $100. If the buy and sell both occur within a one-year period, the tax hit will likely be 25 percent, 28 percent, or whatever your normal marginal income tax rate happens to be. If your buy and sell span a period of more than one year, you need to pay long-term capital gains, which for most folk amounts to 15 percent.

(The tax rules governing municipal zero-coupon bonds bought at a discount and then sold at a lesser discount or a premium can be complicated; talk to your tax advisor.)

What pertains to individual bonds also pertains to municipal bond mutual funds. Sell your shares for more than you purchased them for, and you'll have to pay capital gains. Of course, if you sell at a loss, whether a bond or a bond fund, you may then declare a capital loss, which is usually used to write off capital gains.

Introducing the fully taxable muni

Huh? Say whaa?

At first glance, a taxable muni seems about as sensible as a race horse running in a yoke, but in fact, taxable munis offer potential return comparable to investment-grade corporate bonds, and sometimes they may make for an excellent bond choice. Taxable municipal bonds exist on the market because the federal government doesn't give a break to the financing of certain activities that it perceives do not offer a significant benefit to the public. The funding of a new hockey stadium or the refunding of a municipality's ailing pension plan are two examples of muni bond issues that would be federally taxable. They barely existed a couple of decades ago but are becoming more and more popular.

Build America Bonds (known as BABs) are a special category of taxable muni. These bonds were issued in 2009 and 2010 as part of President Obama's plan to revive the sagging economy. They allow local governments to raise capital, and the Treasury subsidizes 35 percent of the municipality's interest costs. Most of these bonds carry top ratings but tend to be especially volatile due to their lengthy maturity dates (sometimes as high as 30 years). If you have room only in your retirement accounts, and you want munis that pay about as much as corporate bonds, then a position in BABs or other taxable munis may actually make good sense.

Buying Munis Made Easier

Perhaps because the muni bond market is made up mostly of individuals rather than institutional buyers, the number of sharks in fancy suits out to rip the hide off unwary investors is highest in the muni bond market. Buyer beware! I've seen examples of people paying markups on individual bonds in some cases exceeding a full year's interest.

If you're interested (and can stomach it!), check out http://muniadvocate. com, a website created by Kevin Olson, a former muni bond trader turned independent investor advocate. Olson delights in cataloging municipal bond trades that should never have happened: trades with ridiculously high spreads between buys and sells where individual investors got hurt. Some of these trades, as you'll note if you visit Olson's site, are clipping as much as 20 percent off the value of the bond! (Beware: Olson feels strongly that municipalities across the nation are too deeply in debt to fulfill their obligations to bondholders and that defaults in the future will be much more common.)

If you're buying individual munis on your own, you want to take full advantage of all the latest consumer tools that allow you, in many cases, to get a pretty good idea what kind of markup the bond broker is shooting to make. You don't want one of your trades to appear on Olson's web list! If you go to websites such as www.investinginbonds.com, www.finra.org, or www.emma.msrb.org, you can research individual bonds to see the prices paid for past transactions. If the bond was traded recently, that should give you some idea whether a broker is offering you a fair price. The easiest way to research an individual bond is to ask the broker for its *CUSIP number* (an identification number assigned to bonds, as well as stocks), and then plug that number into the website's search function.

You can avoid getting pinched too badly on trading individual bonds by going with primary issues (buying directly from the municipality) rather than secondary issues (buying on the open market). I discuss that topic in Chapter 15.

You may also evade these somewhat nefarious brokers by visiting another website from Kevin Olson, who has launched www.munimarket.com, which Olson foresees as someday becoming an eBay for muni bond investors. At the time of this writing, the site had just gone live. If it catches on, you may find numerous prospective buyers and sellers of individual muni bonds looking to connect directly. If this baby is successful, it could provide a breakthrough in bond trading.

In the meantime, bond funds, rather than individual issues, may make better sense altogether for the majority of investors. By buying in bulk and using their professional prowess, fund managers can often get better deals than you can get on your own. Of course, funds charge you a yearly management fee, and given the low yields of munis, you don't want to pay too much for a fund. In fact, you want to pay as little as possible.

Whichever way you decide to go — individual bonds or municipal bond funds — Chapters 15 and 16 give you all the practical advice you need to build your muni bond portfolio wisely.

Chapter 9

Le Bond du Jour: Global Bonds and Other Seemingly Exotic Offerings

. . . .

In This Chapter

▶ Investing in bonds issued in other countries

▶ Letting your conscience be your guide

▶ Walking on the wild side with Bowie, catastrophe, and death bonds

▶ Dipping into the dangerous waters of derivatives and defaulted bonds

▶ Introducing exchange-traded notes

. . . .

I once saw a cartoon showing an American-looking couple standing in a street in what looks like Mexico, watching a group of small children at play. The cartoon husband turns to the cartoon wife and cartoonishly says, "Isn't it amazing how these kids can conjugate all those verbs?"

What's amazing is how something that appears exotic to one person in one part of the world can be so run-of-the-mill to another. Consider that more than two-thirds of all fixed-income offerings come from outside the borders of the United States. To the hordes of Europeans and Asians who invest in them, these bonds are about as exciting as bread and rice. Yet to the average Yank, an investment in a foreign bond may be considered something exotic.

In this chapter, I talk not only about foreign bonds but also about some rather unusual and, in some cases, even somewhat quirky bond offerings to be found closer to U.S. shores. None of the bonds discussed in this chapter are a must for your portfolio (some I would consider almost must-nots), but sprinkled throughout are a few bond choices possibly worth your consideration.

Traveling Abroad for Fixed Income

The ratio between what we Americans invest in domestic bonds and what we invest in foreign bonds is somewhere in the ballpark (cricketfield) of *30 to 1*. Given the gargantuan size of the foreign bond market, you may find that a bit surprising — especially because foreign bonds sometimes make very sensible investments. And although it was once difficult to invest in this arena, it's very easy today, especially since the advent of exchange-traded funds; dozens of foreign-bond funds have materialized just in the past couple of years.

When most investments professionals look at the world of global fixed income, they see two large categories of bonds: developed-world bonds and emerging-market bonds.

Dipping into developed-world bonds

Just as the U.S. government and corporations issue bonds, so too do the governments and corporations of Canada, England, France, Italy, Germany, Sweden, Japan, Switzerland, and many other countries, large and small, hot and cold, rich and not-so-rich. True, it may be difficult to find a decent sirloin in some of these distant lands, but that doesn't mean their fixed-income offerings are all chopped meat. Foreign bonds, just like domestic bonds, come with varying maturities, risk levels, and peculiar characteristics. Some are callable, others not. Some are inflation-adjusted, others not. Some are fixed-rate, others have floating rates. Some, like U.S. bonds, tend to pay interest semiannually. Others — most European bonds, for example — pay interest annually.

Needless to say, not all foreign bonds yield the same return. As you can see in Table 9-1, the current yield on the day I'm typing these words varies considerably.

Table 9-1	Current Yield on Various Developed-World Government Bonds (10-Year Maturities)
Japan	0.98
Germany	1.92
United States	1.99
United Kingdom	2.14
France	2.92
Australia	4.07
Italy	5.62
Greece	33.12

What are they?

Whether they're issued by corporations or by governments, foreign bonds may be dollar-denominated; these are often called *Yankee bonds*. But most are denominated in the currency of their home countries, be it euros, pounds, yen, or krona.

Over the long run, you can expect that bonds of similar credit quality and duration, bearing similar risk, should yield roughly equal returns, no matter in which country they are issued or sold. After all, if British bonds consistently paid higher rates of interest than U.S. bonds, investment money would start to float eastward across the big pond. U.S. bond issuers, such as the Treasury, the State of California, and Exxon Mobil, would eventually either have to up their coupon rates or raise capital another way, such as bake sales or bingo games.

In the short run, however, interest rates can vary among bond markets, and more importantly, exchange rates can fluctuate wildly. For that reason, U.S. investors putting their money into foreign fixed income in developed nations are generally looking at a fairly volatile investment with modest returns. (All fixed-income investments generally see modest returns.) On the flip side, foreign bonds, especially non-dollar-denominated bonds, tend to have limited correlation to U.S. bonds (meaning their value is independent of U.S. bonds), so owning some foreign fixed income in developed countries can be a sensible diversifier. Figure 9-1 offers a nice snapshot of the performance of U.S. versus foreign fixed-income securities from 1992 through the end of 2011.

Difference in Return (%)

Figure 9-1: The rolling 12-month returns of developed-nation versus U.S.-issued bonds.

Illustration courtesy of Vanguard based on data from Barclays Capital

Should you invest?

Investing in individual bonds is tricky. Investing in individual foreign bonds is trickier — kinda like buying a villa in Venice as opposed to a condo in Connecticut. To tap into the foreign fixed-income market, you're better off looking at investing through a mutual fund or exchange-traded fund. Most foreign-bond funds are pricier than their U.S. cousins — by a long shot. My Morningstar Principia software can readily show me more than 100 domestic bond funds with net annual management expenses of less than one-quarter of 1 percent. Not a single foreign-bond fund is that economical, and only a handful have management expenses less than 0.60 percent. In this low interest rate environment, that kind of cost difference matters. A lot.

Is the diversifying power of foreign bonds worth that added expense? Just as importantly, is the added volatility due to currency flux that accompanies most foreign fixed-income investments worth the ride?

The answer (I apologize; please don't hate me): It depends.

If you are still going to work every morning, still in the accumulation phase of your investing career, and already have a good percentage of your portfolio in foreign currency-based investments, such as foreign stock mutual funds or exchange-traded funds, then holding foreign bonds of developed-world nations won't serve all that much purpose. If, however, you have a large bond portfolio (say $200,000 or more), and especially if you are living off those bonds, then putting a certain amount of your bond portfolio into foreign bonds — maybe a fifth or a quarter — may make a lot of sense. The diversification effect could help smooth out your total portfolio returns and possibly boost performance.

Please don't make the assumption that you can predict currency fluctuations and start loading up on foreign bond (or stock) funds as a way to speculate on a falling dollar. Currency exchange is as unpredictable as ordering the Thursday Night Fish-Extravaganza-Special at a cheap diner. Don't try it. You'll likely lose. If you buy into a foreign bond fund, do it only for the diversification benefit, and keep the allocation modest.

In Chapter 16, I provide the names of various mutual funds that offer exposure to foreign developed-world bonds at a relatively reasonable price. Most of these funds offer pure unhedged exposure. A few are dollar-hedged. When a fund is *dollar-hedged,* that means the manager is using sophisticated financial tools (usually currency forwards) to offset any currency flux. These hedged funds (not to be confused with hedge funds) are less volatile than the currency unhedged funds, but you lose a lot of the diversification power.

Embracing the bonds of emerging-market nations

Emerging markets is something of a euphemism for "poorer countries of the world." Those who invest in them *hope* that these nations are emerging, but no one can say with any certainty. In any case, if you want to buy bonds issued in Brazil, Turkey, Russia, Venezuela, Mexico, or Argentina, the opportunities are out there. The interest rates can be considerably higher than the interest rates you find in the developed world; the volatility can be enough to make your stomach contents start emerging.

What are they?

The majority of emerging-market bonds are so-called *sovereign* bonds. That title sounds like it may have something to do with kings and queens, but all *sovereign* means is that these bonds are issued by national governments. U.S. Treasury bonds are sovereign bonds.

Unlike the bonds issued by developed nations, such as Germany and Japan, most emerging-market bonds are denominated in U.S. dollars (although that's slowly changing over time). Still, given the poverty, tsetse flies, and other problems of these nations, the governments can be shaky. To get enough people to lend them money, they must pay high rates of interest. At the time I'm writing this chapter, the Fidelity New Markets Income Fund has enjoyed an average annualized return since inception in May 1993 of slightly over 12 percent a year. Woooahhh. Find *that* anywhere else in a fixed-income investment.

Of course, with the high return, as always, comes high volatility. In 1998, when Russian government bonds went into defaultski, investors in the Fidelity New Markets Income Fund, like investors in most emerging-market funds, quickly saw about a quarter of their investments disappear overnightski. The following year, 1999, most emerging-market bond funds sprung back rather nicely, even though Ecuador defaulted on its bonds that year.

By the way, certain dollar-denominated bonds issued by Latin American countries are often referred to as *Brady* bonds, named after former U.S. Treasury Secretary Nicholas Brady. The bonds were part of a scheme developed in the late 1980s to figure out a way for Latin American countries to deal with their giant-sombrero-sized debt burdens.

Entering an Alice-in-Wonderland world

In more recent years, emerging-market bonds took a serious hit in 2008 when investors in the Fidelity New Markets Income Fund, as well as most similar funds, lost nearly one-fifth of their investment value. (Treasuries were just about the only investment that actually made money that year.) But once again, the next year, 2009, was a gangbuster year, and investors who stayed put in their emerging-market bonds recouped nicely.

And then . . . a very strange thing happened. We saw a debt crisis emerge in Europe. Bonds across the continent took a swan dive, with yields in certain nations like Spain and Italy reaching yields similar to most emerging-market bonds. In January 2012, for example, just as S&P lowered its ratings on the government bonds of eight European nations, bonds issued by Italy were yielding more than bonds issued by Mexico, and bonds issued by Spain were yielding more than bonds issued by the Philippines. Bonds in Greece that month (see Table 9-1) were yielding more than 30 percent — way more than most emerging-market bonds.

As a whole, however, developed-world bonds, even immediately following the S&P (and later, Moody's) downgrades in Europe, never approached yields offered by the emerging-market nations. (Many, many more bonds are issued by Germany and France than by Italy, Spain, and Greece.) Most developed nations still maintain high S&P ratings: Germany and the Netherlands are still AAA; France and Austria are AA (same as the United States); Spain is A; Italy is BBB+. Most emerging markets have lower ratings: Russia and Brazil are BBB; Turkey and the Philippines are BB; Columbia is BBB-.

While there has been lots of talk lately about how the ratio of debt to gross domestic product has reached higher levels in many developed-world nations (including the United States) than in many emerging-market nations, that ratio is not the only determinant of a nation's default risk. And the ratings firms know this. Emerging-market nations — because of unstable governments, economies that are often reliant on commodity prices, and lack of infrastructure — are riskier places in which to invest and likely will remain such. Emerging-market bonds, therefore, must offer higher interest rates in order to remain attractive to investors.

Should you invest?

I like emerging-market bonds, and I think they belong, in modest amounts, in most portfolios larger than $100,000 or so. If you're going to have high-yield bonds in your portfolio, emerging-market bonds make sense. When recession hits the United States and the Dow and S&P have a rough year, U.S. high-yield (junk) bonds usually tank. That makes sense. As companies hit hard times, marginal companies are most likely to default. Emerging-market bonds, however, have little correlation to the U.S. stock market (despite their synched tumble in 2008). That's why I advocate a small allocation — perhaps 3 to 5 percent — of a well-diversified portfolio in emerging-market bonds.

But, given the volatility of these bonds and the potentially high returns, I look at them more like stock investments than bond investments; in fashioning portfolios, I put emerging-market bonds on the equity side of the pie. There's only one practical way to invest in emerging-market bonds, and that's through a fund. I suggest some good fund options — both mutual funds and exchange-traded funds — in Chapter 16.

Some of the newer emerging-market funds available — which I do not recommend to you in Chapter 16 — offer a way to invest in "local currency" emerging-market bonds. These are bonds not only issued by countries with lots of inherent risks but also denominated in those countries' inherently risky currencies, rather than in U.S. dollars. These funds are double-daring you. I wouldn't go there unless you have an exceptionally hearty appetite for risk, and even then, I'm not sure these funds make sense. As one financial industry colleague said to me recently, "Oh my! When my grandparents left Russia 80 years ago, they couldn't wait to get rid of their rubles. To think that there are investors today actually going out of their way to sink their savings in rubles — it boggles the mind!"

Bond Investing with a Conscience

Whatever your religion, whatever your political leanings, you may find a bond or bond fund out there waiting for you to express your beliefs. No one ever said that making money has to be all about making money.

Having faith in church bonds

Talk about good deeds. Churches in the United States have issued bonds for more than a century now. The bonds are most often secured by a deed of trust on church real estate or other property. Traditionally, most of these bonds have been sold as private offerings to bona fide members of the church congregation only. But in the past decade or so, a market has been growing for church bonds offered to the general public — believer and heathen alike. Yes, a church-bond mutual fund even exists for those who seek holy diversification.

What are they?

Church bonds look and feel something like corporate bonds, but they have a certain advantage in that they are almost always backed by the issuer's real property. For that reason, when property held stable value, as it did for many years, church bonds rarely defaulted. But that situation changed when the real estate market starting tumbling. Since 2008, some church bonds have gone under.

Because most of these bonds are still sold under private offerings, and because the ratings agencies— the same people who generally produce default statistics— don't rate church bonds, there's no way to say exactly how many church bonds have defaulted. But according to Scott Rolfs of B.C. Ziegler and Company (in the business of issuing church bonds since 1913), only 4 of the nearly 500 bond issues his firm has managed over the past 30 years have failed to pay investors back their promised interest and principal.

As for yield, says Rolfs, church bonds generally pay 65 basis points (65/100 of a percentage point) higher than BBB corporate bonds. At the time of this writing, in early 2012, the typical 10-year church bond was yielding about 6 percent, according to Rolfs.

Keep in mind a few caveats when buying church bonds:

- Church bonds, which are usually issued in denominations of $1,000, tend to be rather *illiquid*; you could have a hard time selling a church bond that you don't plan to hold to maturity.
- All church bonds are *callable,* meaning that the church may give you your money back and retire the bond before it matures.

> ✔ Because church bonds are generally too small to be rated by the major rating agencies, you've really got to trust your broker to do due diligence (that means homework in financial-speak) and make you an honest deal.

Don't for a minute believe that church bonds are somehow divine creations. In 2010, a former Indiana pastor was sentenced to 54 years in prison for his role in selling more than $120 million in bogus church bonds. His main selling point, according to trial testimony, was an appeal to the Christian faith. The vast majority of church bonds, however, are legitimate financial instruments . . . if not divine.

Should you invest?

Church bonds are viable alternatives to corporate bonds, especially if you care where your money is going and reap emotional reward from knowing that you are helping to fund the growth of a church. But the offerings are limited, and most are restricted to residents of certain states.

One church-bond mutual fund — Capstone Church Bond Fund (XCBFX) — founded in 2005, is available to any investor in any state. Unfortunately, the yearly management fee of 1.82 percent is too high for me to recommend this fund. Nonetheless, for more information on the fund, you can contact Capstone Church Bond Fund at www.capstonechurchcapitalfund.com or 1-800-262-6631. The five-year return of this fund is currently a very unimpressive 0.83 percent. Because of the high management fee, I doubt you'll ever see returns too spectacular.

You may also try two other outfits devoted to the offering of individual church bonds:

> ✔ B.C. Ziegler and Company at www.ziegler.com or 1-800-366-8899
>
> ✔ The American Investors Group at www.churchbondsusa.com or 1-800-815-1175

If you shop for church bonds, don't do it on a prayer; shop as you would for any other bond. Make sure you read the prospectus and understand the risks involved. Note especially the collateral offered on the bond. Then get competitive bids, and be sure that you are not paying an unreasonable markup to the broker. As of 2009, church bonds have been listed on the TRACE system that allows you to see recent buys and sells. Chapter 15 provides a list of commandments for dealing in individual bonds of any faith.

Adhering to Islamic law: Introducing sukuk

According to the classical laws of Islam, paying or charging interest is a definite no-no. You'd think, therefore, that bond investing would be as sinful as slugging Jack Daniels while eating pork rinds and watching a swimsuit contest.

Well, it depends on the bond. Some very special bonds, called *sukuk* (pronounced *soo-cook*), actually allow for virtuous investing . . . at least according to some followers of Islam. Other followers see the sukuk as smoke and mirrors. But while the controversy continues, there are likely at least $100 billion — some say considerably more — in sukuk floating around the world. In fact, you can even track their performance with the Dow Jones Sukuk Index.

Most of these bonds are being issued in Islamic countries and sold to Middle Eastern and European investors. But sukuk sales in the United States have begun to take hold. In June 2006, Houston-based East Cameron Partners, an oil development company, issued $166 million in sukuk. Most of the buyers were U.S.-based hedge funds. They didn't buy the sukuk for religious reasons; these particular sukuk were paying 11.25 percent. In late 2009, General Electric Capital Corp. issued $500 million in sukuk with five-year maturities. Buyers responded, in part because the issue, rated AA+, offered to pay 1.75 percent more than comparable Treasuries were paying at the time.

What are they?

Traditional bonds pay you a fixed interest amount over the life of the bond, and then you get your principal back upon maturity. Sukuk may also pay you a fixed rate, but it isn't called interest, and the money is said to come not from the lending itself but rather from the sale or leasing of certain tangible assets, such as property, or (in the case of East Cameron) oil profits, or (in the case of GE) aircraft assets. A sukuk in full compliance with Islamic law also cannot guarantee your principal; the return of your initial investment, as with your share of profits, may depend on whatever returns are garnered from the assets backing the bond.

Note that Islamic law, like the law of many other religions (as well as governments, for that matter) is often subject to interpretation. Just ask the bankers at Goldman Sachs who announced a $2 billion sukuk deal in late 2011 that, months later, was still being widely debated, with some Islamic scholars blessing the proposed deal and others objecting to it.

The central tenet of Islamic law is that money cannot have any real value in and of itself, explains Eric Meyer, chairman and CEO of Shariah Capital, a Connecticut-based financial product development firm specializing in Islamic offerings. "Returns from an investment must stem from a hard asset that is both real and substantial," he says.

Like a traditional bond, a sukuk has a maturity date and a certain rate of return, but that rate of return may be either fixed or floating and is always backed by some hard ("real and substantial," as Meyer says) asset.

Should you invest?

So far, the sukuk market in the United States is pretty small. But keep your eyes and ears open; more likely be coming. I have no direct experience with sukuk, so all I can say is to do a lot of research before investing. (*Islamic Finance For Dummies* by Dr. Faleel Jamaldeen [Wiley] is a good place to start.) If you are Muslim, you may want to check with your mullah to ascertain whether a particular offering meets your religious needs. The website of Shariah Capital, www. shariahcap.com, should bring regular updates on the development of sukuk in this country, as well as abroad.

Investing for the common good: Socially responsible bonds

Socially responsible investing (SRI) can mean different things to different people, but for most, the goal of SRI is to shun bad-thinking-and-doing companies and embrace good-thinking-and-doing companies. Typically, companies that produce tobacco and alcohol, engage in gambling activities, produce lethal weapons, pollute the environment, discriminate in employment, or violate human rights are shunned. Companies that are helping to create a safer, cleaner, healthier, and more just world are embraced.

Most SRI investing is done through stock mutual funds. Steve Schueth, president of First Affirmative Financial Network, a Colorado-based independent advisory firm specializing in SRI, finds that somewhat ironic. "Doing social action from the debt [bond], as opposed to the equity [stock] side of the portfolio is potentially much more powerful," he says.

Schueth points out that most stock transactions occur on the secondary market. After the initial public offering of stock by a company, people generally don't buy stock directly from the firm but rather from a third party through an impersonal exchange. Not so with bonds. Bonds are much more often purchased directly from the issuer. "As a lender of money, you actually have considerable power to affect a company's actions," says Schueth. Of course, he admits, only really big lenders have really big power. For the rest of us, a handful of SRI bond mutual funds allow us to exert our influence in communal fashion.

What are they?

These mutual funds put companies through a social screen. Only those companies that act in accordance with the social guidelines of the fund managers get to sell their bonds to the fund. Examples of SRI bond funds include the following:

- **Calvert Social Investment Fund (CSIBX):** www.calvertgroup.com or 1-800-368-2748
- **Domini Social Bond Fund (DSBFX):** www.domini.com or 1-800-762-6814
- **Pax World High Yield Fund (PAXHX):** www.paxworld.com or 1-800-767-1729

All three of these funds use somewhat similar social criteria. From the people at Pax World:

> Pax World offers mutual funds dedicated to promoting peace, protecting the environment, advancing equality, and fostering sustainable development. We seek to invest in companies that meet positive standards of corporate responsibility and that provide products or services that improve the quality of life.

The somewhat similar Calvert and Domini funds consist of mostly higher quality, intermediate-term bonds. The Pax fund, as the name implies, includes bonds of lesser quality but potentially fatter returns.

Should you invest?

None of these funds is terrible; none (from a strictly financial viewpoint) would likely make it to the top of my buy list. But some things in life matter more than money, more than even some of the things that money can buy, such as chocolate. If your values jibe with those of the managers of these funds, I would recommend that you consider these funds, carefully, for the fixed-income side of your portfolio. You could do a lot worse.

Playing with Bond Fire: Potentially Risky Bond Offerings

When rock star David Bowie decided in 1997 to produce his own bonds using his considerable talent (and future song royalties) as collateral, it struck some as a rocking good idea. Bowie got $5.5 million out of the deal, but some investors haven't fared as well as they thought they would. In this section, I introduce a few types of bonds that fall a few notes shy of being totally safe investments but nonetheless may make a reasonable addition to some people's portfolios.

Bonds with big hearts

Calvert Foundation Community Investment Notes are sort of like any other individual bonds in the sense that they have a maturity date, pay a steady rate of interest, and can be purchased through many brokers. But the similarity ends there. You select the term — between one and ten years — and you select the interest rate (up to a modest limit). The money you lend goes to fund affordable housing, make small business loans to people who otherwise couldn't get them, and build community facilities that provide healthcare and education to the underserved.

The Calvert Foundation began the project 15 years ago, no investor has yet to lose a dime, and the loans have undoubtedly helped to alleviate poverty worldwide. The notes are available to U.S. residents of all states, with the exceptions of Arkansas, Pennsylvania, South Carolina, and Washington (subject to change). The sliding rate scale (the less you earn, the more altruistic your investment), purchase instructions, and more information on the various anti-poverty projects funded by the foundation can be found at `www.calvertfoundation.org` or by dialing 800-248-0337.

For *accredited* investors (generally speaking, those with more than $1 million in net worth, not including the home) willing to sink in at least $25,000, somewhat similar, low-risk, low-interest loans to help combat poverty can be made through Root Capital. Find them at `www.rootcapital.org` or 617-661-5792.

Rocking with Bowie Bonds

David Bowie was the first artist to issue bonds using his future royalties as collateral. The bonds, issued in 1997, carried a coupon rate of 7.9 percent. Not too shabby. But in 2004, given some changes in the music industry, including the advent of file sharing on the Internet, Moody's downgraded the bonds to junk status. The price of Ziggy Stardust's bonds fell to earth. Those who needed to sell lost a good deal. But the concept of Bowie Bonds — raising cash with talent — caught on nonetheless, and other artists soon followed.

What are they?

Since the original Bowie Bonds (sometimes called *Pullman Bonds* after David Pullman, the financier who pulled the Bowie deal together), other artists have followed suit. James Brown, The Isley Brothers, Iron Maiden, Ashford & Simpson, and Rod Stewart all closed similar deals, raising cash with bonds backed by future song royalties. The music-makers get their money up front, and bondholders get to collect interest (they hope). Similarly, a few small bond issues have been backed by future revenues of Hollywood film sales and a handful of sporting events.

Should you invest?

These are all very modest bond issues, rather *illiquid* (meaning that should you wish to sell your bond, you may not be able to), and backed by assets of wavering value. I wouldn't go out of my way to purchase Bowie Bonds. Bond manager Marilyn Cohen, a California-based colleague of mine who knows the bond world inside and out, wisely suggests that if you do buy a Bowie-type bond, at least try to find a rocker in the grave! That way you know he or she is beyond scandal.

Cashing in on catastrophe bonds

Call it strange (I think it is), but in past years several billion dollars have poured into bonds that pay higher-than-market rates of interest, but only if the weather cooperates.

What are they?

Known as *catastrophe bonds,* they are issued mostly by insurers, pay juicy rates of return, and are backed by revenues from true moneymakers. That may sound great, but here's the catch: The issuer reserves the right to use the cash behind the bonds if a hurricane or tsunami or tornado or earthquake results in many people suddenly making claims against the insurance company. If the catastrophe results in massive claims, bondholders can wind up seeing their principal cast into the wind.

In November 2010, for example, insurer Mariah Re Ltd. issued a $100 million, three-year "U.S. tornado catastrophe bond" on behalf of American Family Mutual Insurance Company. The bond paid 6.25 percent — or, more accurately, it promised to pay that amount. In late 2011, following a year of heavy twister activity, Mariah defaulted on the bonds. Investors lost everything to the tornadoes, just as Dorothy's aunt and uncle lost their Kansas farm — only it wasn't a dream. The bonds became worthless.

Should you invest?

Are you kidding? A few extra dollars in possible interest in exchange for risking your principal? No way. That's not what bonds are all about — or should be about. These bonds may possibly make sense for institutional buyers with huge resources but not for mere mortals like you and me, who hope to retire someday and live on more than peanut butter sandwiches.

Dealing in death

If catastrophe bonds weren't morbid enough, some of the world's biggest insurance companies have begun to issue *death bonds.* You stand to gain higher-than-market rates of interest, but only if a certain number of people don't die.

You read that right.

What are they?

These bonds are somewhat similar to catastrophe bonds. The bonds are issued by insurers and pay raucous rates of interest, but the insurer reserves the right to tap the money behind the bonds if more people than expected die. Some of these bonds directly tie your return to the death rates of a pool of the insured. If the insurance company's customers eat their vegetables, wear their seatbelts, and don't play with guns, you win. If an epidemic strikes or a volcano erupts, you lose, and your investment may turn to ash.

American International Group has pushed other strange bonds lately, which may also be called death bonds, "blood pools," or "collateralized death obligations." These bonds are backed by insurance policies on the elderly, and they pay off when the insured dies. It's sort of the opposite of the more traditional death bond. So far, AIG has been having a hard time pushing these bonds, as the major ratings agencies have refused to play along.

Should you invest?

Yuck. These investments are both risky and morbid. As with the catastrophe bonds, institutional investors may have some reason to take a risk on such a thing. For living, breathing individuals, these bonds make little to no sense.

Dancing in the Flames: Derivatives and Default Bond Products

Whooooeeee! If you think of debt securities as safe and boring, cast a gander on some of these investments, which are built on derivatives and defaulted bonds. You could double or triple your money overnight . . . or see it shrink and fade faster than the bankroll of a drunken gambler in Vegas on a not-so-hot night.

Daring to delve into derivatives

In general, a *derivative* is a financial something-or-other whose value is based on the price of some other financial something-or-other. (I apologize for the highly technical definition.)

Examples of derivatives include futures and options. Entire fun books are written on futures and options (such as *Futures & Options For Dummies* by Joe Duarte, MD, published by Wiley). Suffice to say that they allow you to leverage your money and make big plays on just about anything, including the price of pork bellies, orange juice, most stocks, and — yes — even "conservative-investment" bonds, too.

Futures and options allow investors to purchase a contract that says on such-and-such a date, you're going to buy (in the case of a future) or you have the option of buying (in the case of an option) such-and-such a bond. The price is set today, not knowing what the price of the bond will be at that date in the future (the *expiry date*). If, on that day, the price of the bond is 110 and you have a contract to buy it at 100, BINGO — you win! If, however, the price of the bond has dropped to 95, ZINGO — you lose! Futures and options allow you to put up relatively little money (the price of the contract) and possibly profit a lot . . . or lose every penny.

Warren Buffett has called derivatives (such as futures and options) "weapons of financial mass destruction." And they certainly can be.

Lehman's downfall

One derivative product, specific to bonds, is called the *collateralized debt obligation* (CDO), of which the most common is the *collateralized mortgage obligation* (CMO). Talk about weapons of financial mass destruction . . .

A CMO is a complicated beast created by a brokerage house. It is a certificate that represents partial ownership of a huge pool of mortgage bonds, such as Ginnie Maes, Fannie Maes, and Freddie Macs (see Chapter 7). Different owners in the pool get paid at different times, and the payments are contingent on the performance of the pool and the payoff of other partial owners. Prior to the credit crisis that brought down such institutions as Lehman Brothers, many CMOs were created using pools of subprime mortgage bonds. The subprime mortgage bonds, in turn, were bonds issued on the mortgages of huge homes sold to people with small paychecks. When the people with small paychecks realized that they could not afford the huge homes, the pools cracked. And you know what happened then. If only the executives at Lehman Brothers had read the first edition of *Bond Investing For Dummies*!

Should you invest?

All derivatives are risky investments. In my mind, that's not the purpose that bonds serve in this universe. I wouldn't suggest dabbling in either CMOs or bond futures. Professional traders, who live-breathe-and-die this stuff, will very likely clean your clock. Heck, sometimes the professionals, as we saw in the case of Lehman Brothers and Bear Stearns, clean their own clocks!

Banking on losses with defaulted bond issues

In Chapter 6, I talk about junk bonds: bonds that offer high yields but carry high risk. Some bonds — bonds *in default* — are even junkier than junk.

What are they?

Bonds in default are almost always corporate bonds (very, very rarely municipal bonds). *In default* usually means that the company is bankrupt or very close to being bankrupt, coupon payments on the bonds have stopped, and there is an extremely high likelihood that investors' principal — or a good portion of principal — will never be returned.

But miracles do happen. Companies that seem to be going under or are forced into reorganization sometimes make surprising comebacks. And when they do, or even if it looks like they might, big profits can ensue. Defaulted bonds sell, as you would imagine, at very deep discounts. Those who purchased the defaulted bonds of Delphi, the bankrupt auto parts producer, saw their investments double in price within several months. The defaulted bonds of Calpine, the bankrupt energy company, quadrupled in value in a three-month period. Most other defaulted bonds, however, fade into oblivion, and investors looking to make a quick buck are left with little to nothing to show.

Should you invest?

Hmmm. I spoke with Martin Fridson, CEO of FridsonVision LLC (an independent investment research firm in New York City) and something of an expert on defaulted bonds. Here's what he says:

> Buying a bond in default is the polar opposite of ordinary bond investing. You get no income. No security. You're purely speculating that the price will shoot up and you'll have a capital gain. Most people who buy these never see any gain.

> They [people who buy defaulted bonds] may have been talked into buying the defaulted bond by a fast-talking broker, and that *broker* will make a nice gain. But the person who bought the bond will generally see nothing.

I'm inclined to agree. Play the horses . . . roll some dice . . . go to Spain and bet on the bull to kill the matador . . . buy defaulted bonds. Have fun, but don't call any of them investing. They are gambling.

Ah, but what if you are *already holding* a bond that goes into default? Should you keep it or sell it? That depends, says Richard Lehmann, publisher of the *Forbes/Lehmann Income Securities Investor* newsletter (www.incomesecurities.com). If you're holding a municipal bond, keep it, he says. The recovery rate on munis is very high, in part because bondholders are usually the creditors with the most clout — more than, say, retired schoolteachers and librarians lining up for their pension benefits.

If you're holding a corporate bond that goes into default, that's another story. Powerful banks and other creditors tend to get their money before you do. Defaults usually begin with an announcement from a company that it will cease coupon payments on its bonds. Most often, such announcements come in November or December for tax reasons, says Lehmann. As soon as the announcement is made, the price of the bond will tumble as the market starts to panic.

After the initial panic, prices on defaulted corporate bonds usually, but not always, creep up. If you can get your hands on a corporate balance sheet, note what percentage of the company's assets are intangibles, such as goodwill and brand names, says Lehmann. "The higher the percentage of intangible assets versus hard assets, the lesser your chance of recovery [getting back any of your principal], and the more incentive you have to sell the bond as soon as possible," he says. "The greater the percentage of hard assets, such as land and property, the greater your odds of recovery, and the more incentive you have to hold onto the bond."

Evaluating Exchange-traded Notes

They sound like *exchange-traded funds* (investments similar to mutual funds, usually indexed mutual funds that trade like stocks), but exchange-traded notes (ETNs) are as different from ETFs as jellyfish are different from fish. ETNs are debt instruments, bonds of sorts, but the income they produce is far from fixed. In fact, unlike most other debt securities, they offer no coupon rate, and the maturity date, although it exists, is rather inconsequential.

What are they?

ETNs were first issued in 2006 by Barclays, and Barclays iPath ETNs continue to dominate the market. ETNs trade on the major exchanges, just like ETFs. You can buy as little as one share (under $100), or many shares. But instead of buying a basket of stocks or bonds as you do when you buy a mutual fund or ETF, the purchase of an ETN represents a direct loan to its purveyor, be it Barclays, PowerShares, Direxion, ProShares, or whoever. If the firm were ever to go under, you could lose your money, just as you might if you were holding a coupon-paying bond issued by one of these companies.

Instead of promising you a steady rate of interest on your loan, as you'd get with a traditional bond, Barclays, for instance, promises to pay you in accordance with the performance of a particular index. So, for example, if you were to purchase shares in the (Barclays) iPath Goldman Sachs Crude Oil

Total Return Index (the ticker is OIL), your return would be commensurate with any rise (or fall) in the price of crude oil. If you were to purchase shares in the iPath Dow Jones-AIG Commodity Index Total Return ETN (DJP), your returns would be commensurate with the rise (or fall) in the value of an index that tracks a variety of commodities, from silver and gold to cotton futures and natural gas.

These are but two examples of dozens of ETNs that allow you to track the prices of commodities, stocks, bonds, or currencies. At present, the IRS is taxing ETNs (other than the currency ETNs) very gingerly, asking only for capital gains tax if profits result from a sale of shares. But the IRS is known to be looking at ETNs with a magnifying glass, and the current favorable tax status may not last forever.

Should you invest?

If you're going to invest in oil or gas or Indian stocks, or any investment that is difficult to buy directly, ETNs may make sense. They are fairly low-cost, tax-efficient (for the moment) securities. They can also be highly volatile investments depending on the type of asset or derivative they are tracking, so be sure you know what you're getting into. These are not your father's debt instruments! Always keep in mind that in addition to the market risk you take on, there is also default risk, just as with any bond. Be certain to investigate the credit worthiness of the issuer!

Part III
Customizing and Optimizing Your Bond Portfolio

The 5th Wave   By Rich Tennant

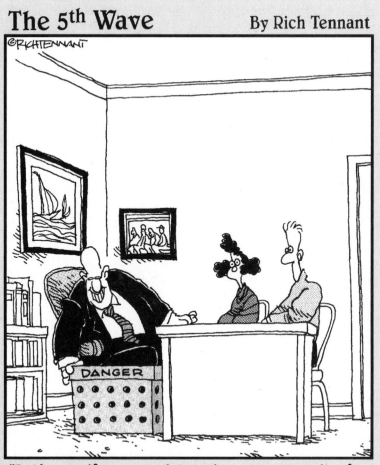

"Let's see if we can determine your capacity for assuming risk. Now, how familiar are you with snake handling?"

In this part . . .

*I*f portfolio construction were done in the kitchen, Part II would be our list of ingredients, and Part III is where I begin to divulge the secret family recipes. In the four chapters that follow, I ask you to join me in mixing together various investments to build a delicious savings buffet. I focus, of course, on the bond side of the portfolio. But I don't want you to look at bonds in a vacuum, so I discuss other kinds of investments as well.

Before you step into the kitchen to begin the actual portfolio-cooking process, your first step is to look at investment risk and potential return: the yin and yang of wealth-building. I introduce you to something called Modern Portfolio Theory that explains how to balance your yin and yang for maximum yield and minimal insomnia. I explain the concept of correlation and how you want to incorporate into your portfolio some investments that zig while others zag (and preferably a few that zog).

Finally, I serve as official matchmaker, matching you with particular kinds of bonds that make sense for you — the kinds of bonds with which you can live happily ever after.

Chapter 10

Risk, Return, and Realistic Expectations

● ●

In This Chapter

▶ Accepting a risk-return tradeoff — like it or not!

▶ Recognizing the seven different kinds of bond risk

▶ Looking back in time to see how well bonds have done

▶ Using bonds to adjust your portfolio's volatility and growth

● ●

Dear Russell: I am 8 years old. Some of my little friends say there is no tradeoff between risk and return. Papa says, "If you see it in Bond Investing For Dummies, it's so." Please tell me the truth: Is there a tradeoff between risk and return?

VIRGINIA O'HANLON
115 WEST NINETY-FIFTH STREET

*Y*es, Virginia, there is a tradeoff between risk and return.

Your little friends are wrong. They have undoubtedly been thumbing through too many paperback books in airport kiosks that say you can get rich quick with absolutely no risk to your principal by following some crazy scheme or another.

That is all fantasy, Virginia. In this great capitalist system of ours, the individual investor is a mere insect, an ant, whose hope to get rich quick is fed by the mass media and the greed of Wall Street and then squashed under the heel of financial reality.

Alas! How dreary would be the world if there were no tradeoff between risk and return. It would be as dreary as if there were no Virginias. You and your Papa and all your little friends might simply invest in money-market funds and retire rich tomorrow. Variable-annuity salesmen would be out on the street. CNBC, instead of hyperventilating 24 hours a day over the stock market, would be airing reruns *of Star Trek.*

Not believe in the tradeoff between risk and return?! You may as well not believe in compound interest, or the miracle of modern orthodontics.

No tradeoff between risk and return?! A thousand years from now, Virginia, nay, ten times ten thousand years from now, there will STILL be a tradeoff between risk and return. This chapter explains why that is so, why understanding that tradeoff is integral to building a successful portfolio, and why trying to do so without bonds is as silly as . . . well, questioning the existence of Santa Claus.

Searching, Searching, Searching for the Elusive Free Lunch

Just in case you want to know the explanation, Virginia (Virgil, Vinny, Vicky . . . whoever is reading this page), a tradeoff between risk and return exists for roughly the same reason that a shiny new Lexus costs more than a 2003 Honda Civic. If both vehicles cost the same, everyone except maybe Ralph Nader would buy a new Lexus. Similarly, if you thought you could earn as much investing in FDIC-insured CDs as you could earn investing in shiny tech stocks, backed only by the capriciousness of the market, would you invest in the tech stocks? No, I don't think so.

A risk-free investment that paid high returns would be the equivalent of a free lunch. Sorry, Charlie, but free lunches are very hard to find. No stable investment should be expected to pay a high rate of return. No luxury car should be expected to sell for the same amount as an old jalopy. The capitalist market, as Adam Smith once said (and even Ralph Nader can't deny), has an invisible hand.

Making a killing in CDs . . . yeah, right

What I'm saying, and what Professor Smith was saying (sort of), is that risky investments — or at least investments perceived as risky — tend to return more than less risky investments for the very same reason that old jalopies sell for less than new luxury cars: at least over the long run, they *must.*

Look: If you could invest in the stock market, commodities, real estate, or money-market funds and CDs, all returns being equal, you'd invest in money-market funds and CDs, right? Everyone would invest in money-market funds and CDs. There'd be no market for more volatile investments. Similarly, if luxury cars and old jalopies were available at the same price, there'd be no market for old jalopies.

Only because of differing rewards (higher return potential or greater price bargain), there is a market for both. Honk honk. Ka-ching ka-ching.

Defining risk and return

In just a moment, I talk of the particular risk and return characteristics of bonds. But first, I want to make clear what risk and return really are. (No, it isn't obvious to everyone.)

Risk is the potential of losing money. Although you can lose (or gain) money a lot more easily in certain investments than others, all investments carry some risk . . . including the safest of bonds, and even including cash. When most people think of risk, they think of wild market swings such as those that often occur in the market for, say, cocoa bean futures. They think of how much money they could potentially lose in a week, a month, or a year. But you can lose money in an investment in other ways, which I address in the next section.

Return is the potential of making money. Most of the money made in bonds is made in the form of interest payments. Sometimes, bonds also appreciate (or, alas, depreciate) in value. Overall, the return potential of bonds is modest compared to certain other investments, like an investment in the S&P 500 or a dry-cleaning franchise in the local strip mall. As I make clear, I hope, throughout this book, the benefit of bonds is more to temper risk and provide steady, predictable income than to capture huge gains.

Appreciating Bonds' Risk Characteristics

In Chapter 9, I talk about bond derivatives, defaulted bonds, and a few other bond investments that most people would consider wild and crazy by fixed-income standards. But the vast majority of bond offerings are rather staid investments. You give your money to a government or corporation. You receive a steady flow of income, usually twice a year, for a certain number of years. Then, typically after a few years, you get your original money back. Sometimes you pay taxes. A broker usually takes a cut. Beginning and end of story.

The reason for bonds' staid status is not only that they provide steady and predictable streams of income, but also that as a bondholder you have first dibs on the issuer's money. A corporation is legally bound to pay you your interest before it doles out any dividends to people who own company stock. If a company starts to go through hard times, any proceeds from the business or (in the case of an actual bankruptcy) from the sale of assets go to you before they go to shareholders.

However, bonds offer no ironclad guarantees. First dibs on the money aside, bonds are not FDIC-insured savings accounts. They are not without some risk. For that matter, even an FDIC-insured savings account — even stuffing your money under the proverbial mattress! — also carries some risk.

Following are seven risks inherent in bond investing. As a potential bond-holder, you need to know each of them.

Interest rate risk

Interest rates go up, and interest rates go down. And whenever they do, bond prices move, almost in synch, in the opposite direction. Why? If you're holding a bond that pays 5 percent, and interest rates move up so that most new bonds are paying 7 percent, your old bond becomes about as desirable to hold as a pet scorpion. Any rational buyer of bonds would, all things being equal, choose a new bond paying 7 percent rather than your relic, still paying only 5 percent. Should you try to sell the bond, unless you can find a real sucker, the price you are likely to get will be deeply discounted.

The longer off the maturity of the bond, the more its price will drop with rising interest rates. Thus long-term bonds tend to be the most volatile of all bonds. Think it through: If you have a bond paying 5 percent that matures in a year, and the prevailing interest rate moves up to 7 percent, you're looking at relatively inferior coupon payments for the next 12 months. If you're holding a 5 percent bond that matures in ten years, you're looking at potentially ten years of inferior coupon payments.

No one wants to buy a bond offering ten years of inferior coupon payments unless she can get that bond for a steal.

That's why if you try to sell a bond after a period of rising interest rates, you take a loss. If you hold the bond to maturity, you can avoid that loss, but you pay an opportunity cost because your money is tied up earning less than the prevailing rate of interest. Either way, you lose.

Of course, interest rate risk has its flip side: If interest rates fall, your existing bonds, paying the older, higher interest rates, suddenly start looking awfully good to potential buyers. They aren't pet scorpions anymore — more like Cocker Spaniel puppies. If you decide to sell, you'll get a handsome price. (I discuss the formulation of bond prices in Chapter 4.)

This "flip side" to interest rate risk is precisely what has caused the most peculiar situation in the past three decades, where the longest-term Treasury bonds (with 30-year maturities) have actually done as well as the S&P 500 in total returns. The yield on these babies has dipped and dipped and dipped . . . from over 14 percent in the early 1980s to just a little over 3 percent today. Hence, those old bonds, which are now maturing, have turned to gold. Will this happen again in the next 30 years? Not unless long-term Treasuries in the year 2042 are being issued with a negative 8 percent interest rate. Of course, that isn't going to happen. More likely, interest rates are going to climb back to historical norms.

You can probably figure out now why I am putting interest rate risk first on this list. Interest rate risk has perhaps never been greater than it is today. You would be foolish to put your money into 30-year Treasuries and assume that you are going to get 11.5 percent a year annual return, as some very lucky investors have done over the last 30 years. Chances are, well . . . anything can happen over 30 years, but keep your expectations modest, please.

Inflation risk

If you are holding a bond that is paying 4 percent, and the inflation rate is 4 percent, you aren't making anything. You are treading water. And that's only if your interest is coming to you tax-free. If your bond is paying 4 percent, and inflation moves up to 5 percent, you are losing money. Inflation risk is perhaps the most insidious kind of bond risk because you can't really see it. The coupon payments are coming in. Your principal is seemingly intact. And yet, when all is said and done, it really isn't intact. You are slowly bleeding purchasing power.

Although inflation rarely hits you as fast and hard as rapidly rising interest rates, it's the fixed-income investor's greatest enemy over the long run. Interest rates, after all, go up and down, up and down. But inflation moves in only one direction. (Well, we could have *deflation,* where prices fall, but that hasn't happened since the Great Depression — except for a month or two here and there. I don't believe deflation is likely to happen again anytime soon.) Inflation takes its toll slowly and steadily, and many bondholders don't even realize that they are losing ground.

Some bonds — Treasury Inflation-Protected Securities — are shielded, at least theoretically, from the risk of inflation. (It's complicated. See Chapter 5.) Most bonds (and bondholders), however, suffer when inflation surges.

Reinvestment risk

When you invest $1,000 in, say, a 20-year bond paying 6 percent, you may be counting on your money compounding every year. If that is the case — if your money does compound, and you reinvest all your interest payments at 6 percent — after 20 years you'll have $3,262.

But suppose you invest $1,000 in a 20-year bond paying 6 percent and, after four years, the bond is *called.* The bond issuer unceremoniously gives back your principal, and you no longer hold the bond. Interest rates have dropped in the past four years, and now the best you can do is to buy another bond that pays 4 percent. Let's suppose you do just that, and you hold the new bond for the remainder of the 20 years. Instead of $3,262, you are left with $2,387 — about 27 percent less money.

The risk I describe here is called *reinvestment* risk, and it's a very real risk of bond investing, especially when you buy callable or shorter-term individual bonds. Of course, you can buy non-callable bonds and earn less interest, or you can buy longer-term bonds and risk that interest rates will rise. Tradeoffs! Tradeoffs! This is what investing is all about.

Note that one way of dealing with reinvestment risk is to treat periods of declining interest rates as only temporary investment setbacks. What goes down usually goes back up.

Default risk

Default risk is what most people think of when they think of investment risk. Even many bond investors focus on default risk . . . sometimes, too much. In fact, most bond investors worry so much about default risk that it often blinds them to the more common and more insidious risks of bond investing, such as those I mention in the previous sections.

What is default risk? Simple: The issuer of your bond starts to go under; limited or no money is left to pay creditors; and not only do your interest payments stop coming in the mail every six months, but also you start to wonder if you'll ever get your principal back. If the issuer actually declares bankruptcy, your mailbox, instead of offering you interest payments, will be flooded with letters from lawyers explaining (in explicit Latin) that you are a sucker and a fool.

With Treasuries and agency bonds, a default has never happened. Rarely do municipal bonds or investment-grade corporate bonds default. Default risk is mostly an issue when you invest in high-yield (junk) corporate bonds. When the economy is humming along, defaults are rare. When the economy slides and even companies that make hotcakes can't sell their wares, default rates jump. That's an especially nasty time to be losing money on your bonds because chances are good that your other investments are doing poorly.

Certain foreign bonds, especially emerging-market bonds, carry default risk as well. But emerging-market bonds (bonds issued mostly by the governments of poor countries), unlike U.S. junk corporate bonds, have limited correlation to the U.S. stock market. For that reason, although emerging-market bonds have somewhat higher volatility than U.S. junk bonds, I often recommend them first for a portfolio (see Chapter 9).

Downgrade risk

Even if a bond doesn't go into default, rumors of a potential default can send a bond's price into a spiral. When a major rating agency, such as Moody's, Standard & Poor's, or Fitch, changes the rating on a bond (moving it from, say, investment-grade to below investment-grade), fewer investors want that bond. This situation is the equivalent of *Consumer Reports* magazine pointing out that a particular brand of toaster oven is prone to explode. Not good.

Bonds that are downgraded may be downgraded a notch, or two notches, or three. The price of the bond drops accordingly. Typically, a downgrade from investment-grade to junk results in a rather large price drop because many institutions aren't allowed to own anything below investment-grade. The market therefore deflates faster than a speared blowfish, and the beating to bondholders can be brutal.

On occasion, downgraded bonds, even those downgraded to junk (sometimes referred to as *fallen angels*), are upgraded again. If and when that happens (it usually doesn't), prices zoom right back up again. Holding tight, therefore, sometimes makes good sense.

But trust me when I tell you that bond ratings and bond prices don't always march in synch. Consider, for example, that when U.S. Treasuries were downgraded by Standard & Poor's in 2011 from an AAA to an AA rating, the bonds did not drop in price but actually rose, and rose nicely. Why? In large part, it was because of the credit crisis in Europe and the realization of Japan's rising debt. In other words, although the United States appeared to be a slightly riskier place to invest vis-à-vis other nations, it actually started to look safer.

Tax risk

When comparing taxable bonds to other investments, such as stocks, some investors forget to factor in the potentially high cost of taxation. Except for municipal bonds and bonds kept in tax-advantaged accounts, such as an IRA, the interest payments on bonds are generally taxable at your income-tax rate, which for most people is in the 25 to 28 percent range but could be as high as 35 percent . . . and, depending on the whims of Congress, may rise higher.

In contrast, stocks may pay dividends, most of which (thanks to favorable tax treatment enacted into law just a few years back) are taxable at 15 percent. If the price of the stock appreciates, that appreciation isn't taxable at all unless the stock is actually sold, at which point, it's usually taxed at 15 percent. So would you rather have a stock that returns 5 percent a year or a bond that returns 5 percent a year? From strictly a tax vantage point, bonds lose. Paying even 25 percent tax represents a 67 percent bigger tax bite than paying 15 percent. (Of course — getting back to the whims of Congress — these special rates are also subject to change.)

Tax risk on bonds is most pronounced during times of high interest rates and high inflation. If, for example, the inflation rate is 3 percent, and your bonds are paying 3 percent, you are just about breaking even on your investment. You have to pay taxes on the 3 percent interest, so you actually fall a bit behind. But suppose that the inflation rate were 6 percent and your bonds were paying 6 percent. You have to pay twice as much tax as if your interest rate were 3 percent (and possibly even more than twice the tax, if your interest payments bump you into a higher tax bracket), which means you fall even further behind.

I don't believe that inflation will go to 6 percent. But if it does, holders of conventional (non-inflation-adjusted) bonds may not be happy campers, especially after April 15 rolls around.

Keeping-up-with-the-Joneses risk

Despite all the other risks I mention, bonds, when chosen wisely, and well diversified, usually make good, safe investments. But the return on bonds generally isn't going to be anything to write home about. From a strictly financial point of view, that may not be so bad. Some people who live within their means and already have good nest eggs don't need, and really should not take, much risk with their investments. But if you're not taking that risk and your neighbors are, and the markets are good, and the economy is humming, your neighbors (those pesky Joneses) may be making much more on their investments than you are. Ouch.

Studies show that *relative* wealth (making more than your neighbors) is more important to many people than *absolute* wealth (how much you actually have in the bank). Can you handle dinner with your neighbors and friends as between bites they boast about their major gains in the markets?

Regarding all these risks . . .

Please don't think that I'm trying to convince you not to buy bonds! Despite all the risks I mention, bonds still belong in your portfolio. Stay tuned for the numerous reasons why.

And in the meantime, check out Figure 10-1. To the left, see where bonds tend to fit into the investment risk spectrum as compared to other kinds of investments. To the right and the far right, see where different kinds of bonds rank in order of relative risk.

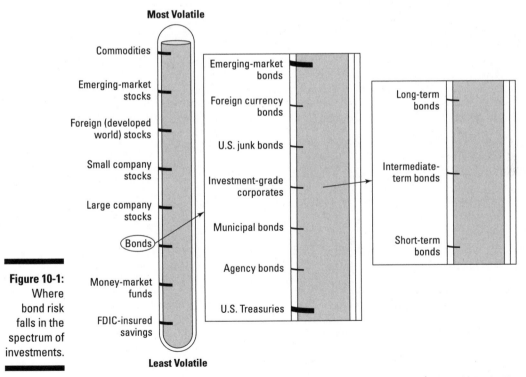

Figure 10-1: Where bond risk falls in the spectrum of investments.

Understanding standard deviation

When comparing different kinds of bonds — or any investments, for that matter — it helps to know the *standard deviation*. This is the most oft-used measure of risk when comparing investments.

What does it mean? An investment with a standard deviation of, say, 3 will give you a return that is within one standard deviation (in this case, 3 percentage points) of the mean about two-thirds of the time. So suppose you have a bond fund that has an historical average annual return of 6 percent, and you know that the standard deviation is 3. What that means is that two-thirds of the time, the return from this bond fund will fall somewhere between 9 percent (6 percent average return + 3 percent standard deviation) and 3 percent (6 percent average return − 3 percent standard deviation). If that same bond fund had a standard deviation of 5, the returns you could expect would generally fall between 11 percent and 1 percent.

Is a high standard deviation good or bad? That depends on how much volatility you can stomach and how much return you need to get.

Thanks to Morningstar Principia software, I can readily find the ten-year standard deviation for any bond fund (which means how volatile the funds have been for the past ten years). Following are a few examples. The higher the number, the greater the price swings in years past and the greater the price swings, most likely, in years to come. In the world of bonds, the greatest factors affecting volatility are the maturity of the bonds and the stability of interest rates. The price of long-term bonds tends to be much more volatile than the price of short-term bonds. But the quality of the bonds matters, too. High-yield (junk) bonds tend to be more volatile. And foreign bonds, denominated in other currencies, also tend to be more volatile due to currency flux.

To help put things in perspective, the ten-year standard deviation for the stocks of the S&P 500, an index of the 500 largest companies in the United States, stands at 15.9. As you can see, not even the most volatile categories of bonds are as volatile as that. And the S&P 500 is considerably less volatile than certain other investments, such as tech stocks, small-company stocks, and oil futures.

Name of Fund	Type of Bonds in Fund	Ten-Year Standard Deviation
Fidelity New Markets Income	Emerging-market bonds, dollar denominated	11.15
Vanguard Long-Term U.S. Treasury	Government bonds with average maturity of 20 years	11.13
T. Rowe Price International Bond Fund	International bonds with average maturity of 8 years	9.12
Vanguard High-Yield Tax-Exempt	Municipal bonds of various grades with average maturity of 8 years	5.33
Vanguard GNMA	Government-backed bonds with average maturity of 7 years	2.96
Vanguard Short-Term Bond Index	Investment-grade corporate bonds with average maturity of 3 years	2.24

Reckoning on the Return You'll Most Likely See

If all bonds were the same, this would be a very short book indeed. Bonds differ greatly as far as risk, expected return, taxability, sensitivity to various economic conditions, and other factors. Up until now, this chapter has focused more on risk than on expected return. (Yes, Virginia, I do believe that I already mentioned there's something of a connection between the two!) I now discuss expected returns.

I can hear you say with confidence, "But a bond yielding 5 percent can be expected to return 5 percent over the life of the bond, and a bond yielding 6 percent can be expected to yield 6 percent. How hard can this be?"

HA! Ha ha ha ha!

Calculating fixed-income returns: Easier said than done

So you invest in a $1,000 bond that yields 6 percent and matures in 20 years. What do you do with the $30 coupon payments that you receive every six months? Do you reinvest them or spend them on Chinese dinners? Do you keep the bond for the entire 20 years or cash it out beforehand? (If the bond is callable, of course, you may have no choice but to take back your principal before maturity.) And if you do cash out before maturity, what kind of price will you be able to get for the bond?

And what about the *real* (after-inflation) rate of return — the return that really matters? If inflation runs at 2 percent, your real return will be a lot greater than if inflation runs at 8 percent. But how can future inflation be predicted?

And what if you invest in a bond fund? Just because the fund yielded, say, 5 percent annually over the past seven years, does that mean it will yield that much moving forward?

And (sorry, just a couple more questions here . . . I'm almost done) what about *after-tax* real return (return after both inflation *and* taxes)? Ultimately, that's the return that matters the most of all. That's the return that moves you ahead financially or sets you back. Do you know what your tax bracket will be in ten years? Do you know what *anyone's* tax bracket will be in ten years?

These are just some of the questions that make bond investing — or any kind of investing — so much fun! I now pull out my crystal ball.

Measuring risk a simpler way

An outfit called RiskMetrics offers a new, easier way of comparing investment risk. Instead of using standard deviation (the most common way of measuring risk, as I explain in the preceding sidebar in this chapter), the folks at RiskMetrics have come up with a scale that allows for much simpler understanding of risk.

I recommend that you check out the following URL: www.nasdaq.com/symbol/abmd/risk. Plug in any of the various bond (or stock or commodity) exchange-traded fund symbols, and voilà, you are given a number. The higher the number you receive, the greater the risk. The lower the number, the lesser the risk. Unlike standard deviation numbers, RiskGrade numbers are logical and to scale (just like the metric system of measuring distance or weight). In other words, an investment with a RiskGrade of 20 is twice as volatile as an investment with a RiskGrade of 10, and half as volatile as an investment with a RiskGrade of 40.

Unfortunately, I suppose because mutual funds don't trade on exchanges such as the NASDAQ but exchange-traded funds do, this nifty tool doesn't work for mutual funds — only for ETFs.

But many mutual fund companies can, I'm sure, if you ask them very nicely, provide you with RiskGrade numbers. The free tool on the NASDAQ site allows you to compare and contrast any of the dozens upon dozens of bond ETFs, including those I list below.

RiskGrades takes into consideration various kinds of risk, including interest rate risk, currency fluctuation, and default risk. Theoretically, at least, the RiskGrades methodology could prove to be a truer measure of future risk than the always backwards-looking standard deviation. Check with me in about 20 years, and I'll have the definitive answer! In the meantime, you may wish to compare and contrast the two measures, and take them both into consideration when choosing a bond fund.

The following ETFs are somewhat similar to the mutual funds that I give standard deviations for in the "Understanding standard deviation" sidebar. As a point of comparison, the RiskGrade for the S&P 500 is 113. Notice that the first fund, made of all "risk-free" U.S. Treasury bonds, is nearly as risky as an all-stock fund!

Name of Fund	Type of Bonds in Fund	RiskGrade
iShares Barclays 20+ Year Treasury Bond (TLT)	U.S. government bonds with very long maturities	100
iShares JPMorgan USD Emerging Markets Bond Fund (EMB)	Emerging-market bonds, dollar denominated	36
iShares S&P National AMT-Free Muni Bond (MUB)	Intermediate-term municipal bonds	27
iShares Barclays Agency Bond Fund (AGZ)	Government agency bonds	14
Vanguard Short-Term Corporate Bond Index (VCSH)	Investment-grade corporate bonds with short maturities	11

Looking back at history: An imperfect but useful guide

Not to tickle a dead horse or anything, but I said something earlier about the markets pretty much assuring that in the long term investors are appropriately rewarded for the risks they take. And so it stands to reason that if we know what kind of returns a certain kind of bond has seen in the past, oh, 30 years, that information may give us a pretty good indication of the kind of returns that kind of bond is likely to provide in the next 30 or so years — at least relative to other bonds. Granted, history is only a guide. (Repeat: *History is only a guide.*) But aside from tea leaves and Tarot cards (which I don't put a whole lot of faith in), history is one of the only guides we have.

I've nabbed a couple charts from Vanguard that show *nominal* (before inflation) bond returns over the past 30 years. You'll note that the past 30 years have been particularly good ones for long-term government bonds, which, despite their lesser risk, have returned almost as much as long-term corporate bonds. (In fact, the past 30 years, because of declining interest rates, have been a good period for nearly all kinds of bonds.)

Figure 10-2 shows the nominal returns of $1 invested in long-term government bonds from 1982 through 2012.

Figure 10-2: The 30-year nominal returns of long-term (10+ years) government bonds.

Illustration courtesy of Vanguard based on data from Barclays Capital

Figure 10-3 shows the nominal returns of long-term corporate bonds from 1982 to 2012.

Figure 10-3:
The 30-year nominal returns of long-term (10+ years) corporate bonds.

Illustration courtesy of Vanguard based on data from Barclays Capital

And now for a couple big-picture visuals. Figure 10-4 shows the nominal returns of $1 invested in the Barclays Capital U.S. Aggregate Bond Index, which reflects the total U.S. bond market, during those same 30 years. Figure 10-5 represents the real (after inflation) returns of that same $1.

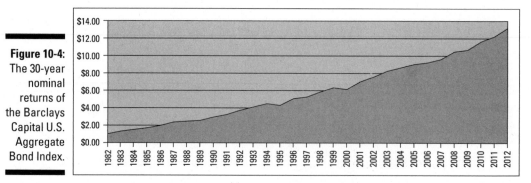

Figure 10-4:
The 30-year nominal returns of the Barclays Capital U.S. Aggregate Bond Index.

Illustration courtesy of Vanguard based on data from Barclays Capital

Figure 10-5:
The 30-year real returns of the Barclays Capital U.S. Aggregate Bond Index.

Illustration courtesy of Vanguard based on data from Barclays Capital

Okay, so much for the past 30 years. Now I invite you to look at bond returns over an even longer period.

As it happens, we have pretty good data about bond returns over the past 86 years, largely thanks to Ibbotson Associates, a Morningstar company. Here are the figures for the average annual *nominal* (before inflation) return of three categories of bonds since 1926:

- ✔ One-month Treasury bills: **3.6 percent**
- ✔ Long-term government bonds: **5.5 percent**
- ✔ Long-term corporate bonds: **5.9 percent**

And here are those same figures translated into *real* (after inflation) returns for the same time period:

- ✔ One-month Treasury bills: **0.6 percent**
- ✔ Long-term government bonds: **2.4 percent**
- ✔ Long-term corporate bonds: **2.8 percent**

Um, I suppose as the author of *Bond Investing For Dummies* I'm not supposed to point this out, but quite honestly, the numbers aren't too awe-inspiring, are they? Keep in mind that they don't even factor in taxes, and you are taxed on the nominal (pre-inflation) returns of your bonds, not the real (post-inflation) rate of return.

Investing in bonds despite their lackluster returns

So what would you have earned, after taxes, investing in long-term government bonds over the past eight decades or so? Well, compared to stocks, which have returned about 9.5 percent a year before inflation and 6.5 percent after inflation, you would have earned squat. With corporate bonds, you would have earned slightly more than squat. And with short-term government bonds, you would have earned less than squat.

Keep in mind that all squat figures are rough approximations. If you force me to get technical, the long-term return on all bonds, judging by the past eight decades, is about half that of all stocks. The real return on bonds (after inflation but before taxes) is about one-third that of stocks. For the average taxpayer, the after-tax, long-term return on bonds is very roughly one-quarter that of stocks. (I *told* you this wasn't a book on getting rich quick!)

So why even bother to invest in bonds? There are several *very* good reasons:

- ✔ Even squat adds up when compounded year after year. Start with $10,000. Give yourself a mere 2 percent annual return, and — voilà — within a century, you'll have $72,450. Granted, you're not going to live another century unless you're from extremely good stock and you're reading this in diapers, but you get the point, right?

- ✔ In the last 80-plus years, stocks clearly clobbered bonds, but the next 80-plus years could be entirely different. Data from the 1800s show that the returns of stocks and bonds weren't all that different way back when.

- ✔ Investment-quality bonds have little — practically no — correlation to stocks, so they provide excellent balance to a portfolio. If you want to make sure that you're holding investments that don't all crash at once, stocks and bonds are a sweet mix to have.

- ✔ At certain times when stocks have tanked, bonds (especially long-term Treasury and high-quality corporate bonds) have rallied, providing comfort to investors when comfort was most needed. See Figure 10-6. Remember 2008.

- ✔ Unlike just about any other kind of investment, bonds provide steady income for people who need it.

- ✔ Bonds' limited volatility, as compared to many other investments, makes them good bets for people who can't afford to take much short-term risk.

- ✔ Even though bonds have earned squat compared to stocks, they are virtual money machines compared to keeping your money in a savings account or money market fund. Passbook savings accounts and money market funds are generally not going to pay you enough to even keep up with inflation. These days, they don't even come close.

- ✔ Because you're going to take my advice on regularly rebalancing your portfolio (see Chapter 12), the "drag" of bonds on total portfolio performance will likely be much less than you think.

Figure 10-6:
When stocks have declined, bonds have typically generated positive returns.

Finding Your Risk-Return Sweet Spot

Portfolio A is as volatile as a 3-year-old child but offers high return potential. Portfolio B is as volatile as a three-toed sloth (it hangs in trees) and offers modest return potential. Portfolio C is halfway between the two. Without knowing anything else about these three hypothetical portfolios, I'd say that Portfolio A is made up mostly of stocks; Portfolio B is constructed mostly of bonds; and Portfolio C is a more even mixture of both.

Allocating your portfolio correctly

Deciding how to split your portfolio between fixed income (bonds, cash, CDs) and equity (stocks, real estate) is usually going to affect your risk-return profile more than any other decision. For that reason, I have an entire chapter — Chapter 12 — designed to help you make that one crucial decision. Do you want a 70/25/5 (stocks/bonds/cash) portfolio? A 50/45/5 portfolio? A 30/55/15 portfolio? Silly formulas abound. I want you to get it right . . . which you will.

But certainly, what *kind* of equity (large-company stocks, small-company stocks, foreign stocks, dry-cleaning franchise) and what *kind* of fixed income (Treasuries, corporate bonds, junk bonds, munis) you choose for your portfolio plays very much into your risk-return profile as well. In Chapter 13, I ask you to tell me something about yourself so I can help you decide what kinds of bonds are best for you. For now, I want you to start thinking about your risk-return "sweet spot."

Tailoring a portfolio just for you

Your age, your income, your wealth, your expenses, your retirement plans, your estimated Social Security, and your health all come into play when deciding where your risk-return sweet spot should fall.

As far as choosing your bonds, the less volatile bonds (short-term, high quality) naturally edge your portfolio toward safety but more modest returns. The higher volatility bonds (long-term, high-yield) move your portfolio toward greater risk but potentially higher return. (Ask Virginia O'Hanlon if this isn't self-evident; she can explain it.)

Ah, but at times choosing even a very volatile bond or bond fund may make perfect sense, even for someone looking to avoid risk. You'll understand why after reading about *Modern Portfolio Theory,* which tells us that new investments added to a portfolio must take into consideration existing investments within the portfolio. It's not as complicated as it sounds. Honest! Read all about Modern Portfolio Theory in Chapter 11.

Chapter 11

The Science (and Pseudoscience) of Portfolio-Building

No man is an island.

> — John Donne (Devotions Upon Emergent Occasions, "Meditation XVII")

No bond is an island, either.

> — Russell Wild (Bond Investing For Dummies, Chapter 11)

People sometimes ask me, "Russell, is such-and-such a good investment?" My response is always the same: "It depends largely on what other investments you have in your current portfolio." Wishy-washy? Nah.

Some investments are so horrible that no one should ever touch them. (Your brother-in-law will be happy to recommend several to you, I'm sure. If he can't, mine will!) Somewhere, I suppose, there may be an investment so perfect that anyone who doesn't jump on it is a fool. (I've never seen such an investment, but presumably one exists somewhere.) Most investments are neither horrible nor perfect; they may be good for you but not good for me, or vice versa.

Take John Hypothetical Investor, whose entire portfolio consists of bonds in the ChickenLickin' Corporation. John needs yet another ChickenLickin' bond about as badly as I need water in my basement. But just because another ChickenLickin' bond isn't right for John doesn't make it a fixed-income pariah. Such a bond may be just the perfect addition to the portfolio of Jane Hypothetical Investor, whose present wealth consists of a few randomly chosen tech stocks and a dozen mayonnaise jars filled with loose change.

Starting with the next chapter, I explain the mechanics of building a portfolio, including which kinds of bonds may fit in best and how to go about buying and selling them. But before I get there, I need to discuss a few of the theoretical underpinnings that can help you understand how intelligent portfolios are constructed. In this chapter, I explain some of the modern science that allows smart investors, like you, to construct the leanest and meanest portfolios possible — portfolios that minimize risk and maximize potential return.

What do such portfolios look like? Here's a hint: Bonds, be they ChickenLickin' or any other variety, are an essential ingredient.

Mixing and Matching Your Various Investments

So, what kinds of investments go well together, and which kinds clash?

If you already have a portfolio that looks like John Hypothetical Investor's — a portfolio filled with ChickenLickin' bonds — the last thing you need is another ChickenLickin' bond. That's because putting all your eggs in one basket is the surest way to wind up with scrambled eggs (or fried chickens). You want to include different kinds of investments in any portfolio, preferably investments from different asset classes and, best of all, investments that have little or no correlation.

Dreaming of limited correlation

An *asset class* is a group of investments that share common characteristics. Long-term, investment-grade corporate bonds would be an example. Small cap growth stocks would be another example. United States–based real estate investment trusts (REITs) would be a third.

For a good, basic education on asset-class investing and why it makes so much sense, I highly recommend two books:

- *All About Asset Allocation,* Second Edition by Richard Ferri (McGraw-Hill)
- *The Intelligent Asset Allocator* by William Bernstein (McGraw-Hill)

One distinguishing characteristic of an asset class is that it tends to perform in cycles, and those performance cycles tend to be different than the performance cycles of other asset classes. In other words, two distinct asset classes have *limited correlation:* They won't move up and down at the same time. And so, having them together in a portfolio helps make for smoother sailing.

Let me illustrate how lack of correlation works to lessen a portfolio's ups and downs. Figure 11-1 shows the performance of two investments, which we'll call "Volatile Investment A" and "Volatile Investment B." Both investments offer high long-term positive returns and equally high volatility; they move up and down like pogo sticks under a hyperactive child. However, notice that they don't move up and down at the same time. In fact, these two investments move in opposite directions. They are said to have *negative correlation.*

Figure 11-1:
Investments A and B each offer high returns and high volatility.

Illustration by Wiley, Composition Services Graphic

Because of that negative correlation (easy to find in textbooks, very difficult to find in the real world), Volatile Investment A and Volatile Investment B combine to create a portfolio with socko returns but not a wee bit of volatility. Figure 11-2 shows what happens when you put them together into the same portfolio: You get the perfect result of high returns and no price swings!

Figure 11-2:
The ideal portfolio: The price (represented by the dotted line) rises steadily.

Illustration by Wiley, Composition Services Graphic

Unfortunately, this is only a model. Finding two investments that offer high long-term positive return potential with negative correlation is almost impossible in the real world (although finding one without the other isn't difficult at all).

Seeking zig and zag with Modern Portfolio Theory

What I'm talking about is diversification: combining an investment that zigs with another that zags, and possibly a third that zogs. In the investment realm, diversification is your very best friend.

Most investment pros are familiar with something called *Modern Portfolio Theory.* You should be, too. Modern Portfolio Theory is the key to maximizing return with minimal risk. What the theory says is that if you combine asset classes that zig and zag (and possibly zog) in a portfolio, even though each asset class by itself may be quite volatile, the volatility of the entire portfolio can be quite low. In fact, in some cases, you can add a volatile investment to a portfolio and, as long as that investment shows little correlation to everything else, you may actually *lessen* the volatility of the entire portfolio!

Translating theory into reality

Correlation is measured on a scale of –1 to 1. Two investments with a correlation of 1 are perfectly correlated: They move up and down in synch, like two Rockettes. Two investments with a correlation of –1 have perfect negative correlation: When one goes up, the other goes down, like pistons. A correlation of zero means that there is no correlation between two investments: When one goes up, the other may go up or down; there's simply no predicting.

In the real world, negative correlations of two productive investments are hard to find, but you *can* find investments that have close to zero correlation. Perhaps the best example from history is stocks and bonds. Bonds as a whole generally move up and down independent of stock prices. Some bonds — such as long-term Treasuries — tend to have negative correlation to stocks, generally climbing during times of recession (often in response to dropping interest rates in combination with stock-investor panic that drives up demand for security). But other bonds, such as U.S. high-yield bonds, tend to move more in synch with the stock market.

When choosing a bond or bond fund, you always want to consider the correlation that your new investment is going to have with your existing investments. High-yield bonds throw off considerably more interest than Treasuries, but they aren't going to give you nearly the same diversification power if your portfolio is made up mostly of U.S. stocks.

In Figure 11-3, you can see how the performance of the entire bond market (as reflected in the share price of the Vanguard Total Bond Market Index Fund) and the performance of stocks (as reflected in the share price of the Vanguard Total Stock Market Index Fund) exhibit little correlation. Sometimes they go up together and sometimes down together, but often they move in opposite directions.

Daily closing prices January 2002-December 2011

Figure 11-3: Bonds and stocks: Two paths that often diverge.

Illustration courtesy of Vanguard

Appreciating Bonds' Dual Role: Diversifier and Ultimate Safety Net

Okay, okay, so diversification is a good thing, but why must a diversified portfolio include bonds? After all, there are many investments to choose from in this world.

True enough: There are many investments to choose from in this world. And I encourage you, if your portfolio is large enough, to do some *gonzo investing*, as I like to call it. Go ahead, invest in commodities and foreign real-estate funds and emerging-market stocks and stocks in small value international companies and hedge funds and emerging-market debt. All these asset classes are imperfectly correlated, so you will likely get extra return while shaving off some volatility.

But invest with caution. Even when you use sophisticated portfolio-building tools to take maximum advantage of Modern Portfolio Theory, diversification isn't foolproof. It's no guarantee that you won't lose money.

Sometimes, even historically noncorrelated asset classes can move in the same direction. We're seeing more examples of increased correlation these days. Thank globalization, which has tied many markets together. Thank hedge funds and exchange-traded funds, which have taken previously obscure asset classes, such as coffee-bean and palladium futures, and turned them into frequently traded investments.

Protecting yourself from perfect storms

Lately, the markets have seen several *perfect storms:* times when all the economic conditions are lined up in such a fashion that practically everything everywhere loses money. You may recall a few very ugly days on the markets in late February and early March 2007.

Tuesday, February 28, 2007 was one of the worst days the market has ever seen. As reported in *The Wall Street Journal* on March 1, 2007, "Not only did all 30 stocks of the Dow Industrial Average fall, so did all but two of the stocks in the Standard & Poor's 500-stock index." The article goes on to explain that of 51 nations' stock markets, only two — the tiny stock markets of Jordan and Morocco — did not swoon with all the rest. The article continues, "Emerging-market and junk-bond prices fell sharply. Even the price of gold, where investors typically run in times of trouble, fell."

That day in early 2007, of course, was just a precursor to the market freefall that began later that year and continued until early 2009. At one point, the major indexes (such as the S&P and the Dow) were down about 50 percent. For the entire calendar year of 2008, the major indexes, both U.S. and foreign, were down nearly 40 percent. Almost nothing was left unscathed: Asian stocks, European stocks, small caps, large caps, REITs . . . even commodities took a big tumble, as did — yes — many bonds, including municipals and high-yield corporate bonds. It was indeed the perfect storm.

But Treasuries and the highest quality corporate bonds more than held their own. Once again, these particular asset classes provided portfolios with some cushion during the hardest of times.

Eyeing a centuries-old track record

Not only do high-quality bonds, such as Treasuries, have a proven track record of slightly negative correlation to the stock market, but they also have a long history of stability and positive returns. So they provide two vital roles in a portfolio: diversification and (just in case diversification doesn't work) a solid floor that will keep your portfolio from falling past a point of no return.

You can't say that about many other asset classes. You couldn't say it prior to 2008, and you certainly can't today. Here's why:

- ✔ **Foreign stocks:** With the globalization of markets, foreign stocks, although they still offer limited correlation to U.S. markets, are beginning to have less diversification power. And foreign stocks, like all stocks, can be very volatile, especially with currency fluctuations.

- ✔ **Gold:** The precious metal, a hedge against stock market gyrations for generations, has lost some its diversifying glimmer. Lately, for a number of reasons, gold has moved in synch with the stock market more often than not. It's also unclear whether gold, silver, oil, or any other nonproductive commodity is going to produce gains in the long run. Over the past 100 years, the price of gold has risen just about the same as the rate of inflation.

- ✔ **Hedge funds:** They are expensive. Terribly expensive. They are opaque (it's 11 p.m. — do you know where your money is?). They are volatile. They are *illiquid* (meaning it's sometimes hard to unload your shares). They may or may not give you the diversification you seek.

- ✔ **Cash:** Nothing in the short run is as safe as cash. The price of cash is, well, the price of cash! But over the long run, cash is inevitably eaten up by inflation. Keep too much of your portfolio in cash, and you are taking a real risk of losing purchasing power over time. (Say, for example, your grandfather earned about $12,000 a year during the 1930s, stored an entire year's salary in cash, and left it under the mattress for you. You could use that money today to perhaps buy a very cheap used car.)

 On the other hand, quality bonds — Treasuries, agencies, and investment-grade corporate bonds — seem to have lost none of their diversifying power. They held up well in 2008, when nothing else did. Plus, they earn enough return (generally) to stay ahead of inflation, and they are stable. In fact, because bonds offer a steady stream of income, which tends to offset any price depreciation, and because those bond payments are not contingent on company profits (as are stock dividends), quality bonds very rarely lose money. Occasionally, when interest rates rise, long-term investment-quality bonds may lose value for a year or two. By year three, however, you are virtually assured of at least breaking even (at least if history is your guide).

Recognizing Voodoo Science

Although Modern Portfolio Theory has its limitations, the science behind the theory is sound, and its real-world applications are profound. Given that just about all asset classes fell in 2008, some people have claimed that MPT is dead. Not so. Far from it. First, 2008 was a once-in-our-lifetimes (so far) event. And even though all asset classes went down, they went down to different degrees, and they recouped at very different speeds. MPT is still alive and well . . . and very much legitimate.

The same cannot be said for other common theories on investing. Now is as good a time as any for me to blow a couple of these common deceits out of the water.

Here's deceit number one: Timing the markets, finding "hidden" bond deals, and predicting changes in interest rates are the ways to manage a bond port-folio. And deceit number two: Successful buying and selling of bonds can boost your portfolio yields considerably.

Comparing actively managed funds to index funds

The Oppenheimer Champion Income mutual fund's latest prospectus explains that the fund's manager, in choosing bonds for the fund, seeks a "'bottom up' approach, focusing on the performance of individual securities while considering industry trends. . . . He evaluates an issuer's liquidity, financial strength and earnings power... [and] analyzes the overall investment oppor-tunities and risks in different market sectors, industries and countries." The prospectus goes on to explain that the esteemed fund manager uses a slew of very sophisticated and complicated investment strategies and instruments, including options, futures contracts, swaps, structured notes, and mortgage-related securities. The prospectus is downright intimidating, even to someone like me who knows an awful lot about bonds. How can anyone read this prospectus and fail to be dazzled?

Keep reading. And stop being dazzled.

The Oppenheimer Champion Income Fund, C Shares (*C shares* means you pay a load or commission when you sell the fund), as of early 2012, boasts a ten-year annual return of –8.63 percent. That's a full 14.41 percent lower than the ten-year annualized return for the Barclays Capital Aggregate Bond Index (a popular index that estimates the return of all bonds in the United States), and a full 17.47 percent lower than the Merrill Lynch U.S. High Yield Master II Index. The Oppenheimer Champion Income Fund is one of the more than *85 percent* of actively managed bond mutual funds that failed to beat the Barclays Capital Aggregate Bond Index over the past ten years.

Forecasting the future — and getting it wrong

So few actively managed bond funds succeed at beating the index because timing markets, predicting changes in interest rates, and finding "hidden" bond deals are very, very hard things to pull off. Even the highly educated and handsomely paid managers who run the nation's largest bond funds consistently fail to do it.

Just as is the case in the stock market, bond markets tend to be *efficient.* Because so many investors are out there looking for a good deal, good deals are very, very hard to find.

Fund managers who spend hours and hours poring over company documents (so-called *fundamental analysis*) to find "hidden" deals usually fail to beat the market. Those who read charts that show the price of bonds going up and down and try to predict their future direction (so-called *technical analysis*) usually fail to beat the market. Those who read *The Wall Street Journal* every day and can list all the leading economic indicators, from employment figures to the latest on the trade deficit, usually fail to beat the market.

Those few mutual fund managers who succeed at beating the market often succeed to such a small degree that they typically don't add enough value to offset their high fees and the many costs of constant trading.

Of course, most people buy into the belief that investment professionals, including bond mutual fund managers and bond brokers, know what they are doing and can pull off miracles. Millions and millions are spent on advertising each year so that people continue to believe. And yet year after year, those who buy and hold *index funds* — funds that simply track stock or bond indexes and charge little in fees — come out ahead.

Ignoring the hype

I'm not saying that a good bond broker or bond mutual fund manager can't be an asset to you. A handful of good bond mutual fund managers are out there, and I've occasionally invested in their funds.

Good bond brokers, who can help you structure a portfolio, build good bond ladders for regular income, and gauge a proper level of risk for your investments, are also out there. But please don't believe the broker who says that he is privy to information that will help you score big in the bond world. Such inside scoops, legally or illegally obtained, are extremely rare.

Beware especially of the bond broker who pats herself on the back for never having sold you a bond that went into default. No Treasury or agency bond has ever defaulted. Defaults among municipal bonds are almost as uncommon as penguins in the Caribbean. And defaults in the corporate bond universe are fairly easy to avoid if you select top-rated quality bonds.

Bonds are ballast to a portfolio; they aren't meant to make a killing. How to pick the best individual bonds is the subject of Chapter 15. How to pick the best bond funds is covered in Chapter 16. None of it is magic. None requires secret decoder rings. The best bonds are bought with common sense, frugality, and the knowledge that no bond is an island.

Chapter 12

Dividing Up the Pie: What Percentage Should Be in Bonds?

In This Chapter

▶ Weighing the importance of the bond side of your portfolio

▶ Estimating your future need for cash flow

▶ Considering a variety of fixed income and equity investments

▶ Understanding why — and when — to rebalance your portfolio

As a teenager, I had a boat. It was 15 feet from bow to stern, yellow with two white vinyl bucket seats up front and a small bench in the back. I kept it behind my home on Long Island, tied to a floating dock in an inlet that led to the Atlantic Ocean. It was propelled (if you can even use that word) by a 25-horsepower engine. The boat, when it had the currents running against it, moved at a snail's pace. When I had three passengers in the boat, it was lucky to move at all.

Mind you, I am *not* looking for sympathy. I know darned well that other kids growing up had to deal with much, much tougher things in life, but this alleged power boat would lose a race to a paddle boat. Sometimes the other teenage boys on the water would throttle their engines, do vicious circles around me, point in my direction, and scream "Slooow down, Russell!" while laughing themselves sick.

My father, you see, bought that boat from an elderly gentleman who used it for lake fishing. Dad purposely wanted a boat with little horsepower because he figured the severely limited speed might keep his son safe. Dad's motivation was good, but his reasoning wasn't so good. A boat that size with a 25-horsepower engine may be perfect for lake fishing, but out in the ocean it was something of a floating deathtrap, prey to strong currents and the wakes of behemoth yachts.

After such a wake blew me into the side of a concrete bridge and cracked the hull, I was finally able to convince my father to up the horsepower a bit . . .

for safety's sake. I wasn't exactly going *vroom vroom* with my new 35-horse-power engine, but I ceased having to listen to "Slooow down, Russell!" from my boating schoolmates. And that felt awfully good.

Funny how some things never change. Many years later, I would become an investment advisor. And my Dad, by then retired from years as a New York City attorney, was living (along with my Mom) off a portfolio of mostly bonds and CDs. It took some doing, but I was finally able to convince them to "up the horsepower" of the portfolio by adding some stocks. Like many retirees I've worked with, especially those who lived through the Great Depression, my parents had the notion that bonds and other slow and steady fixed-income investments, such as bank CDs, mean safety.

True, a bond portfolio, unlike a stock portfolio, tends to move at a steady pace. But as with an underpowered boat in a large ocean, lack of horsepower can be as dangerous as too much horsepower. Bond portfolios lack volatility, but they are easy prey to the currents of the economy and the tides of infla-tion. The truly safest portfolios, as we've seen in both the Great Depression and the high inflation of the 1970s and 1980s, have both the horsepower of stocks *and* the stability of bonds.

Ah, but how much horsepower and how much stability? How do you find that perfect blend? Well, that depends on whether, investment-wise, you are an elderly lake fisherman, a youngster with a hankering for speed, a retired attorney and his wife, or a yachtsman leaving a big wake. In this chapter I ask you some questions about your life and, by examining your answers, help you determine the proper allocation of bonds for your portfolio. In other words, I help you find just the right *vroom-vroom/slooow-down* ratio.

Why the Bond Percentage Question Is Not As Simple As Pie

I may as well cut right to the chase. Here's how to figure out what percent of your portfolio should be in bonds, in Seven Easy Steps. Simply pull out a blank piece of paper, and pencil in the appropriate numbers. Ready?

1. Start with the number 100.   <u>100</u>
2. Subtract your current age from 100.   ____
3. Divide line 2 by the number of years between now and retirement. ____
4. Do you have a pension? If so, add 5.   ____
5. Does your boss have freckles? If so, subtract 3.   ____
6. Do you have a cousin named Pablo? If so, subtract 6.   ____
7. Add the number of feet between you and the closest garbage can. ____

All done? Good! Now wad up the piece of paper and see if you can sink a three-pointer in the basket. My point?

There are no simple formulas.

A 28-year-old with $2,800 in savings should not invest his money the same way as a 56-year-old with $620,000 in savings. A 67-year-old with a $500,000 nest egg and no pension should invest differently than a 67-year-old with the same nest egg but a generous pension. A gazillionaire with spouse and kids and a desire to leave half a gigillion to charity may invest differently than a gazillionaire whose greatest interest is throwing big parties in Morocco with dozens of camels in drag. These are only some of the factors ignored by simplistic formulas. They will *not* be ignored in this chapter!

Minimizing volatility

If I may briefly recap what I say about bond returns in Chapter 10, the long-term return on all bonds, judging by the past 80-plus years, is about *half* that of all stocks. The real return on bonds (after inflation but before taxes) is about a *third* that of stocks. For the average taxpayer, the after-tax, long-term return on bonds is roughly a *quarter* that of stocks. So what percent of your portfolio do you want in bonds? If an easy formula existed, it would be this:

> *Ideal percent of your portfolio in bonds =*
> *The necessary amount and no more (or less, for that matter)*

The "no more" part, in my book (hey! — this *is* my book!), is the easier part of the formula. The answer is *75 percent.* No kidding. Except perhaps in very rare circumstances, no one needs or wants a portfolio that is more than 75 percent bonds. Why? Because stocks and bonds together provide diversification. With all bonds and no stocks, you lack diversification. Diversification smooths out a portfolio's returns.

Believe it or not, even though stocks are much more volatile than bonds (see Figure 12-1), a modest percent of stocks added to a portfolio of mostly bonds can actually help lower the volatility of the portfolio. (I discuss this fact when I explain Modern Portfolio Theory in Chapter 11.) To include less than that (or more than 75 percent bonds) raises volatility and lowers the odds of favorable returns both over the short run and long run. So why would anyone ever want to go there? Unless you have good reason to expect an economic apocalypse anytime soon (you don't), it doesn't make a whole lot of sense to invest only in bonds.

Figure 12-1:
Stocks are much more volatile than bonds, offering significantly higher return in most years but chillingly lower returns in others.

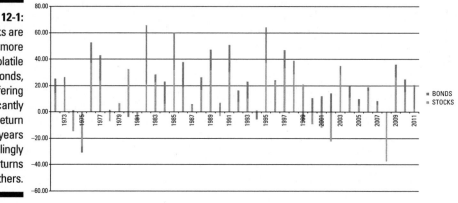

Illustration courtesy of Vanguard based on data from Barclays Capital

Maximizing return

The highest returning portfolios over the past few decades — over any few decades, for that matter — are made up predominantly of stocks. But those are also the portfolios that go up and down in value like popcorn on a fire. So the question "How much do you need in bonds?" is largely a question of how much short-term volatility you can or should tolerate.

How much volatility you can or should stomach, in turn, is largely a factor of time frame: Are you investing for tomorrow? Next year? A decade from now? Five decades from now? If you run an endowment fund, or if you happen to be immortal, your timeframe may be infinite. Most of us human-being types will want to tap into our treasured nest egg at some point. But when?

To compare the volatility of bonds versus stocks, take a look at Figure 12-2. Bonds' long-term gains pale in comparison to stocks, but when things get rough, bonds don't take it on the chin as stocks do. The figure shows the best and worst returns for stocks and bonds (as measured by the S&P 500 Index and the Lehman Brothers [which later became the Barclays] U.S. Aggregate Bond Index) since the Great Depression.

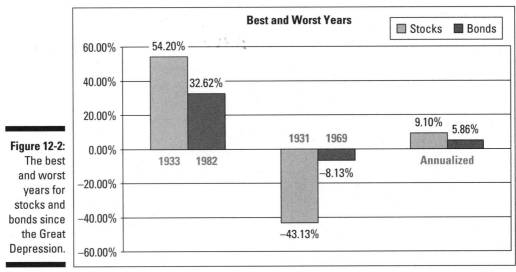

Figure 12-2:
The best and worst years for stocks and bonds since the Great Depression.

Illustration courtesy of Vanguard

Peering into the Future

You may be saving and investing to buy a new home, to put your kid(s) through college, or to leave a legacy for your children and grandchildren. For most people, however, a primary goal of investing (as well it should be) is to achieve economic independence: the ability to work or not work, to write the Great (or not-so-great) American Novel . . . to do whatever you want to without having to worry about money. In this section, I help you start thinking about how to achieve your investment goal, whatever it may be.

In Chapters 17 and 18, I discuss in some depth how big a nest egg you'll likely need for economic independence and how much you'll be able to withdraw from your portfolio, should you stop working, without running out of money. I'll save the nitty-gritty for those later chapters (or you can jump ahead and then return here, if you wish). For now, the pertinent question is this: Just how far along are you toward achieving your nest-egg goal?

Estimating how much you'll need

For reasons I divulge in those two upcoming chapters, please think of how much you will need to withdraw from your nest egg each year when you stop getting a paycheck. Whatever that number is ($30,000? $40,000?), multiply it by 20. That is the amount, at a minimum, I would like to see you have in your total portfolio when you retire. (I'd prefer 25 times, however.) Now multiply that same original-year withdrawal figure ($30,000? $40,000?) by 10. That is the amount, at a minimum, that I'd like to see you have in fixed-income investments, including bonds, when you retire.   3 м .

I'm assuming here a fairly typical retirement age, somewhere in the 60s. If you wish to retire at 30, you'll likely need considerably more than 20 times your annual expenses (or else very wealthy and generous parents).

Assessing your time frame

Okay. Got those two numbers: one for your total portfolio, and the other for the bond side of your portfolio at retirement? Good. Now how far off are you, in terms of both years and dollars, from giving up your paycheck and drawing on savings?

If you're far away from your goals, you need lots of growth. If you currently have, say, half of what you'll need in your portfolio to call yourself economically independent, and you are years from retirement, that likely means loading up (to a point) on stocks if you want to achieve your goal. *Vroom vroom.*

If you're closer to your goals, you may have more to lose than to gain, and stability becomes just as important as growth. That means leaning toward bonds and other fixed-income investments. *Slooow down.*

For those of you far beyond your goals (you already have, say, 30 or 40 times what you'll need to live on for a year), an altogether different set of criteria may take precedence.

Factoring in some good rules

As I hope I made clear at the onset of this chapter (with my silly example of the boss's freckles and good cousin Pablo), no simple formulas exist that determine the optimal allocation of bonds in a portfolio. That being said, there are some pretty good rules to follow. Here, I provide you with a few, and then I ask you to join me for a few case studies to help clarify:

- ✔ **Rule #1:** You should keep three to six months of living expenses in cash (such as money market funds or online savings bank accounts like www. ally.com or www.emigrantdirect.com) or near-cash. If you expect any major expenses in the next year or two, keep money for those in near-cash as well. When I say *near-cash,* I'm talking about CDs or very short-term bonds or bond funds, such as those I introduce in Chapter 16.

- ✔ **Rule #2:** The rest of your money can be invested in longer-term investments, such as intermediate-term or long-term bonds; or equities, such as stocks, real estate, or commodities.

✔ **Rule #3:** A portfolio of more than 75 percent bonds rarely, if ever, makes sense. On the other hand, most people benefit with some healthy allocation to bonds. The vast majority of people fall somewhere in the range of 70/30 (70 percent equities/30 fixed income) to 30/70 (30 percent equities/70 fixed income). Use 60/40 (equities/fixed income) as your default if you are under 50 years of age. If you are over 50, use 50/50 as your default. Tweak from there depending on how much growth you need and how much stability you require.

✔ **Rule #4:** Stocks, a favorite form of equity for most investors, can be very volatile over the short term and intermediate term, but historically that risk of loss has diminished over longer holding periods. Over the course of 10 to 15 years, you are virtually assured that the performance of your stock portfolio will beat the performance of your bond-and-cash portfolio — at least if history is our guide. (It shouldn't be our only guide! History sometimes does funny things.) Most of the money you won't need for 10 to 15 years or beyond could be — but may not need to be — in stocks, not bonds.

✔ **Rule #5:** Because history does funny things, you don't want to put all your long-term money in stocks, even if history says you should. Even very long-term money — at the very least 25 percent of it — should be kept in something safer than stocks.

Recognizing yourself in a few case studies

Different strokes for different folks. The following vignettes are all based on real, live clients who have asked me to massage their portfolios. All names and most identifying information have been changed to protect the identities of these good people. Perhaps you will see some similarities between their situations and yours.

Jean and Raymond, 61 and 63, financially quite comfortable

Married in 1982, Jean and Raymond raised three children; the third is just finishing up college. Jean and Raymond are both public school teachers and both will retire (he in two years; she in four) with healthy traditional pensions. Together, those pensions, combined with Social Security, should cover Jean and Raymond's living expenses for the rest of their lives. The couple will also likely bring in supplemental income from private tutoring. Jean's mother is 90. When Mom passes away, Jean, an only child, expects to receive an inheritance of at least $1.5 million. Mom's money is invested almost entirely in bonds and CDs. So what should Jean and Raymond do with the $710,000 they've socked away in their combined 403(b) retirement plans?

Jean and Raymond are in the catbird seat. Even if they were to invest the entire $710,000 nest egg in stocks, and even if we were to see the worst stock market crash in history, Jean and Raymond would likely still be okay. The couple certainly doesn't need to take the risk of putting their money in stocks because they don't need to see their portfolio grow in order to accomplish their financial goals. But given their pensions, is investing in stocks really that risky? No. If Jean and Raymond desire to leave a large legacy (to their children, grandchildren, or charity), a predominantly stock portfolio may be the way to go. Because equities tend to be so much more lucrative than fixed income in the long run, a greater percentage in equities would likely generate more wealth for the future generations.

Ignoring for the moment a slew of possibly complicating factors from the simple scenario above, I would feel comfortable suggesting an aggressive portfolio: perhaps two-thirds in equity (stocks and such) and one-third in fixed income (bonds and such). I show this breakdown in Figure 12-3. It's not what most people think of as appropriate for an "aging" couple, but to me, it makes a whole lot of sense, provided Jean and Raymond are fully on board and promise me that they won't cash out of stocks (as many investors do) the first time the market takes a dip.

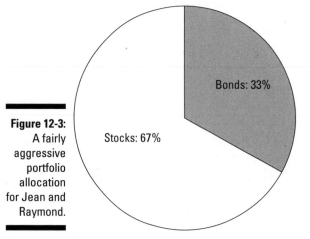

Figure 12-3:
A fairly aggressive portfolio allocation for Jean and Raymond.

Bonds: 33%

Stocks: 67%

Illustration by Wiley, Composition Services Graphics

Kay, 59, hoping only for a simple retirement

Kay, divorced twice, earns a very modest salary as a medical technician. She scored fairly well in her last divorce. (Hubby was a condescending jerk, but a well-paid condescending jerk.) Thanks to a generous initial cash settlement, as well as having made a good profit on the sale of her last home, Kay has a portfolio of $875,000. Kay doesn't hate her work, but she isn't crazy about it, either; she would much rather spend her days doing volunteer work for stray animals. After careful analysis, she figures that she can live without the paycheck quite comfortably if allowed to pull $45,000 a year from savings. Her children are grown and self-sufficient.

I use Kay to illustrate why simple formulas (such as *your age = your proper bond allocation*) don't work. Kay is roughly the same age as Jean in the previous example. And Kay, like Jean, is financially comfortable. But it would be a great mistake for Kay to take the same risks with her money. Unlike Jean, Kay does not have a spouse. Unlike Jean, Kay does not have a pension. Unlike Jean, Kay is not expecting a big inheritance. Unlike Jean and Raymond, Kay cannot afford to lose any significant portion of her nest egg. She is dependent on that nest egg to stay economically afloat.

At her current level of savings and with a fairly modest rate of growth in her portfolio, Kay should be able to retire comfortably within four to five years. In Kay's case, she has more to lose than to gain by taking any great risk in the markets. On the other hand, if things work out as she plans, Kay may be spending 30 or more years in retirement. So an all fixed-income portfolio, which could get gobbled up by inflation, won't work. In Kay's case, I would likely recommend a portfolio, somewhat depending on Kay's tolerance for risk, of 50 to 55 percent stocks and 45 to 50 percent bonds (see Figure 12-4).

Figure 12-4:
A more conservative portfolio allocation for Kay.

Stocks: 50%   Bonds: 50%

Illustration by Wiley, Composition Services Graphics

Juan, 29, just getting started

Three years out of business school with an MBA, Juan, single and happy in his city condo, is earning an impressive and growing salary. But because he has been busy paying off loans, he has just started to build his savings. Juan's 401(k) has a current balance of $3,700.

Juan — yet another example of why simple formulas don't work! — should probably tailor his portfolio to look something like Jean and Raymond's, despite the obvious differences in age and wealth. Juan is still many years off from retirement and doesn't see any major expenses on the horizon. Juan's budding 401(k) is meant to sit and grow for a very long time — at least three decades. History tells us that a portfolio made up of mostly stocks will likely provide superior growth. Of course, history is history, and we don't know what the future would bring. So I would still allocate 25 percent bonds to Juan's portfolio (see Figure 12-5).

Figure 12-5:
A very
aggressive
portfolio
allocation
for Juan.

Bonds: 25%

Stocks: 75%

Illustration by Wiley, Composition Services Graphics

Before moving any money into stocks or bonds, however, I would want Juan to set aside three to six months' worth of living expenses in an emergency cash fund, outside of his 401(k), just in case he should lose his job, have serious health issues, or become subject to some other unforeseen crisis.

Miriam, 53, plugging away

Never married, with no children, Miriam wants to retire from her job as a freelance computer consultant while still young enough to fulfill her dreams of world travel. Her investments of $75,000 are growing at a good clip, as she is currently socking away a full 20 percent of her after-tax earnings — about $20,000 a year. But she knows that she has a long way to go.

Miriam is right; she has a long way to go. To fulfill her dreams of world travel, Miriam needs considerably more than a nest egg of $75,000. In this case, the bond allocation question is a tough one. Miriam needs substantial growth, but she isn't in a position to risk what she has, either. Cases like Miriam's require delicate balance. I would likely opt for a starting portfolio of mostly stocks and about 25 to 30 percent bonds (see Figure 12-6), but as Miriam gets closer to her financial goal in coming years, I would urge her to up that percentage of bonds and take a more defensive, conservative position.

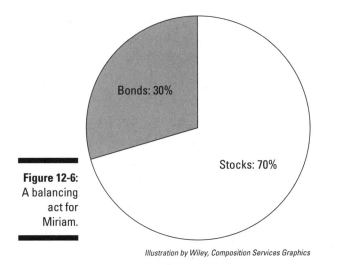

Figure 12-6:
A balancing
act for
Miriam.

Illustration by Wiley, Composition Services Graphics

Do you have a "bond" career or a "stock" career?

Part of your entire net worth, most likely the largest part, is your own human capital — in other words, your present and your future earnings. Some people have argued that you must factor in this human capital when fashioning your optimal investment portfolio. If, for example, you are firmly entrenched in a staid and steady career in a staid and steady industry (you are an actuary for a life insurance company, or an x-ray technician at the local hospital, or a bill collector for the utility company), the human potential part of your portfolio may be seen as more bond-like than stock-like. If, however, you are in a potentially very lucrative but unpredictable career in an unpredictable industry (you are a high-ticket and high-tech

commissioned salesperson, or a Hollywood producer, or a fashion model with string-bean legs), the human potential part of your portfolio may be seen as more stock-like.

To achieve the best diversification, individuals with bond-like careers should tilt their investments more toward stocks, while those with stock-like careers should tilt their portfolios the other way, with more bonds. Of course, the kind of personality that would choose a staid and steady career could also be the kind of personality to choose a staid and steady investment portfolio. In other words, in fashioning your optimal investment portfolio, it may serve you well to fight your gut instinct to go in one direction or the other.

Noticing the Many Shades of Gray in Your Portfolio

Although the world of investments offers countless opportunities — and dangers! — all investments qualify as one of these two types:

- **Equity:** Something you own (such as stocks, real estate, or gold)
- **Fixed income:** Money you've lent in return for interest (such as bonds, CDs, or money market funds), or possibly money you've given up in return for steady payments (annuities)

For the sake of simplicity, my portfolio discussion thus far has dealt largely with "stocks" and "bonds," ignoring the many shades of gray that define both of these large umbrella terms. I've also ignored other forms of fixed income, such as annuities, and other forms of equity, such as real estate and commodities. It's time now to stop ignoring and start addressing.

Bonds of many flavors

If the point of investing in bonds is to smooth out the returns of a portfolio that also includes stocks (Yes! That *is* the point!), it makes sense to have bonds that tend to zig when stocks zag. By and large, you're looking at Treasuries, including Treasury Inflation-Protected Securities (see Chapter 5), corporate investment-grade bonds (see Chapter 6), or agency bonds (see Chapter 7). If you're in the higher tax brackets and have limited space in your retirement accounts, you may consider municipal bonds (see Chapter 8). If you have a very large bond portfolio, you may consider a smattering of international bonds (see Chapter 9).

High-yield bonds (addressed in Chapter 6) may also play a role in your portfolio, along with other forms of more exotic bonds (see Chapter 9), but they need to be added with some finesse. As alluring as high-yield bonds can be, they don't offer the same diversifying power as do quality bonds. When stocks sink, high-yield bonds tend to sink as well, for the very same reason: Companies are closing doors.

Don't be a "yield-chaser"! Higher returning bonds always carry more risk.

Whatever your choice in bonds, it's best to seek some diversification: different issuers, different maturities. I make specific recommendations for diversifying the bond side of your portfolio in Chapter 13, again in Chapter 15 where I discuss individual bonds (diversification mandatory!), and yet again in Chapter 16 where I talk about bond funds. You can probably tell that I'm something of a stickler when it comes to diversification!

Stocks of all sizes and sorts

This is a book about bonds, so I won't dwell on what you should do with the stock side of your portfolio. In this chapter on portfolio-building, however, it seems fair to devote at least a few paragraphs to the subject. So here goes:

Because stocks can be so volatile, you must diversify. The best way to diversify is with low-cost, no-load mutual funds (index funds are often best) or exchange-traded funds (almost all of which are index funds).

Just as stocks and bonds tend to correlate poorly, different kinds of stocks and different kinds of bonds have limited correlation. That's especially true on the stock side of the portfolio. Smart investors make sure to have domestic and foreign stocks, stocks in large companies and small companies, and growth and value stocks. (*Growth* stocks are stocks in fast-moving companies in fast-moving industries, such as technology. *Value* stocks are stocks in companies that have less growth potential; you may be able to get these stocks on the cheap, at times making them better investments than growth stocks.)

Just as you get more bang for your buck but also more bounce with stocks versus bonds, you also get more potential return and additional risk with small-company stocks versus large-company stocks. Although international stocks aren't any more volatile than U.S. stocks, *per se,* differences in exchange rates can make them much more volatile to U.S. investors. The greater your tolerance for risk, the more small-company stocks and the more international stocks you may want to incorporate.

After your portfolio grows and you have all the broad asset classes covered, you may consider branching out into narrower (but not too narrow) kinds of investments. Possibilities include certain industry sectors, especially those that tend to have limited correlation to the market at large, such as real estate, timber, and energy. And beyond that, perhaps think about certain high-yield bonds that offer the potential for stock-like growth.

For more tips on investing in stocks, do *not* go to your local pub or to various and sundry get-rich-quick websites! Instead, see *Stock Investing For Dummies,* 3rd Edition by Paul Mladjenovic; *Mutual Funds For Dummies,* 6th Edition by Eric Tyson; or my own entertaining and highly educational *Exchange-Traded Funds For Dummies,* 2nd Edition. (All are published by Wiley.) Sure, there are many other good books out there (and lots of bad ones too), but the Dummies series is a darned good place to start.

Other fixed income: Annuities

For some people, sticking an annuity on the fixed-income side of the portfolio makes sense. When you purchase an annuity, you typically surrender your principal to the annuity issuer. You then receive cash at regular intervals at a principal to the annuity issuer. You then receive cash at regular intervals at a rate of return that's (sort of) considerably higher than you receive by buying a Treasury or municipal bond. (I say "sort of" because part of the "return" is actually your own money being given back to you. It's complicated.)

Let me be clear: I'm not talking about *variable* annuities, most of which are pretty terrible investment products sold by people who make outrageous commissions and conveniently forget to mention that most of the money you'll be seeing is your own money being returned to you. Rather, I'm talking about *fixed* annuities. The difference? With a variable annuity, you receive payments that are largely based on the performance of some piece of the market, such as the S&P 500 or another stock index. A fixed annuity gives you a certain fixed amount of income (which may be inflation-adjusted) at fixed intervals. Your payments are not contingent on the performance of the markets or anything else. And the interest earned may be tax-deferred.

With either kind of annuity, the rate of return usually is largely determined by your age. The fewer years the annuity provider thinks he'll be sending you checks, the more generous he'll be with his payments.

At the time I'm writing this, a 65-year-old man with $100,000 could get about 7 percent on an immediate fixed annuity for the rest of his life. Treasuries are currently paying 2 to 3 percent. But keep this in mind: If the investor dies tomorrow after taking out an annuity today, his estate loses $100,000. He could get an annuity with a death benefit (so his spouse continues to get payments should he die), but that lowers the rate of return.

The best candidates for annuities are generally healthy people with good genes in their 60s or 70s who don't mind dying broke and don't care about leaving behind any chunk of money. And you must remember that an annuity is only as good as the company issuing it. Don't even consider buying an annuity from anything less than a huge and stable issuer. (However, each state has a guaranty association that provides annuity protection plans up to a certain sum; go to www.immediateannuities.com/guaranty_liability/guaranty.htm to check the limits in your state.) I would generally recommend inflation-adjusted annuities for anyone under 70; otherwise, you risk seeing your income get swallowed up by inflation to the point that your monthly checks will seem like pin money.

Some investment houses, Vanguard and Fidelity included, have begun to broker very modestly priced fixed annuities without the horrible surrender charges that plague this industry. Typically, if you sign up for an annuity and then change your mind and want your principal back, you'll be penalized to the tune of 7 percent if you try to withdraw your money within a year, 6 percent if you try to withdraw within two years, and so on.

For more on annuities, check out *Annuities For Dummies* (Wiley), written by a friend of mine (and fellow resident of Allentown, Pennsylvania), Kerry Pechter.

Other equity: Commodities and real estate

Equity is investment-speak for "something you own." It doesn't have to be a share in a company. You can own real estate, silver, gold, or corn futures. Real estate, if it refers to your own home, should generally not be considered part of your nest egg, simply because you will always need a place to live. Selling your home and downsizing or moving to an apartment may someday add to the size of your nest egg, and you always have the option of a reverse mortgage (although it is expensive), but you should not count on your home as your main retirement fund.

Investment real estate can indeed be profitable, but only if you know what you're doing and are willing to clock some serious hours landlording. It helps to know something about plumbing. And my own personal nightmare a number of years ago involving a property in Maryland tells me that no one should *ever* be a long-distance landlord! (If you want to learn about buying houses for a profit, check out *Real Estate Investing For Dummies,* 2nd Edition by Eric Tyson and Robert S. Griswold [Wiley].)

 Commodity investing was once a sticky business, with high fees and complicated strategies. Lately, with the advent of exchange-traded funds and exchange-traded notes that allow you to buy into commodities without a lot of mess, commodity investing has become much like investing in stocks or bonds. Commodities have limited correlation to both stocks and bonds, and I recommend a modest position in commodities for many people's portfolios. I discuss some of these funds at the end of Chapter 9.

Making Sure That Your Portfolio Remains in Balance

Say you've decided that you want a portfolio of 60 percent equities and 40 percent fixed income (commonly expressed as a *60/40* portfolio). You have $100,000, so you aim to construct a portfolio that is $60,000 in stocks and $40,000 in bonds. Over the ensuing months, the stock market takes off. At the end of a great year, you count your blessings and realize that you now have not $60,000, but $75,000 in stocks. Your bonds, however, have hardly budged. Let's say you have $41,000 in bonds. Your entire portfolio is now worth ($75,000 + $41,000) $116,000. But you no longer have a 60/40 portfolio. You have a 65/35 portfolio. Funny how that happens.

What to do? It's time to rebalance.

Rebalancing means getting your investment house back in order. Unless your life circumstances have changed, you probably still want a 60/40 portfolio. That means that your new $116,000 portfolio should be ($116,000 × 60 percent) $69,600 in stocks, and ($116,000 × 40 percent) $46,400 in bonds. In order to get to that point, you're going to have to sell ($75,000 − $69,600) $5,400 in stocks and buy ($46,400 − $41,000) $5,400 in bonds.

It won't be easy. You've seen your stocks go up while your bonds have languished. But rebalancing is the smart thing to do. Let me explain why.

Tweaking your holdings to temper risk

The primary reason to rebalance is to keep you from losing your shirt. If your personal situation a year ago warranted a 60/40 portfolio, then a 65/35 split is going to be more volatile than the portfolio you want. If you continue to leave the portfolio untouched and stocks continue to fly, you'll eventually wind up with a 70/30 portfolio, and then a 75/25 portfolio. And what happens if the stock market reverses at that point, moving as quickly backwards as it was moving forwards a year or two before? You'll see a much larger loss than you ever bargained for.

Wouldn't you rather lock in some of your profits and start afresh with the proper portfolio mix?

Savoring the rebalancing bonus

Rebalancing also helps you to realize larger returns over time. Think about it: Most investors buy high, choosing whatever asset class is hot, and sell low, getting rid of whatever asset class is lagging. The financial press is continually pushing us to do this; "10 HOT FUNDS FOR THE NEW YEAR!" inevitably focuses on ten funds that have risen to new heights in the past months, largely because of the kind of asset class in which they invest (U.S. stocks, foreign stocks, long-term bonds, or whatever).

Studies show that, as a result of continually buying high and selling low, the average investor barely keeps up with inflation. It's sad. But you, by rebalancing regularly, are destined to wind up ahead. Rather than buying high and selling low, you will continually be selling high and buying low. In the preceding example, you were selling off your recently risen stocks, for example, and buying more of your lagging bonds.

Over the long run, not only will rebalancing temper your risk, but your long-term returns, if we're simply talking about rebalancing stocks and bonds, will tend to be about ½ percent higher. Need proof?

Consider the ten-year average annual return of the Vanguard Total Stock and the Vanguard Total Bond Index funds. They currently clock in at 4.4 percent average annual return for the stock fund and 5.5 percent for the bond fund. Adding the two together, giving the stocks a 60-percent weighting and the bonds a 40-percent weighting, you would expect the average annual ten-year return of the two to be 4.84 percent. But when you look at the Vanguard Balanced Index fund, which combines the total stock market with the total bond market and continually rebalances, the average annual return for the same period (ending January 31, 2012) is not 4.84 percent — it's 5.27 percent, despite an expense ratio slightly higher than either the stock or bond index fund.

If you invest in multiple asset classes (including commodities, foreign and domestic stock, and so on), regular rebalancing may add a full percentage point or more each year to your long-term returns.

Scheduling your portfolio rebalance

With the miracle of modern technology, Excel spreadsheets and whatnot, rebalancing can be easy — too easy! Rebalancing your portfolio every week, or even every month, is most likely going to be counterproductive. You may get hit with transaction costs, as well as potential capital gains taxes, with every sale you make. But another important (and often overlooked) factor is the *momentum* of markets: When an asset class shoots up, all those yokels who like buying something that is up will often, by the very fact that they are buying, force the price a bit higher.

The question of how often to rebalance has been studied to death, and those studies show that someone who rebalances as often as he brushes his teeth tends to lose out to momentum — in addition to paying more in transaction costs and taxes.

So, what's the perfect time to rebalance? There is no perfect time. It depends on the volatility of the markets, the correlation of the securities in your portfolio, the cost of your personal transactions, and your tax status. In general, however, rebalancing should be done once every year or two. If you are retired and pulling cash from your portfolio, you may want to rebalance twice a year in order to make sure your cash reserve doesn't dip too low. But do be careful whenever selling securities to watch your trading costs and monitor your potential tax hit.

The division between stocks and bonds, be it 70/30 or 50/50 or 30/70, is often the most important risk-and-return determiner in your portfolio. Even if you allow everything else to get out of balance, keep your balance of stocks and bonds on an even keel.

Such balance, grasshopper, will keep you afloat and spare you from getting slammed into financial bridges or swamped by the wake of inflation.

Chapter 13

Which Kinds of Bonds Make the Most Sense for You?

● ●

In This Chapter

▶ Choosing among government, corporate, and municipal bonds

▶ Selecting the right maturities for your portfolio

▶ Weighing your need for fixed-income diversification

▶ Knowing how to mix and match your bond holdings

▶ Selecting securities that provide for your current and future needs

● ●

*E*ach spring, as the crocuses sprout and the song birds return to my yard, I face the difficult question of whether to call Mike. Mike is a guy in my town with a truck who, for a flat price, will drop an entire truckload of mulch — *ka-chunk* — onto my driveway. Given the cost savings, and the fact that I don't particularly enjoy lugging home big plastic, leaking bags of mulch in my car, it seems like a slam-dunk decision. It isn't.

Most years, I simply can't use as much mulch as Mike's required minimum. So I wind up shoveling mulch on mulch, begging the neighbors to take some, watching the dregs biodegrade on my driveway, and then waiting for the summer rains to flush the rest away.

Of course, the question of how much mulch to buy goes hand-in-hand with what *kind* of mulch to buy. There's hardwood mulch. Pine mulch. Cypress mulch. There are big chips. Little chips. Shredded mulch. Finely pureed mulch. And then there's the more exotic cocoa-bean mulch, which comes largely from The Hershey Company in nearby Hershey, Pennsylvania. Yup, it smells like chocolate.

This chapter is about picking the kinds of bonds you're going to put into your portfolio. It's just like buying mulch. You look first at the quantity of fixed income you need. You then decide on the particular kinds of bonds:

Treasuries, corporates, munis, or maybe something more exotic. Finally, you need to decide where and how to purchase them.

Mike the mulch guy doesn't sell bonds (as far as I know), but The Hershey Company sells them by the truckload. Unfortunately, they don't smell like chocolate.

Reviewing the Rationale behind Bonds

In Chapter 12, I present a plan for dividing a portfolio largely between stocks and bonds. Stocks and bonds are yin and yang, Fred and Ginger, cookies and milk, tequila and taxi rides home — they go together perfectly. Stocks are where you're likely to get your growth. Bonds provide predictability and stability. Any other reasons for having bonds in your portfolio — such as getting a stream of income — are nice, but secondary. (If it seems that I'm too lightly kissing off the importance of bond income, read Chapter 17.)

Some bonds are more volatile than others. That matters. But what also matters, perhaps more, is the extent to which the price of bonds tends to rise and fall with the price of stocks. The kinds of bonds that historically zig when stocks zag are by and large the kinds of bonds that should dominate most people's bond portfolios. And those kinds of bonds are government and agency bonds, high quality (investment-grade) corporate bonds (like Hershey's), and perhaps tax-exempt bonds from stable municipalities.

Making your initial selection

In Part II, I outline the different kinds of bonds I mention here, and I review their most distinguishing characteristics. But in choosing types of bonds to put in your portfolio, you also need to look at your *personal* characteristics.

For example, what may your need for funds be over the next several years? What is your tax bracket? Are you subject to the sneaky alternative minimum tax? How much room do you have in your retirement accounts? How heavily is the stock side of your portfolio invested overseas? How subject are you to the ravages of inflation? These are some of the things that make me different from you and may make my "perfect" bond portfolio very different from your "perfect" bond portfolio.

As I do in Chapter 12, here I give you the best rules I can. Then, toward the end of this chapter, I provide a few case studies to help sharpen your sights on what kinds of bonds may best match your investment goals.

Following a few rules

These guidelines should begin to give you an idea of the kinds of bonds you may want. They are quick and a bit dirty. I clean them up — and get more specific in my recommendations — as this chapter rolls along.

✔ **Rule #1:** It's best to keep three to six months of living expenses in cash (a savings account or money market fund) or near-cash for emergencies. For any major expenses you anticipate in the next couple years, you may want to keep that money in near-cash as well. By *near-cash,* I mean very short-term, high-quality bonds or bond funds with bond portfolios maturing in one to three years. Short-term bonds generally pay slightly higher rates of interest than savings accounts and money market funds but less interest than longer-term bonds. Correspondingly, they can be a wee bit more volatile than a money market account but far less volatile than longer-term bonds.

✔ **Rule #2:** Money you won't need in the next few years should be invested in higher yielding securities for greater income and growth. These securities include bonds with maturities of three years and greater.

✔ **Rule #3:** The majority of your bond holdings should be high-quality, mid-term (3- to 10-year maturity) bonds, be they Treasuries, agency bonds, corporates, or munis. If you're looking for higher return and can take the risk, you're usually going to be better off moving into stocks rather than into either high-yield or ultra-long-term bonds.

Go with tax-free munis if your tax bracket warrants it and if you are investing in a taxable account. See Chapter 8 for all the muni formulas you need. As for the other bonds, it's preferable to mix and match both issuers and maturities.

✔ **Rule #4:** Whatever your allocation to fixed income, but especially if you have a large fixed-income allocation, a portion of it should be inflation-adjusted, either with an inflation-adjusted annuity or with special bonds called Treasury Inflation-Protected Securities (TIPS). TIPS are a nice complement to other bonds because they tend not to correlate to other bonds in their price movements. If inflation takes off, or even if people think inflation is about to take off, traditional bonds tend to suffer, but TIPS tend to flourish. If inflation is less than expected, however, TIPS won't do as well.

Sizing Up Your Need for Fixed-Income Diversification

As you know, some stocks can double or triple in price overnight, while others can shrink into oblivion in the time it takes to say "CEO arrested for fraud." Unless you are investing in individual high-yield bonds (not a good idea), your risk of default — and the risk of your investment shrinking to oblivion — is minimal. But diversifying your bonds is still a very good idea.

Although you can minimize your risk of default by simply buying Treasury and U.S. agency bonds, you still incur other risks by having too concentrated a bond portfolio.

Diversifying by maturity

Regardless of whether you invest in Treasuries, corporate bonds, or munis, you always risk swings in general interest rates (which can depress bond prices) and reinvestment risk (the fact that interest or principal invested in a bond may not be able to be reinvested in such a way that it can earn the same rate of return as before). Both risks can be greatly ameliorated with the fine art of *laddering,* or staggering your individual bond purchases to include bonds of differing maturities. I discuss laddering in Chapter 15. You can also lessen risks by investing in (the right) bond funds, discussed in Chapter 16.

Diversifying by type of issuer

In addition to diversifying by maturity, you also want to divide up your bonds so they represent different kinds of bond categories, such as government and corporate. This is true with both individual bonds and bond funds. Different kinds of bonds do better in certain years than others. Holding various types of bonds helps to smooth out your total bond portfolio returns.

Let's take two years — 2008 and 2009 — as examples.

The year 2008 was an extraordinarily bad year for the economy, and the stock markets worldwide plummeted. Investor confidence fell, and fell hard. As is always the case in hard economic times, money rushed to safety . . . primarily U.S. Treasuries. At the same time, inflation came to a standstill. Interest rates also fell, as the Fed attempted to pump-prime the failing economy. All of this meant good times for owners of conventional Treasuries and U.S. agency bonds, whereas other bondholders didn't fare quite as well. That year, from January to December, we saw the following returns:

- ✔ Long-term conventional government bonds: +25.8 percent
- ✔ Investment-grade corporate bonds, all maturities: +8.8 percent
- ✔ Treasury Inflation-Protected Securities: –2.40 percent
- ✔ Municipal bonds, all maturities: –2.47 percent

By 2009, investor confidence had improved, the stock market shot up, the yearning for a safe harbor dissipated, and inflation was back in the picture. Many investors bid *au revoir* to Treasuries and moved back into stocks and higher-risk, higher yielding bonds. Munis and corporates fared better that year than Treasuries, except for inflation-protected securities, which led the pack:

- Treasury Inflation-Protected Securities: +11.4 percent

- Municipal bonds: +12.47 percent

- Investment-grade corporate bonds: +3.0 percent

- Long-term conventional government bonds: –14.90 percent

Generally, investment-grade corporate bonds do better than government bonds when the economy is strong. When the economy is in trouble (and people flock to safety), government bonds — especially conventional long-term Treasuries — tend to do better. If you think you can tell the future, buy all one kind of bond or the other. If you are not clairvoyant (you're not), it makes the most sense to divide your holdings.

Diversifying by risk-and-return potential

The returns on high quality corporate bonds, Treasuries, and munis (after their tax-free nature is accounted for) generally differ by only a few percentage points in any given year. (The years 2008 and 2009 saw unusually high spreads, given the tumultuousness of the times.) But some other kinds of bonds, such as high-yield corporates, convertible bonds, and international bonds, can vary much, much more.

In general, because the potential return on stocks is so much higher than just about any kind of bond, I favor stomaching volatility on the stock side of the portfolio. For some people, however, more exotic, "cocoa-bean" type bonds make sense. High-yield bonds, for example, act like a hybrid between stocks and bonds. They often produce high returns (higher than other bonds, lower than stocks) when the economy is growing fast, and they tend to dive (more than other bonds, less than stocks) when the economy falters. Because of this hybrid nature, they make particular sense for relatively conservative investors who need the high yield but can't take quite as much risk as stocks involve.

Emerging-market bonds (issued by the governments of lesser developed countries) also can produce very high yields but can be very volatile. Unlike U.S. high-yield bonds, they tend to have limited correlation to the U.S. stock market. For this reason, I often include a small percentage of emerging-market bonds in many people's portfolios.

Diversifying away managerial risk

Where I discuss bond funds in Chapter 16, I suggest that you put most of your bond money into *index* funds: funds run by managers who work on the cheap and do not attempt to do anything fancy. But occasionally, taking a bet on a talented manager may not be such a terrible thing to do. And regardless of what I say, you may turn your nose up at index funds anyway. You may attempt to beat the market by choosing bond funds run by managers who try to score big by rapid buying and selling, going out on margin, and doing all sorts of other wild and crazy things.

Whenever you go with an actively managed fund (as opposed to a passively managed fund, otherwise known as an index fund), you hope that the manager will do something smart to beat the market. But you risk that he will do something dumb. Or, perhaps your manager will get hit by a train, and the incompetent junior partner will wind up managing your fund. That is called *managerial risk.*

Managerial risk is real, and it should always be diversified away. If you have a sizeable bond portfolio and are depending on that portfolio to pay the bills some day, you shouldn't trust any one manager with that much responsibility. Recall the numbers from the "Diversifying by type of issuer" section, which reflect the differences among returns of different kinds of bonds in a couple of sample years? That is *nothing* compared to the differences you find between well-managed and poorly managed active bond funds.

According to Morningstar Principia,

- ✔ The ten-year cumulative return on the well-run Loomis Sayles Bond Fund is **169.08 percent** (meaning $10,000 invested 10 years ago would now be worth $26,908).

- ✔ The ten-year cumulative return on the not-so-well-run Oppenheimer Champion Income fund, Class C is **-58.46 percent** (meaning $10,000 invested 10 years ago would now be worth $4,154).

If you're going to take a shot at beating the market by giving your bond money to managers who tinker and toy (yes, even Dan Fuss, the very talented manager at Loomis Sayles — see Chapter 21), do it in moderation, please.

Weighing Diversification versus Complication

Most individual bonds sell for $1,000. But buying individual bonds (not Treasuries, but most other bonds) means paying a broker, and that can be very expensive. You can't very well build a diversified bond portfolio — different maturities, different issuers — out of individual bonds unless you have quite a few grand sitting around.

Diversifying with funds isn't the easiest thing in the world, either. Many bond funds have minimums, often in the $1,000 to $10,000 range. And exchange-traded funds, even though they have no minimums, often carry trading fees. In other words, if you haven't got a fair chunk of change, building a diversified bond portfolio can be a challenge. But I do have a few suggestions for all you non-millionaires.

Keeping it simple with balanced funds (for people with under $5,000)

If you have under $5,000 to invest, you are going to find little choice if you want a balanced portfolio. Forget about individual stocks and bonds. Even building a fund portfolio, given the minimums of most funds, will be tough.

Best solution: Consider a *balanced fund,* a one-stop-shopping fund that allows you to invest in stocks and bonds in one fell swoop. Some balanced funds are static; they allocate, say, 60 percent of your money to stocks and 40 percent to bonds, and that is how it will always be. Others are dynamic; these are often called *life cycle* funds. A life cycle fund has a target retirement date and, as you move toward that date, the fund shifts your money, usually from the stock side to the bond side, to become more conservative. See my recommendations for several all-in-one funds in Chapter 16.

Moving beyond the basic (for people with $5,000 to $10,000)

In the ballpark of $5,000 to $10,000, you may be looking to invest several thousand in stocks and several thousand in bonds. Your best bet for building a diversified portfolio would be a handful of low-cost, no-load mutual funds or exchange-traded funds. Perhaps you want one total market bond fund, one total U.S. stock fund, and one diversified foreign stock fund. See Chapter 16 for my recommendations for total market bond funds.

Branching out (with $10,000 or more)

When you pass the $10,000 mark, you can begin to entertain a more finely segmented portfolio of either mutual funds or exchange-traded funds. But you'll probably want more than $10,000 in the bond side of your portfolio before you sell your total market bond fund and start diversifying into the various sectors of the bond market.

I wouldn't suggest dabbling in individual bonds unless you have a bond portfolio of $300,000 or so. Otherwise, the trading costs will eat you alive. The exception would be Treasury bonds because you can buy them at `www.treasurydirect.gov` without any markup. Even some large brokerage houses allow you to buy Treasuries without a markup.

Finding the Perfect Bond Portfolio Fit

In Chapter 12, I introduce four portfolios, belonging to Jean and Raymond, Kay, Juan, and Miriam. In that chapter, I suggest what percentage of their portfolios should be in bonds. I revisit our friends here to suggest what specific kinds of bonds they might consider.

Case studies in bond ownership

You'll notice that just as there are no hard and fast rules for the percentage of a portfolio that should be in bonds, there are no absolutes when it comes to what kind of bonds are optimal for any given investor.

Jean and Raymond, 61 and 63, financially fit as a fiddle

These folks have a solid portfolio of nearly three-quarters of a million dollars. A fat inheritance is likely coming. They are both working in secure jobs, and when they retire, their (inflation-adjusted) pensions and Social Security should cover all the basic bills. With their children and grandchildren in mind and having little to risk with any volatility in the markets, Jean and Raymond have decided to invest about two-thirds of their savings (all in their retirement accounts) in equities — mostly stocks, with some commodities. They have chosen to invest the other third (about $235,000) in fixed income.

What to do with the fixed income? Financially fit as they seem, Jean and Raymond still could use an emergency kitty. Because both are older than 59½ and are allowed to pull from their retirement accounts without penalty, I would suggest three months' living expenses ($15,000) be kept in cash or in a very short-term bond fund, of the kind I suggest in Chapter 16.

That leaves them with $220,000. Chances are this money won't be touched for quite some time — perhaps not until after Jean and Raymond have passed to that great teachers' lounge in the sky, and their children and grandchildren inherit their estate. That being the case, it warrants investing in higher yielding bonds. Just in case the economy takes a real fall and the lion's share of the estate goes with it, these bonds should be strong enough to stand tall.

Tax-free munis make no sense in this case because Jean and Raymond have room in their retirement accounts, and munis, which pay lower rates of interest than bonds of comparable quality and maturity, *never* make sense in a tax-advantaged retirement account.

I would suggest that about 30 percent of the remaining pot (approximately $66,000) be put into intermediate-term conventional Treasuries, either in a bond fund or individual bonds. Another 30 percent should go into a fund of investment-grade corporate bonds. The corporate bonds over time will tend to return higher interest than the government bonds but may not do quite as well if the economy hits the skids. And another 30 percent of the bond allocation should go to Treasury Inflation-Protected Securities (TIPS), again either in a TIPS fund (see my recommendation in Chapter 16) or individual TIPS purchased free of markup on the Treasury's own website.

Then, Jean and Raymond might devote 10 percent of their bond allocation to a foreign bond fund. These funds have their pros and cons, as I discuss in Chapter 9. Whether Jean and Raymond go with a foreign bond fund would depend on how much exposure they had to foreign currencies on the equity side of their portfolio. I present some good international bond funds in Chapter 16.

See Figure 13-1 for a chart that reflects my recommendations to Jean and Raymond.

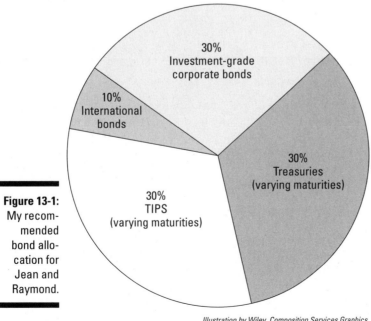

Figure 13-1: My recommended bond allocation for Jean and Raymond.

Illustration by Wiley, Composition Services Graphics

Kay, 59, approaching retirement

Kay, our divorced medical technician, is currently on her own. She needs a larger emergency fund than do Jean and Raymond. Having no pension, she will also be reliant on her portfolio when she retires and can't take quite as much risk as the older married couple. (Simple formulas that say you need to take less risk as you get older simply aren't very helpful much of the time.) Kay's healthy portfolio of $875,000 is divided 50/50 between equities and fixed income. That equates to $437,500 in fixed income.

Where to put it?

Kay needs a somewhat larger cash cushion for emergencies than do Jean and Raymond. She is, after all, on her own, although her adult children could help her in a real emergency. I would allot four to five months of her fixed income to either a money market fund or a very short-term bond fund. That would still leave $418,000 or so to invest in higher yielding instruments.

Kay doesn't care about leaving an inheritance. Her kids are grown and doing very well. She is also of good genes, eats low-fat granola and grapefruit for breakfast, and expects to live a long life. In four or five years, when Kay plans to retire, she will be a good candidate for an inflation-adjusted fixed annuity that will guarantee her an income stream for the rest of her life.

I would set up a bond portfolio for her with the intention of making the move to an annuity when Kay is in her mid-60s (provided interest rates at that time are favorable). Kay needs a bond portfolio that will be there for her in four or five years, providing income and, more importantly, providing the cash she'll need to live on in retirement should the other 50 percent of her portfolio — the stocks — take a dive. With $418,000 to invest in bonds, almost twice what our teacher couple has to invest, I would suggest a somewhat more diversified bond allocation.

Kay may start by taking a third of her bond money ($139,000) and buying either a Treasury Inflation-Protected Securities (TIPS) fund or individual TIPS through www.treasurydirect.gov. These bonds offer modest rates of return but adjust the principal twice a year for inflation. If inflation goes on a rampage, Kay will have some protection on the fixed-income side of her portfolio. As a rule, people with higher allocations to fixed-income should have more inflation protection on that side of the portfolio, as they'll have less inflation protection from stocks.

With the other two-thirds of her bond portfolio ($279,000 or so), I would suggest equal allocations to intermediate-term traditional Treasuries, short-term Treasuries, long-term investment-grade corporate bonds, intermediate-term investment-grade corporate bonds, international bonds, and high-yield bonds (see Figure 13-2).

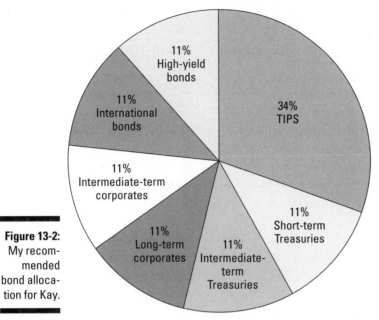

Figure 13-2:
My recommended bond allocation for Kay.

Illustration by Wiley, Composition Services Graphics

Juan, 29, building up his savings

Juan's 401(k) has a current balance of just $3,700, but he's making a good salary. I would first encourage Juan to save up enough so he can set aside three to six months' living expenses in an emergency cash fund.

Given that his 401(k) money is (we hope) not going to be touched until Juan is at least 59½ (and able to make withdrawals without penalty), he has decided to allocate only 20 percent of his retirement fund to bonds — just about right. The purpose of those bonds is to somewhat smooth out his account's returns, provide the opportunity to rebalance, and be there just in case of an economic apocalypse. Juan, of course, is prisoner to his 401(k) investment options, whatever they may be.

If his employer's plan is like most, he may have the option of one mixed-maturity Treasury fund and one mixed-maturity corporate-bond fund. Because we're talking about only 20 percent of his portfolio, whichever way he goes shouldn't make a huge difference over the next few years. I'd suggest splitting the baby and going half and half (see Figure 13-3).

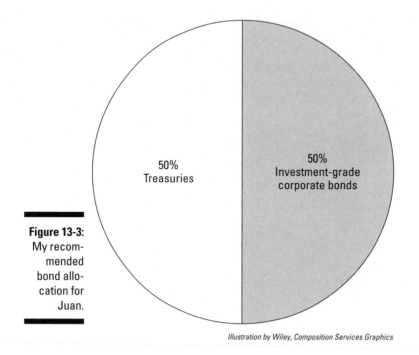

Figure 13-3: My recommended bond allocation for Juan.

Illustration by Wiley, Composition Services Graphics

Should Juan leave his job, he may be able to transfer his 401(k) to his new place of employment, or he may be able to roll it into an individual retirement plan (IRA). I would usually advise the latter because IRAs typically offer better investment choices at lower costs. At that point, should Juan open an IRA, and should the balance grow beyond several thousand dollars, I would encourage greater diversification of his bonds.

Miriam, 53, behind on her goals

With $75,000 in savings and the good majority in stocks, Miriam's 25 percent in bonds ($18,750) must serve two purposes: First, it must provide ballast to smooth out the year-to-year return of her investments. Second, it may well help provide cash flow when (within a decade, we hope) Miriam is able to retire and fulfill her dreams of world travel.

Miriam is currently making serious bucks in her job as a freelance computer consultant — about $160,000 a year. But she lives in New York City, paying high city and state taxes. She rents rather than owns her home, so she gets no mortgage deduction. Most of her $75,000 in savings sits in a taxable brokerage account.

Given Miriam's relatively high tax bracket and the fact she pays a boatload in taxes, it would make most sense for Miriam to have her $18,750 of bonds in her taxable account socked away in high-quality municipal bonds. Locally issued munis would offer income exempt from federal, state, and local taxes, and these would be good candidates. But for the sake of diversification, I'd like to see a mix of both local and national muni bonds. With less than $20,000 to invest in munis, she would be chewed up and spit out by the markups should she start dabbling in individual issues. Fortunately, there a number of good funds in which she might invest in both New York and national munis. I give examples in Chapter 16. (See Miriam's allocation in Figure 13-4).

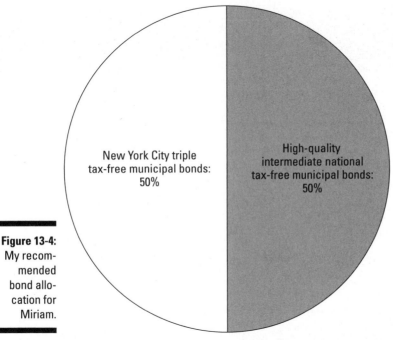

New York City triple tax-free municipal bonds: 50%

High-quality intermediate national tax-free municipal bonds: 50%

Figure 13-4:
My recommended bond allocation for Miriam.

Illustration by Wiley, Composition Services Graphics

Seeking out the more exotic offerings

You may have noted that none of these case scenarios calls for more exotic ("cocoa-bean" type) bonds. Sometimes, I like exotic. High-yield bonds from abroad, for example, have very handsome historical returns and, unlike U.S. high-yield bonds, tend to rise and fall _somewhat_ independently of the U.S. stock market. That is especially true of so-called _emerging-market_ bonds (bonds from countries where many people don't have toilets). Because of their extreme volatility, however, I recommend putting emerging-market bonds, in modest allocations, on the equity side of the portfolio.

Ditto for *exchange-traded notes,* bond-like instruments that don't pay a steady rate of interest but rather offer a yield tied to a certain benchmark, such as a commodity index that tracks the fortunes of gold, silver, and corn futures. See further discussion of both emerging-market bonds and exchange-traded notes in Chapter 9.

In Chapter 12, I discuss *rebalancing.* It is crucial, after you set up a properly allocated portfolio, to go in once a year or so and make sure that if you allocated, say, 60 percent to equities and 40 percent to fixed income, those allocations don't go too far astray. At the same time, you want to check once a year or so to make certain that your bond allocations — your division between Treasuries, corporates, munis, and other kinds of bonds — are where you want them to be.

Perhaps you can rebalance your portfolio every spring, just about the same time you spread your mulch. I don't know if Mike-with-the-truck does that, but that's what I do.

Part IV
Bonds Away! Navigating the Fixed-Income Marketplace

The 5th Wave   By Rich Tennant

"We've got several hollow tree options to consider. How many nuts were you looking to invest at this time?"

In this part . . .

In the following three chapters, I turn you into a savvy bond investor. By the time you finish Part IV, you'll be trading bonds like a pro. I promise!

The action starts with Chapter 14. Here, I help you through the crucial first question you need to ask before trading bonds: Are you going to be trading individual bonds or bond funds? While attacking that question, I also address the issue of investment *containers*: whether it makes more sense to store your bonds or bond funds in taxable accounts or in tax-advantaged retirement accounts. I also touch on the timing of your bond purchases: whether it makes sense to wait for the right kind of interest environment, or whether you should just jump in tomorrow.

Chapter 15 shows you the ropes where it comes to buying and selling individual bonds. You find out how to negotiate the best deals and, using some rather revolutionary new tools, lower your transaction costs greatly.

And finally, Chapter 16 gets you up to snuff on bond funds: Which are the best? Which should you avoid? What is the most you should pay?

Ready to set sail?

Chapter 14

Strategizing Your Bond Buys and Sells

In 1497, Vasco da Gama, a man from Portugal with a bushy beard and silly pants, gathered up 170 of his cronies, most of them also sporting bushy beards and silly pants, and set sail for India. Along the way, da Gama and company encountered fierce ocean storms, thirst, hunger, disease, and hostile natives who hated the pants.

But the intrepid travelers, in their four rickety vessels, made it to India, did a bit of sightseeing, picked up a few bags of spices, and headed for home. The trip was deemed a great success, and Mr. da Gama was hailed a hero — despite the pants, two years of misery at sea, half of his boats lost, and 116 dead cronies.

The fact that you could sail from Europe to India was seen as a great advance for humankind. As grueling and treacherous as the seagoing voyage was, it was still preferable to doing the 5,500 miles from Portugal to India on foot, wearing 15th-century footwear.

A short number of years ago, if you wanted to invest in bonds, you had a similarly bitter choice. You could walk into the office of your local bond broker and face fierce markups on individual bonds, or you could sail into the sea of funds and deal with hostile management fees and loads. Whichever option you chose, whatever kind of pants or shoes you were wearing, bond investing was often a perilous journey.

Today's bond market is becoming a friendlier place. Let me introduce you.

Discovering the Brave New World of Bonds

Regardless of which way you decide to invest your money, bond funds or individual bonds, the going is easier and potentially more lucrative today than it was just several years ago. And it's getting easier all the time.

Finding fabulously frugal funds

Expensive bond funds still exist. According to Morningstar Principia, at least 140 of them charge 2 percent or more in annual fees. Imagine. At today's modest interest rates, most bonds yield less than 5 percent a year; I'd say the majority are yielding less than 4 percent. That's a *nominal* — before inflation — 4 percent a year. After inflation, you're looking at a total *real* return of about 1 to 2 percent a year. After taxes, you're looking at less than that. And you're going to fork over 2 percent to a fund manager? Lots of people do! They haven't read this book yet.

But paying such high fees, once a hard thing to avoid, is now strictly optional. Yes, the times they are a changin'. In 1998, 36 bond funds had expense ratios below 0.50 percent. As I write these words, that number is over 700. In the past few years, we've seen a virtual revolution in the world of investment funds. Many of the bond funds I now recommend have annual fees of 0.20 percent or less — a decade or so ago, that was unheard of.

The lowering of fees is largely due to the recent introduction of exchange-traded funds (ETFs). If you want to know more about ETFs, well, I wrote an entire book about them: *Exchange-Traded Funds For Dummies,* Second Edition (Wiley). ETFs are wonderful investment vehicles in their own right — both inexpensive and tax-efficient. They have also given some serious competition to mutual funds, resulting in a lowering of fees across the board.

A lineup of ETFs from Vanguard, State Street SPDRs, BlackRock's iShares, Schwab, and PIMCO, all of which allow anyone with minimal money to buy, allows you to invest in numerous bond index funds — Treasury or corporate, short-term or long-term — for annual fees of a mere 0.11 to 0.20 percent. A number of bond index mutual funds from Vanguard and Fidelity — the two largest U.S. financial supermarkets — are charging annual fees in the same ballpark (although most of these mutual funds have minimums of at least $2,500).

Dealing in individual bonds without dealing over a fortune

The transaction costs on individual bonds, which have traditionally been way higher than stock transaction costs, have been dropping faster than hail.

One 2004 study from the Securities and Exchange Commission found that the average cost of a $5,000 corporate bond trade back then was $84, or 1.68 percent — equivalent to several months' interest. Smaller trades (less than $5,000) tended to whack investors with much higher costs.

Trade costs of municipal bonds (a favorite flavor of bond among individuals in high tax brackets), according to the same study, averaged 2.23 percent — equivalent perhaps to a full year's return after inflation — for trades of $25,000 or less. For trades from $25,000 to $100,000, the average price spread was 1.12 percent.

Since 2004, the cost of bond trading has dropped considerably and continues to do so. Although I haven't seen any recent comprehensive studies, my guess (and the guess of a few industry insiders with whom I speak regularly) is that a savvy bond investor can now buy a typical corporate or municipal bond with half to a third of the trading cost she would have incurred in 2004. But, of course, interest rates are awfully low today. So paying even a markup of half a percent could represent several months of interest.

Bond sales, as opposed to buys, can still be a tougher and more expensive game. That's one reason that I generally recommend buying single bonds only if you plan to hold them until maturity (or until they are called). I discuss individual bond trading in Chapter 15.

The changing environment, which has actually thrown many bond brokers out of business, is due in part to the advent of Internet trading but more so to something called the *Trade Reporting and Compliance Engine* (TRACE), a government and securities industry–imposed national database that allows bond traders — both professional and amateur — to see what other bond traders are up to. Brokers can no longer charge whatever markup they wish. See the sidebar "Peek-a-boo: Bond trades move out of the darkness, into the light" for more details.

Peek-a-boo: Bond trades move out of the darkness, into the light

Once upon a time, you'd go to buy (or sell) a bond, and you'd say to your bond broker, "Hello," and he would say to you, "Hello! How are you? How are the kids?" And you would say, "Good. Good." And then the bond broker would tell you about a real beaut of an A-rated bond, with a maturity of ten years and a coupon rate of 5.46 percent . . . blah, blah, blah. And you would say, "Uh-huh," and you would then fork over $5,000 or so having no idea whether the broker was enjoying a $5 markup, a $50 markup, or even a $500 markup.

Bond trades in those dark but not-so-distant days were done by telephone, one broker to another, and the clients were more or less at their mercy. You couldn't look up bond prices in the daily paper, as you could stock prices. There was no agreed-to commission, as there was with stocks. And there was no Internet. Many bond traders were good people, making a fair living but still looking out for their clients' best interests. Others would never give a sucker an even break, carving off the lion's share of investors' potential profits and hoarding that money for themselves.

Both kinds of brokers still exist, for sure. But thanks to the Trade Reporting and Compliance Engine (and, of course, *Bond Investing For Dummies,* which is clueing people into the Engine), suckers are becoming increasingly rare, and profit-hoarding brokers are seeking new careers.

Known most commonly by its acronym, TRACE, the Trade Reporting and Compliance Engine is a baby of the Securities and Exchange Commission (SEC) and the former National Association of Securities Dealers (NASD), which is now part of the Financial Industry Regulatory Authority (FINRA). TRACE began in July 2002 and was phased in over several years. As of February 2005, every corporate bond trade in the United States — replete with all the information about the trade you could hope for — gets reported into the system and shows up on the web, in living color. The Municipal Securities Rulemaking Board runs a parallel system for municipal bonds.

So now if a broker says that you can get an A-rated bond with a maturity of ten years and a coupon rate of 5.46 percent, you can immediately go online (to www.finra.org or www.investinginbonds.com) and see the most recent trades made on that particular bond. That information often reveals what the broker paid for the very same bond he is now offering to sell you for $5,000. If you can't find that very same bond, you can find similar bonds — other A-rated bonds with similar maturity. If you wish to sell a bond, you can see what other people are getting on the open market for bonds similar to yours. In Chapter 15, I walk you through the system, step by step. You'll like it! And you — not some middleman — will profit from it!

Deciding Whether to Go with Bond Funds or Individual Bonds

Before I get into the nitty-gritty of buying and selling bonds (the next two chapters are nothing but nitty-gritty), you need to make a decision between individual bonds and bond funds. Thanks to the many recent changes in the bond markets that I discuss in the previous sections, either choice can be a good one. My own bias — built on years of experience — is that most investors are better off, most of the time, with bond funds.

Calculating the advantages of funds

I prefer bond funds for a number of reasons, but far and away the largest reason is the diversification that bond funds allow.

Diversifying away certain risks

The obvious appeal of going with a bond fund over individual bonds is the same as the appeal of going with stock funds over individual stocks: You get instant diversification. If you build an entire portfolio of McDummy Corporation bonds (or stocks), and the McDummy Corporation springs a serious leak, you could take a serious hit on the McChin. With bond funds, you don't need to worry so much about the crash of a particular company.

Just as importantly, bond funds allow you to diversify not only by issuer but also by credit quality (you can have AAA-rated bonds and B-rated bonds — see Chapter 6) and by maturity. Some bond funds allow you to diversify even more broadly by including completely different *kinds* of bonds, such as Treasuries, agencies, and corporates, both U.S. and international.

How much money should you be able to invest before you forget about bond funds and build a truly diversified bond portfolio out of individual bonds? "We're talking something in the range of $300,000," says Chris Genovese, executive vice president of Advisor's Asset Management, Inc., a nationwide firm that provides targeted advice on bond portfolio construction to investment advisors.

Making investing a lot easier

Sure, you can own a boatload of individual bonds and *ladder* them (which means to use a diversification technique I discuss in Chapter 15), but owning one or a handful of bond mutual or exchange-traded funds is often a lot simpler. Also, given the numbers that Genovese is talking about, most people don't have nearly enough money to diversify properly with individual bonds.

Individual bonds are also more work than bond funds.

When you own an individual bond, the interest payments generally come to you twice a year. If you reinvest that money rather than spend it, you need to decide how to reinvest. In other words, a portfolio of individual bonds takes ongoing care and maintenance, sort of like an old car that needs to go to the shop every few months. Bond funds, in contrast, can be set up to reinvest automatically and can almost be put on autopilot.

Having choices: Index funds and actively managed funds

If you wish to capture the gains of the entire bond market, bond index funds allow you to do that. If you want to bet (yes, it's always something of a bet) that you can do better than the bond market at large, you can hire an active manager who tries to eke out extra returns for you by looking for special deals in the bond market.

I believe largely in index investing (for both stocks and bonds) because beating the market is very hard to do. Study after study shows that index investors, in both equities and fixed income, wind up doing better than the vast majority of investors. That's largely because index funds tend to be the least expensive funds. Index fund managers take less for themselves, and they incur far fewer trading costs.

Still, if you put the time and effort into finding the right active bond manager, and you pay that manager a modest fee, you may wind up ahead of the indexes. Just know the odds are against it. According to Morningstar, only 27 percent of actively managed bond funds have outperformed the Barclays Capital Aggregate Bond Index over the past 15 years, while many of them take on more risk than the index.

If you wish to try to beat the market using individual bonds, you may be able to find a really good bond broker who knows the markets inside and out and charges you only a reasonable markup for each trade or a reasonable flat fee for his services. Finding such a broker, however, is a lot more difficult than researching bond-fund managers. And most such talented brokers aren't going to work with you if you have chump change to invest.

Keeping your costs to a minimum

For the savvy investor, the cost of trading individual bonds is cheaper than ever. But so, too, is the cost of investing in bond funds. Treasury bonds can be bought online (www.treasurydirect.gov) without any kind of fee or markup. Any other kind of bond, however, costs you something to trade. Given the volume that bond fund managers trade, they can often trade cheaper than you can.

"Institutional buyers can buy and sell bonds and get much better prices than the retail investor," says Helen Modly, CFP, executive vice president of Focus Wealth Management in Middleburg, Virginia. "Because of that, bond funds, especially bond index exchange-traded funds (ETFs), make a lot of sense."

If you pay a fund manager a pittance per year (such as the 12/100 of 1 percent that a Vanguard ETF manager receives), Modly says (and I agree), you are nearly always going to get off cheaper with the fund than with building your own bond ladder.

Note that popular wisdom has it that individual bond investing is cheaper than investing in bond funds. Don't buy it. Except perhaps for Treasury bonds, and maybe new issues on agency bonds or municipals, the small investor dealing in individual bonds is unlikely to wind up ahead.

I should add that many buyers of individual bonds often incur one frequently forgotten cost: the cost of having idle cash. If you collect your semiannual coupon payments and don't spend them, they may sit around in a low-interest money market account. Many of the clients I've seen show me their existing "bond" portfolios, and I immediately notice wads and wads of cash sitting around earning next to nothing. That doesn't happen with bond funds, where the monthly interest can easily be set up to roll right back into the fund, earning money without pause.

Considering whether individual bonds make sense

Individual bonds and bond funds, like politics and money, are even closer than most people think.

Dispelling the cost myth

People who imagine great differences often say that bond funds are more expensive than investing in individual bonds. While this statement is often untrue, the expenses associated with bond funds have traditionally been more *visible* than those associated with trading individual bonds.

Overall, funds tend to be less expensive unless the individual bonds are bought for very large amounts and held till maturity (provided maturity is at least several years away).

Dispelling the predictability myth

Another misconception is that individual bonds are much more predictable than bond funds. After all, you get a steady stream of income, and you know that you are getting your principal back on such-and-such a date. Technically, these things are true. But they're more complicated than they seem.

Say you had all your money in one big, fat bond worth $100,000 with a coupon rate of 5 percent, maturing in 20 years. You would know that you'd get a check for $2,500 once every six months and that, in 20 years, provided the company or municipality issuing the bond is still around, you'd get a final check for $102,500 (your final interest payment, plus your principal returned).

But that's not how things work in the real world. In the real world, investors in individual bonds typically have bonds of varying maturities. As one bond matures, a younger bond takes its place. Except by rare coincidence, the new bond will not have the same maturity period or the same coupon rate. So the argument that the returns on a portfolio of individual bonds are as predictable as the sunrise is weak.

In addition, consider the effects of inflation. Yes, $100,000 invested in individual bonds today will be returned to you in 10, 20, or however many years, depending on the maturity of the bonds. But what will that money be worth in 10 or 20 years? You simply don't know. Because of inflation, it could be worth quite a bit less than the value of $100,000 today. I'm not arguing that inflation wallops the return on individual bonds any more than it wallops the return on bond funds; I'm only arguing that the effect of inflation renders final bond returns kind of mushy — whether we're talking individual bonds or bond funds.

To look at it another way, individual bond *ladders* (which I describe in Chapter 15) fluctuate — in both interest payments and principal value — just as bond funds do. So you won't convince me that individual bonds (except perhaps for short-term bonds that are not as vulnerable to inflation or interest rate fluctuations) are much better than bond funds for reasons of either price or consistency. But that's not to say that individual bonds are never the better choice. They certainly can be, in some cases — most notably, if you plan to hold them to maturity.

Dispelling the interest rate risk avoidance myth

In Chapter 10, I discuss interest rate risk. Interest rate risk — the risk that general interest rates may go up, making the value of your existing bonds (paying what are now no longer competitive rates) go down — can really put a damper on the life of a bond investor. That is especially true when interest rates are so low that they can really only move in one direction: up.

Sometimes, when people get scared, they get stupid. And stupid is, I'm afraid, the word that comes to mind when I hear the argument — and I've heard it *a lot* lately, even from people who should know better — that buying individual bonds is a way of avoiding interest rate risk.

Here's how the argument goes: *Buy an individual bond, hold it until maturity, and you will be immune from interest rate risk. Let those bond fund buyers suffer from depressed prices. You will get your principal back, in full, in 20 (or whatever) years. So the interest rate can go up and down, down and up, and it won't affect you at all!*

Um, yeah. While this argument is technically true, it is, like the predictability argument, more complex than it first seems. Sure, go ahead and buy a bond for $1,000 that pays 5 percent for 20 years. Then let's say that next year, interest rates on similar bonds pop to 7 percent. You, goshdarnit, are going to hold that bond for another 19 years. You aren't going to sell and take a loss like all those idiots who bought into bond funds last year, *are you?*

Introducing funds that act like individual bonds

Any edge that individual bonds may have had over bond funds as far as predictability in getting your money back is quickly losing ground to a new breed of bond fund. For investors who want the diversification of a fund but the knowledge that their principal is coming back to them at a certain date, a lineup of exchange-traded funds from iShares and another from Guggenheim may offer the perfect blend.

Although only a few years old, the iShares series of muni bond funds, such as the iShares 2016 S&P AMT-Free Municipal Series (MUAE) and the iShares 2017 S&P AMT-Free Municipal Series (MUAF), offer instant exposure to a bevy of bonds that all mature at about the same time. The expense ratio is 0.30 percent — quite reasonable. And the predictability of payout is similar to that of a single bond.

Similarly, Guggenheim has a lineup of corporate bond funds they call the BulletShares series. Examples include the Guggenheim BulletShares 2016 Corporate Bond ETF (BSCG) and the Guggenheim BulletShares 2017 Corporate Bond ETF (BSCH). It's the same deal as you get with the iShares munis. As the Guggenheimers say, "By selecting the Funds whose maturities align with your particular time frame, the Fund's final cash distributions may be applied toward each year's expenses." In other words, you get the precision of an individual bond with the diversity of a fund. And with Guggenheim, it'll cost you 0.24 percent, which I also find quite reasonable.

Well, that's your option. But know the cost: For the next 19 years, all things being equal, you will collect 5 percent on your initial investment. Everyone else, perhaps even those bond fund holders, may be collecting 7 percent a year. Sure, you'll get your $1,000 back eventually. But you *are* taking a loss in the form of locking in your principal at the lower interest rate. And that loss could be a very significant one.

Dispelling the tax myth

This one isn't so much a myth: The reality is that bond mutual funds can incur capital gains tax where individual bonds — until perhaps you sell them — do not. When a fund manager sells an individual bond for more than he paid for it, the fund makes a capital gain that gets passed onto the shareholders (if there are no offsetting capital losses). With individual bonds, you often don't incur a capital gains tax unless you yourself sell the bond for a profit — or you buy a bond at a discount to par and you hold it to maturity.

But while capital gains on stock funds can be very large, capital gains on bond funds generally aren't. Most bonds simply don't appreciate in price the way that stocks can. Also, if you are concerned with capital gains on your bond funds, you can always put them into a tax-advantaged retirement account, and your capital gains tax problems disappear. Or, rather than invest in an actively managed bond mutual fund, you can choose a bond index mutual fund or exchange-traded fund (ETF) that rarely sees much in the way of capital gains taxes because less trading is involved. Both index investing and putting your bond funds in retirement accounts are strategies that I recommend. I discuss tax-advantaged retirement accounts more in just a few pages. You find more on ETFs and indexed mutual funds in Chapter 16.

Embracing the precision of single bonds

Neither price nor consistency makes individual bonds all that much a better option than bond funds. What *can* sometimes make individual bonds a better option is control. If you absolutely need a certain amount of income, or if you need the return of principal sometime in the next several years, individual bonds can make sense. For example:

- ✔ If you are buying a house, and you know that you're going to need $40,000 in cash in 365 days, buying one-year Treasury bills may be a good option for your money.

- ✔ If your kid is off to college in two years, and you know that you'll need $20,000 a year for four years, Treasury bills and bonds may be the ticket. (However, it may make more sense to open a 529 College Plan. See *529 & Other College Savings Plans For Dummies* by Margaret A. Munro [Wiley].)

- ✔ If you are comfortably retired and your living expenses are covered by your pension and Social Security, but you need to pay out $500 twice a year for property taxes, it may be wise to put away enough in individual bonds to cover that fixed expense, at least for several years down the road. (Beyond several years, you can't be certain what your property taxes will be.)

- ✔ If you are pulling in a sizeable paycheck and find yourself in the upper tax brackets, and you live in a high-tax city and state, and your reading of Chapter 8 tells you that investing in triple-tax-free munis makes the most sense, then a ladder of triple-tax-free munis may be your best portfolio tool. (*Triple-tax-free* means free from federal, state, and local tax.)

- ✔ If you are getting seriously on in years, and your life expectancy isn't that great, and you suspect that your heirs will inherit your bond portfolio in the next several years, you may want to consider a bevy of individual corporate bonds with death puts, which I discuss in Chapter 6.

Individual bonds allow for a precise tailoring of a fixed-income portfolio, with certain potential estate benefits. Quite simply, most people don't need that kind of precision or insurance, and, therefore, the advantages of funds usually outweigh the advantages of single bonds.

Spotting other scenarios when individual bonds are best

There may be a few instances where precision in payment isn't your main motivation to buy an individual bond rather than tap into a bond fund. If any of the following scenarios apply to you, individual issues may make sense:

But interest rates are almost as unpredictable as the stock market. Yes, the government has more control over interest rates than it does the stock market, but it doesn't have complete control, and the actions it decides to take or not take are not for you to know.

And furthermore, I would argue that even if you *could* predict interest rates (which you can't), and even if you *did* know that they were going to rise (which you don't), now still is a good time to buy bonds.

I'm assuming, of course, that you've done the proper analysis (see Chapter 12), and you've decided that more bonds belong in your portfolio, and you have cash in hand. What do you do with it? You have three savings/investing options, really:

- ✔ Keep it in cash.
- ✔ Invest it in equities.
- ✔ Invest it in fixed income.

If you invest in equities (stocks, real estate, commodities), you mess with your overall portfolio structure, making it perhaps too risky. If you keep cash (a savings or money market account), you earn enough interest to *maybe* keep up with inflation — but after taxes, probably not. In either scenario, you lose.

Now, suppose you choose to go ahead and buy the bonds, and interest rates, as you feared, do rise. That isn't necessarily a bad thing. Yes, your bonds or bond funds — especially those with long maturities — will take a hit. The value of the bonds or the price of the bond-fund shares will sink. In the long run, though, you shouldn't suffer, and you may even benefit from higher interest rates.

After all, every six months with individual bonds, and every month with most bond funds, you get interest payments, and those interest payments may be reinvested. The higher the interest rate climbs, the more money you can make off those reinvestments. Waiting for interest rates to fall — which they may or may not do — just doesn't make sense.

I will concede that when interest rates are very low, as they are these days, it makes sense to lean your bond portfolio more toward the short-intermediate side than the long-term. Yes, you'll get a lesser yield, but you'll take a softer punch when interest rates do rise. I normally aim for an average maturity in my bond portfolios of five to seven years. These days, I'll accept the lower yield that comes with a bond portfolio with an average maturity of three to five years.

✔ **You meet a bond broker extraordinaire.** If you find a b(
is so talented in the ways of bond trading that she can d(
a bond fund manager can do, only better, then I say go f(
brokers are very rare birds, but maybe after reading Cha
have the prowess to spot one.

✔ **You plan to become a bond expert.** If you yourself inten
such an intense study of bonds that you can serve as you
researching individual bond issues and issuers to the po
you have an edge on the market, then individual bonds a
guess is that because you are reading the words on this |
have a *lot* of studying to do before you become a true fixe
warrior.

✔ **You have an inside edge.** If you have inside information
to know that a particular bond is worth more than the m(
worth, you may take advantage of it by investing in that b
true inside information, such as the information available
of a company, is illegal to take advantage of — in stock tr(
trading. And false insider information, the kind of informa
free all over the Internet, is worth every penny you pay fo

✔ **You plan to spend a lot of time and energy on your portfc**
certain strategies to help juice your returns that you can us
ual bonds that you can't use with funds (although a good fu
may very well follow these strategies). One strategy, called
the yield curve, entails holding long-term bonds paying high
until they become intermediate- or short-term bonds, and tl
them and replacing them with other higher yielding long-ter
they become intermediate- or short-term bonds. Such a stra
time, energy, a good head for finance, and strong trading sk(

Is Now the Time to Buy Bonds?

After suggesting a bond portfolio — or any other kind of portfoli
client, I often hear, "But . . . is *now* a good time to invest?"

The answer is *yes.*

Predicting the future of interest rates . . . yeah, right

With stocks, the big concern people have is usually that the mar(
to tumble. With bonds, the big concern — especially these days -
interest rates are going to rise, and any bonds purchased today v
value as a result.

Paying too much attention to the yield curve

Another difficult decision for bond investors putting in fresh money occurs at those rare times in history when we see an inverted yield curve. The *yield curve* refers to the difference between interest rates on long-term versus short-term bonds. Normally, long-term bonds pay higher rates of interest. If the yield curve is *inverted,* that means the long-term bonds are paying lower rates of interest than shorter-term bonds. That situation doesn't happen often, but it happens. The reasons for the yield curve are many and complex, and they include inflation expectations, feelings about the economy, and for-eign demand for U.S. debt.

Whatever the reasons for an inverted yield curve, it hardly makes sense to tie up your money in a long-term bond when a shorter-term bond is paying just as much interest or possibly a slight bit more. Or does it?

Some financial planners would disagree with me on this one, but I am not averse to investing in longer-term bonds even when the yield curve is a slight bit inverted. Perverted? Nah. Remember that a large reason you're investing in bonds is to have a cushion if your other investments (such as stocks) take a nosedive. When stocks plunge, money tends to flow (and flow fast) into investment-grade bonds, especially Treasuries. Initially, the "rush to safety" creates the most demand for short-term bonds, and their price tends to rise.

Over time, however, a plunge in the stock market often results in the feds lowering interest rates (in an attempt to kick-start the economy), which lifts bond prices — especially the price of longer maturity bonds. In other words, long-term Treasuries are your very best hedge against a stock market crash. If that hedge is paying a hair less in interest, it may still be worth having it, rather than shorter-term bonds, in your portfolio.

Consider another reason for investing in longer-term bonds, even if they aren't paying what short-term bonds are paying. What if interest rates drop, regardless of what's going on in the stock market? Sometimes interest rates fall even when the stock market is soaring. If that's the case, once again, you may wish that you were holding long-term bonds, says bond guru Chris Genovese. "If interest rates are falling when your short-term bonds mature, you may be forced to reinvest at a lower rate," he says. "In the context of an entire bond portfolio, having both short-term and long-term bonds, regard-less of the yield curve, may be advisable."

The recent yield curve has not been inverted at all. As of early 2012, longer-term Treasuries in particular are currently paying a good deal more than short-term Treasuries, which are now paying crew-cut rates. By the time you're reading this chapter, however . . . who knows?

Adhering — or not — to dollar-cost averaging

Instead of throwing all your money into a bond portfolio right away, some people say it makes more sense to buy in slowly over a long period of time. As the argument goes, you spread out your risk that way, buying when the market is high *and* when the market is low. And if you invest equal amounts of money each time, you tend to buy more product (bonds or fund shares) when the market is low, potentially adding to your bottom line. This approach to investing is called *dollar-cost averaging*.

Dollar-cost averaging makes some sense if you are taking freshly earned money and investing it. If you have an existing pool of cash, however, it simply doesn't make sense. The cash you leave behind will be earning too little for the whole scheme to make any sense.

If you have a chunk of money waiting to be invested, and you have an investment plan in place, go for it. Buy those bonds you were planning to buy. There's no reason to wait for just the right moment or to buy in dribs and drabs. (I feel a little differently about stocks, but stocks, by and large, are way more volatile than bonds.)

Choosing between Taxable and Tax-Advantaged Retirement Accounts

Yesteryear, when corporations and municipalities were still offering *bearer* bonds — bonds that came with a certificate and were registered nowhere, with no one — you didn't have to concern yourself with keeping them in any particular account. You could keep your bearer bonds in your safe, your glove compartment, or your underwear drawer. Today, it's a different matter.

Chances are that you have both a taxable account where you can store your investments and a tax-advantaged account, such as an IRA, a Roth IRA, a 401(k), or a 529 college savings plan. Think of these as *containers* of sorts, which you fill up with your various investments.

In which container do you keep your bonds?

Balancing your portfolio with taxes in mind

Suppose you've decided that you want a 50/50 portfolio: 50 percent stocks and 50 percent bonds. Suppose, in addition, that you have both a taxable brokerage account and a conventional IRA. You've decided to put all your bonds in the IRA and all your stocks in your taxable brokerage account. Do you really have a 50/50 portfolio?

No, probably not. The IRA bond money, whenever you decide to tap it, will incur income tax. The stocks will be taxable as capital gains — in most cases, 15 percent — only to the extent that they've grown in value.

In other words, $100,000 taken from the stock portfolio in your brokerage account, assuming you originally invested $50,000, will incur a tax of ($50,000 capital gain × 15 percent) $7,500. But $100,000 taken from the bond portfolio in your IRA may incur a tax (assuming you are in the 28 percent tax bracket) of $28,000.

As you can see, your IRA portfolio is worth considerably less (in this case, about 22 percent less)

than the same amount of money in your taxable account.

If you are more than five years from tapping your nest egg, don't concern yourself too much with this discrepancy. You don't yet know what your income tax rate or the capital gains rate will be when you start to withdraw from your savings. Nor can you predict very well the appreciation you'll enjoy in your various accounts. But as you approach retirement, or if you are already in the disbursement phase of your investor life, it makes sense to factor this tax differential into your portfolio allocation.

In the example above, a *true*, after-tax, 50/50 portfolio would need to have more bonds than stocks. If, however, your bonds were in a tax-free Roth IRA rather than in a tax-deferred account, the opposite becomes true, because generally no tax is due on withdrawals from the Roth.

Positioning your investments for minimal taxation

Say you're in the 28 percent federal tax bracket. You'll pay 28 percent tax (plus state income tax) on any bond interest dividends paid from any bonds held in a taxable account — except for tax-free municipal bonds. Plain and simple, tax-advantaged accounts exist to allow you to escape — or at least postpone — paying income tax on your investment gains. It generally makes the most sense to keep your taxable income-generating investments, such as taxable bonds, in your retirement accounts.

Here are some other things to keep in mind:

 ✔ Treasury bonds are free from state tax. Therefore, if you have room in your retirement accounts for only one kind of bond, it makes most sense for it to be corporate bonds.

  ✔ Foreign bonds often require the paying of foreign tax, which usually is reimbursed to you by Uncle Sam, but only if those bonds are kept in a taxable account.

  ✔ Tax-free municipal bonds always belong in your taxable accounts.

Figure 14-1 illustrates where you want to keep your bond holdings.

Figure 14-1:
Where your bonds belong.

Keep in retirement account   Keep in either   Keep in taxable account

Corporate bonds   Treasuries   Foreign bonds   Tax-free munis

Illustration by Wiley, Composition Services Graphics

Factoring in the early-withdrawal penalties and such

Keep in mind that any money withdrawn from an IRA, 401(k), or SEP (self-employed pension) prior to age 59½, except under certain special circumstances, is subject to a 10 percent penalty. (Income tax must be paid regardless of when you withdraw.) So any bonds you are planning to cash out prior to that age should not be put into your retirement account.

On the flip side, at age 70½, you must start taking minimum required distributions from most retirement accounts. That fact should be figured into your allocation decisions, as well. If your minimum required distributions — the amount the IRS requires you to pull from your account each year after age 70½ — are substantial, it can mess with your balance of investments.

As I discuss more in Chapter 18, Roth IRAs are different animals. You pay no tax when you withdraw, and you are not required to withdraw at any particular age. The money grows and grows, tax-free, potentially forever. Imagine. Had Vasco da Gama in 1497 invested a mere $1 in a bond fund that paid 5 percent a year, and had he held that fund in a Roth IRA, that $1 would now be worth $77,857,360,000. Think of all the spices and silly pants *that* could buy!

Chapter 15

Investing (Carefully!) in Individual Bonds

In This Chapter

▶ Assessing recent changes in transparency within bond markets

▶ Picking an honest broker

▶ Doing it yourself (sort of) online

▶ Laddering your bonds to stagger maturities and lessen risk

> *Quit ev'ry surement and ev'ry bond*
>
> *That ye have made to me as herebeforn,*
>
> *Since thilke time that ye were born.*
>
> *Have here my truth, I shall you ne'er repreve.*
>
> — Geoffrey Chaucer, The Canterbury Tales, 14th century

*U*nless you have a PhD in medieval literature, or you're 620 years old, you probably have no more idea what those words mean than I do. (I chose the particular passage above simply because it has the word *bond* in it, although I don't think it has anything to do with finances.) In any case, I'm afraid that Chaucer has become a bit moldy with age.

Alas, I may come to know the same fate. By the time you read these words, this very chapter may well seem antiquated. That's how rapidly the world of individual bond trading is changing.

Ne'rtheless, um, nevertheless, in this chapter I do my best to get you up to current speed. And, should the tales I tell become faded by time, fear not: I give you a few online resources so that with the tap of some keys and the click of a mouse, you can access the most modern methods — the most efficient, friendly, and profitable methods — for buying and selling individual bonds.

Navigating Today's Individual Bond Market

You usually don't pay commissions when you trade individual bonds, as you do when you trade stocks. Instead, someone called a broker (an individual wearing a fancy suit) usually trades your bonds. A broker buys a bond at one price and sells it at a higher price. The difference, known as the *bid/ask spread,* is what the broker brings home. We're sometimes talking *lots* of bacon here. The bid/ask spreads on bonds can be big enough to make the commissions paid on stocks look like greyhound fat.

Once upon a time, and for many decades, commissions on stocks were as fat as spreads on bonds, sometimes fatter. That began to change shortly after Mary Tyler Moore moved to Minneapolis. (Historians who study the 1970s believe the connection is only coincidental.)

In 1975, the Securities and Exchange Commission (SEC) deregulated the stock markets, allowing for open competition and discount brokerage houses. The competition brought prices down somewhat. Internet trading, which allowed the brokerage houses to economize, brought prices down even more. Within a fairly few years, the money that most people spent to make a stock trade was reduced to a fraction of what it had been. In the 1970s, a typical stock trade cost $100 (about $400 in today's dollars). Today, a stock trade may cost as little as $5, and rarely more than $10.

And how has bond trading changed since 1975? It's changed. But it's changed like men's fashions change — not women's. You have to look harder to notice the differences.

Getting some welcome transparency

Bond trading today is, in a sense, about where stock trading was in the early 1980s. You can still spend $300, $400, or way more on the cost of a single trade. But you shouldn't have to anymore. Thanks to a system called the *Trade Reporting and Compliance Engine* (TRACE), bond trading is becoming a bit more like stock trading.

TRACE is a system run by the Financial Industry Regulatory Authority (FINRA) that can be accessed through many financial websites, such as www.investinginbonds.com.

Because of TRACE, bond trading no longer has to be a muddied affair in which individual investors are at the mercy of brokers. This system ensures that every corporate bond trade in the United States is reported, and the details appear on the web. (The Municipal Securities Rulemaking Board runs a similar system for municipal bonds.)

TRACE ensures that trading costs are no longer hidden, bond yields (greatly affected by the bid/ask spreads) are easy to find, and good information is available. Among investment people, access to information is generally referred to as *transparency*. TRACE provides some pretty amazing transparency.

Unfortunately, not everyone knows about the TRACE system, so not everyone realizes that she can find out — for free — the price a broker paid for a bond. In fact, lots of people don't know. The world today is divided more or less evenly, I'd say, between those who know about TRACE and those who don't. Those who don't, pay a heavy price.

Ushering in a new beginning

The new transparency, ushered into practice between 2002 and 2005, has removed much of the mystery from bond trading. You can now go online and, provided your Windows system doesn't crash that particular day, quickly get a pretty good idea of how much a single bond is being bought and sold for — by brokers, institutions, and individuals. You'll also see how far a broker — *your* broker — is trying to mark a bond up, and exactly what yield you'll get after the middleman and all his cousins have taken their cuts, should you purchase that bond.

Unfortunately, the cuts taken on bond trades still tend to be too high, and you can't (except in rare circumstances) bypass the middlemen. But with some tough negotiating on your part, you won't make them terribly rich at your expense, either.

Dealing with Brokers and Other Financial Professionals

As I explain more fully in Chapter 14, you are probably better off investing in bond funds rather than individual bonds unless you have a bond portfolio (not your total portfolio, but just the bond side of your portfolio) of $300,000 or more. Building a diversified bond portfolio — diversified by type of bond, by issuer, and by maturity — is hard unless you have that amount to work with. Negotiating good prices on bonds is also hard when you're dealing with amounts that brokers tend to sneeze at.

Investing in individual bonds also requires substantially more work than investing in bond funds. With individual bonds, you not only need to haggle, but you need to haggle again and again. After all, with individual bonds, you get interest payments on a regular basis, usually every six months. Unless you spend the money right away, you need to concern yourself with constantly reinvesting those interest payments. Doing so can be a real job.

Then there's the risk of default. With Treasuries and agency bonds, you can presume that the risk of default is negligible, and with high quality munis and top corporations, the risk is minimal. With most corporate bonds and some munis, however, the risk of the company or municipality losing its ability to pay you back is very real. Even when issuers don't default, their bonds may be downgraded by the major rating agencies. A downgrade can mean a loss of money, too, if you decide that you can't hold a bond till maturity. Don't start dabbling in individual corporate bonds or munis unless you're willing to put in some serious time and effort doing research.

With these caveats in mind, the first thing you need in order to be an investor in individual bonds is a *dealer*: someone or some institution to place the actual trades for you — without robbing you blind or steering you astray.

Identifying the role of the middleman

Most bond dealers are traders or brokers who buy a bond from Client A at one price, sell it to Client B at another, leave the office for a few rounds of golf, and then come back to harvest more profits. Sorry, I hate to be cynical, but the money some of these Brooks Brothers cowboys make at investors' expense is truly shameful.

Some bond dealers are very knowledgeable about fixed-income investing and can help walk you through the maze, making good suggestions for your portfolio. Some are very talented at finding the best buys in bonds and using certain sophisticated strategies to juice your fixed-income returns.

Unfortunately, the way dealers are paid creates a system where the traditional dealer's financial interests are in opposition to the interests of his clients. The more the dealer makes, the less the client keeps. The more the client keeps, the less the dealer makes. The more the dealer can get you to *flip,* or trade one bond for another, the more the dealer makes. Generally, the more you flip, the less likely you are to come out ahead.

I don't wish to say that dealers are bad people, or greedy people . . . no more so than car salesmen are bad or greedy people. I'm only saying that bond dealers are salespeople (some of them fabulously paid salespeople) and need to be seen as such.

Like the car salesman, the bond trader who acts as *principal* (taking owner- ship of the bond) is not required to reveal what kind of markup he is making. And you won't find this information in *Consumer Reports.* (Fortunately, though, you can find it on TRACE; see the section "Getting some welcome transparency" earlier in this chapter.)

Where bond trading is heading

Some day — I'm not sure when, but some day — traditional bond dealers may disappear. You want to buy a Spacely Space Sprockets ten-year bond maturing in 2080? You'll get an identifying code for the bond (perhaps the CUSIP, which I discuss in another sidebar in this chapter), and you'll put it on a website (something that resembles www.kayak.com, which currently exists for travel deals). People and institutions will offer to sell you their bonds, and you'll be free to pay the lowest price. Want to sell a Spacely Space Sprockets ten-year bond maturing in 2080? You'll advertise it on the same website, and people and institutions will bid. You'll take the highest price you can get.

Kevin Olson, a former bond trader turned investor advocate, currently runs a website called www.munimarket.com, which is a step in the right direction. Buyers and sellers can find each other and post their muni bond desires on a bulletin board. However, both buyer and seller must then find a trader, and the traders transact the deals. Also, the vast majority of muni bond offerings do not appear on Olson's site. "There's no incentive for the big banks to facilitate trading of bonds among individuals," Olson explains. "They want to keep their turf to continue raking in money as the middleman."

Ideally, bonds will eventually wind up trading more like stocks. Instead of a bunch of traders shouting deals at each other over the telephone (as happens today), bonds will be offered on an open exchange, such as the NYSE. Actually, some of the most frequently traded corporate bonds began selling on the NYSE several years ago, but only professionals have access. (Some investment banks, such as Fidelity, can place a NYSE bond trade for a customer, but only through one of their agents.) At some point in the future, an investor may be able to go online and trade a bond just like a stock — with market orders, limit orders, and conditional trades. You want a ten-year bond with an A rating, paying at least 32 percent? (Interest rates are higher in the future!) You'll put the offer into your computer, and it will comb through every bond offer in the land. The first to meet the criteria you're seeking will nail the sale.

Some bond dealers today work as *agents* and charge you a flat fee, an hourly rate, a certain amount per trade, or a percentage of assets under management. A good agent, like a good broker, may know the ropes of bond trading well enough to help you make the best selections and get the best prices.

Agents, unlike brokers, *do* have to reveal exactly what they are charging you. Alas, whereas an agent is generally better to deal with than a broker (simply because the conflict of financial interest doesn't exist), a good one is very hard to find. And even if you do find one, agents often must work with dealers to get trades done.

Do you need a broker or agent at all?

You don't need a broker or agent to buy Treasury bonds. You can do so easily and without any markup on www.treasurydirect.gov.

What the heck is a CUSIP, anyway?

All bonds have a CUSIP that identifies the bond in the same way that a license plate identifies a vehicle. CUSIP stands for *Committee on Uniform Securities Identification Procedures,* which is a part of the American Bankers Association. Although it's often referred to as a CUSIP *number,* that is something of a misnomer because a CUSIP typically contains both letters and numbers. The first six characters of the CUSIP identify the issuer, the next two characters identify the issue itself, and the ninth digit is called a *check digit,* its sole purpose to make computer readers happy. Here's a CUSIP for a General Electric bond: 36966RXR2. Here's one for a Fannie Mae bond: 31396CVP2.

Municipal bonds and corporate bonds must be purchased through an intermediary; you can't buy these securities directly from the issuers. Sure, you can loan your neighbor or brother-in-law $1,000 and demand the money back with interest (good luck!), and that's a bond, of sorts. But if you want to buy and sell marketable fixed-income securities, you must go through a recognized agent.

Going through a financial supermarket, such as Fidelity, T. Rowe Price, or Vanguard, is (generally) cheaper than going through a full-service, markup kind of broker. The supermarket's pricing, which is a *concession* or a fee (more or less), not a markup, is perhaps more clear-cut. But the supermarket agents generally hold your hand only so much, and they won't make actual bond selections for you the way a full-service broker will.

You'll note that I inject some qualifiers in the previous paragraph, such as "generally" and "perhaps." I explain why in the upcoming section "Doing It Yourself Online," where I discuss online bond trading. The financial supermarkets, alas, sometimes make their way of trading sound easier, cheaper, and more transparent than it really is.

Selecting the right broker or agent

Whether you go with a full-service, markup kind of broker or with an agent, I would ask you to do a few things:

- ✔ **Find someone who truly specializes in bonds — preferably the kind you're looking to buy.** If you needed hand surgery, you wouldn't go to a gastroenterologist, would you? If your dealing in individual bonds is going to be any more profitable than, say, investing in a bond index fund, you need a broker or agent who truly knows and tracks the markets carefully — someone who can jump on a good deal. You don't want a broker who deals in bonds, stocks, gold coins, and collector art!

Start by asking people you know and respect for referrals. Make calls. Ask lots of questions about a broker's background, including academic and professional history. Ask for client recommendations. Don't be shy. Ask for numbers: What kind of return figures has this broker been able to garner for clients, and taking what kinds of risks?

✔ **Be on guard.** Always. Whenever you find a broker and agree to buy or sell individual bonds, be certain that you aren't paying an excessive markup. Although different people in the investment business have different concepts of what constitutes "excessive," if you're asked to cough up the equivalent of more than three months' interest, that's excessive, in my humble opinion. Other financial types have their opinions. See the sidebar "Defining 'excessive' in bond markups" later in the chapter.

✔ **Know a dealer's limitations.** Most bond dealers I've known are not the best people to build your entire portfolio. They often have limited knowledge of investments beyond bonds. (And that's probably a good thing; see the first bullet in this list.) If they deal in stocks at all, they often deal in pricy stock mutual funds that you don't want — the kinds that earn them a nice commission.

Checking the dealer's numbers

In a page or two, I discuss online bond trading. If you deal with a full-service broker, you won't have to know every detail about trading bonds online. But I would still urge you, at a minimum, to become familiar with www. investinginbonds.com (the website of the Securities Industry and Financial Markets Association) and www.finra.org (the website of the Financial Industry Regulatory Authority). On these websites, you can plug in information on any bond — either by the name of the issuer or the bond's CUSIP — and you'll experience the type of transparency I discuss earlier in this chapter. (If you don't know what a CUSIP is, see the nearby sidebar "What the heck is a CUSIP, anyway?")

On www.investinginbonds.com, click on <u>See Municipal Market At-A-Glance</u> or <u>See Corporate Market At-A-Glance</u>, and then enter the CUSIP number at the bottom of the first page that pops up, under where it says "Bond History." On www.finra.org, click on the "Investors" link, then go to "Market Data" up on the plum-colored bar, and look to your right for "Quick Bond Search." Another source for an inside look into the trading of munis is the website of the Municipal Securities Rulemaking Board: www.emma.msrb.org.

If a bond has recently been sold, these websites can provide you with lots of information: the bond's selling price; how it's been rated by Moody's, S&P, and Fitch; and its coupon rate, price, and current yield (see Chapter 4). The site www.investinginbonds.com features a nifty bond calculator you can use to plug in the price the bond dealer is offering you (which includes his markup) and see if the yield still makes sense given your objectives and the yields of similar bonds.

Figure 15-1 shows the recent trading history of an everyday bond (from the pharmaceutical company, Merck) as seen at www.investinginbonds.com. You can see the price paid for this bond and the resulting yield. This gives you a pretty good idea of what you should be getting, should you wish to buy or sell . . . provided the particular bond you're interested in has seen recent action.

If you click on Run Calculations, you get something that looks like Figure 15-2.

Figure 15-1:
The recent trading history of a bond, as shown on www. investing inbonds. com.

Trade Details for CUSIP: 589331AK3

Following are recent corporate bond trades reported to the Financial Industry Regulatory Authority, Inc., through its TRACE system. Eligible securities, participants and other information is available from FINRA on their web site, in the Bond Section of the Market Data Center. From the home page navigate through Investors >> Market Data >> Bonds. Trade reports published here are on a real-time basis. Times shown are EST.

RTNGS INS	ISSUER CUSIP SECTOR/ SUBSECTOR		COUPON MATURITY	CALL DATES	CALL PRICES
AA SP Aa3 MDY A+ FTH	MERCK & CO INC 589331AK3 Industrial/Drugs		4.750 03/01/2015		

Graph Trade Data

1 2 3 4 5 6 7 8 9 10 ...

TRADE DATE TRADE TIME	PRICE	YIELD	SIZE	NOTES	MORE INFO SPECIAL PRICE INDICATOR
05/03/2012 09:46:00	111.154	0.737	10K		run calculations
05/03/2012 09:46:00	111.154	0.737	10K		run calculations
05/02/2012 11:52:22	110.890	0.829	1K		run calculations
05/02/2012 10:05:46	111.140	0.745	1K		run calculations
05/02/2012 10:05:46	111.140	0.745	1K		run calculations
05/01/2012 15:37:00	111.008	0.800	50K		run calculations
05/01/2012 15:31:36	111.157	0.750	10K		run calculations
05/01/2012 15:31:36	111.157	0.750	10K		run calculations

Illustration courtesy of the Securities Industry and Financial Markets Association (SIFMA)

Security/Trade Information

⊞ MERCK & CO INC 589331AK3

Security Type	US Corporate Bond ▾
Calculated based on:	Price of ▾
	111.154
Yield	0.737
Trade Date	05/03/2012
Settlement Date	05/08/2012
Maturity Date	03/01/2015
Coupon Rate	4.75

Coupon Frequency

annual ○
semiannual ◉
quarterly ○
monthly ○

[Re-Calculate]

General Calculations

DATA	AMOUNT
Current Yield	4.273
Annual Yield	0.739
Semiannual Yield	0.737
Yield-to-Maturity	0.737
Duration	2.856
Modified Duration	2.846
Convexity	8.556

Cash Flows

DATE	AMOUNT
Accrued Interest	$8.84
09/01/2012	$23.75
03/01/2013	$23.75
09/01/2013	$23.75
03/01/2014	$23.75
09/01/2014	$23.75
03/01/2015	$1,023.75

TIPS

Use this calculator to test different bond transaction scenarios. By adjusting either the price or the yield, determine it's opposite. Or, view yield calculations based on different trade dates. If calls are known they can be entered at the bottom.

Illustration courtesy of the Securities Industry and Financial Markets Association (SIFMA)

Figure 15-2: More detailed information on a bond, as available on www.investinginbonds.com.

To get a bird's-eye view of the bond market, go to Yahoo! Finance at http://finance.yahoo.com/bonds/composite_bond_rates. The chart you find there gives you a pretty good idea of what various categories of bonds are paying on any particular day. If you're in the market for a bond, compare the composite yield to the yield you're being offered. If you aren't being offered at least as much as the average yield, ask why. The Yesterday, Last Week, and Last Month columns show you which way bond yields are headed. But remember that yield trends, just like the wins and losses of your favorite sports team, can reverse direction quickly.

Looking into a broker's record

If you want to make sure that the bond broker you hire isn't going to take your money and buy a one-way ticket to Rio the next morning, check her background before you hand over the check. You can get information on the disciplinary record, professional background, and registration and license status of any properly registered broker or brokerage firm by using FINRA BrokerCheck. FINRA makes BrokerCheck available at no charge to the public. Investors can access this service by linking directly to BrokerCheck at www.finra.org or by calling 800-289-9999.

Hiring a financial planner

Lots of people today, including stock and bond brokers, call themselves financial planners. I suggest that if you hire a financial planner, you seriously consider a *fee-only* planner, who takes no commissions and works only for you. To find one in your area, contact the National Association of Personal Financial Advisors (NAPFA) at 847-483-5400, or go online to www.napfa.org. (I'm a member of NAPFA.)

Some NAPFA-certified financial advisors work with you on an hourly basis. Others want to take your assets under management. Know that if you hire a financial planner who takes your assets under management, you typically pay a fee, usually 1.0 percent a year. I think 1.0 percent is plenty; you shouldn't pay more than that unless you're getting help from that planner that extends to insurance, estate planning, and other matters beyond investing.

If you have a sizeable bond portfolio, a fee-only financial planner who is trading bonds for you can potentially save you enough money to compensate for his fee. Even though the planner will be dealing with a broker, just as you would, planners with numerous clients can bundle their bond purchases, so the broker often settles for a substantially lesser markup.

Here's an example of this type of savings. Matthew Reznik, a NAPFA-certified financial planner with Balasa Dinverno & Foltz LLC of Itasca, Illinois, explains, "If an individual investor is buying a $25,000 bond for his or her portfolio, the markup can be as high as 2.25 percent. If that bond is yielding 5 percent, that's a pretty big haircut. If we buy bonds, we buy the same issue in a $1 million piece. In that case the spread would be reduced to 0.10 percent."

Doing It Yourself Online

A growing number of financial supermarkets and specialty bond shops now allow you to trade bonds online, and they advertise that you can do so for a fixed price. In the case of Fidelity, the supermarket with which I am most familiar, the price is generally $1 per bond.

Whoa, you may say. *That's a great deal!* Well, yes and no. If that were all that Fidelity and the other middlemen were making, it would be a great deal. But what you see and what you get are two different things. The "flat fees" quoted by Fidelity and its competitors are a bit misleading.

"The idea that there are no broker markups is not the case," says financial planner Matthew Reznik. "No matter who sells you a bond, there is always a spread built in to compensate the broker." In other words, Fidelity, or Vanguard, or whomever, may charge you "only $1 to trade a bond," but the price you get for your bond, to buy or sell, has already been marked up from the price that someone else just got to sell or buy. Either your own broker may have marked up the price, or some other broker may have previously done so. Just don't kid yourself into thinking that $1 is all you're paying to trade. It ain't the case.

I've traded a good number of bonds online with Fidelity. The trading process there is similar to other financial supermarkets that offer flat-fee bond shopping. I explain how it works in a moment. First, I want to let you know that, yes, you can get good buys on bonds online, but you can also get zapped hard. Many other investment pros I've talked to have had very similar experiences at other financial supermarkets, such as Vanguard and Schwab.

You are most likely to get a fair deal online when you're *buying* a bond and dealing in large quantities. You are most likely to get zapped when you're *selling* a bond prior to maturity, especially if you're selling a small number of bonds and if those particular bonds are traded infrequently. In such cases, you may let go of your bonds for one price and, using TRACE, find out that they were sold seconds afterward for 3 percent (or more) higher than the price you just got. Someone is making very quick money in that situation, and it isn't you.

In this section, I explain how online trading generally works.

If you're looking to buy

You first choose a bond category: Do you want a Treasury bond, an agency bond, a corporate bond, or a municipal bond? (For reminders about each category, see Part II of this book.) What kind of rating are you looking for? What kind of maturity? What kind of yield? (Chapter 4 contains the goods on ratings, maturity, and yield.)

Buying a primary or secondary bond issue

All bonds are traded through brokers. But some bonds available for sale are new or *primary* issues. Others are *secondary* issues. Yes, it's something like buying a new versus a used car — except the used bond isn't necessarily any cheaper. In fact, according to Bill Conger (a principal and senior portfolio manager with Red Hook Management in Morristown, New Jersey), bonds that are just issued, especially in the municipal-bond arena, quite often offer juicier deals. You still need to be careful and follow all the rules laid out in this chapter. But all things being equal, the odds of a broker nailing you with a ridiculously excessive markup are less in the primary market. That's because new issues are almost universally issued at the same price for all

buyers, says Conger. "If the broker tried to mark up the price of the bond too much, it's doubtful that the bond issue would sell."

Bottom line: Ask your favorite broker — and your favorite broker's competitors — for a listing of all new issues. Then compare and contrast the yields on the newbies versus the oldies. You may be impressed. The mechanics of buying a primary issue differ from one brokerage to the next, but generally, you can place an order at a specific price and yield. If the price goes up and the yield goes down between the time you place the order and the bond goes to market, you have the opportunity to back out of the deal. If you trade stocks, you'll recognize this situation as similar to a limit order on a stock.

Most online bond shops walk you through this process step by step; it isn't that hard. The most difficult piece of the process, and the one I most want to help you with, is making sure that after you know what kind of bond you want, you get the best deal on your purchase.

Here, plain and simple, is what I mean by getting the best deal for a given type and quality of bond: You want the *highest yield.* The yield reflects whatever concession you're paying the financial supermarket, and it reflects whatever markup you're paying a broker.

Comparing yields, however, can be tricky, especially when looking at callable bonds, because you never know how long you'll have them. Keep in mind that in the past, when interest rates were falling, callable bonds were almost always called because the issuers could issue newer bonds at lower interest rates. In the future, that may not be the case. So you need to look at two possible scenarios: keeping the bond to maturity, or having it called.

As David Lambert, founding partner of Artisan Wealth Management in Lebanon, New Jersey, suggests, "When considering callable bonds, be sure to examine whether the bonds are selling at a premium or a discount to the call price. If trading at a premium, consider the yield-to-call first. If trading at a discount, consider the yield-to-maturity first. Both of these will give you your most realistic picture of future performance. You can pretty much ignore just about everything else," says Lambert.

What he is saying is that the yield-to-call on premium bonds and yield-to-maturity on discount bonds both represent _yield-to-worst_ (or _worst-case basis yield_). That yield is what you're likely going to get, so you may as well factor it into your bond purchase decisions.

If two comparable bonds — comparable in maturity, duration, ratings, callability, and every other way — are offering yields-to-worst of 4.1 percent and 4.2 percent, unless you have an inside track and therefore know more about the issuer than the ratings companies do, go with the 4.2 percent bond. Just make sure you've done your homework so you know that the two bonds are truly comparable.

Fidelity has a neat tool on its website called the _scatter graph_; it allows you to see a whole bunch of similar bonds on the same graph and what kind of yield each is paying. You can access it at `www.fidelity.com`. Click on Investment Products and then Fixed Income and Bonds. Get into Individual Bonds and then select the type of bond you're interested in purchasing. Enter your parameters to create the scatter graph you need.

To reiterate: The yield reflects the middleman's cut. _Focus on the yield,_ and especially on the yield-to-worst, to get the best deal. Don't over-concern yourself with the bid/ask spread on the bond.

When you go to place your order, use the "Limit Yield" option. You are telling the brokers on the Fidelity network that you'll buy this bond only if it yields, say, 4.2 percent. Anything less, and you aren't interested. Putting in a "Market" order on a bond can get you chewed up — don't do it.

If you're looking to sell

Selling bonds online can be a much trickier business. You have a particular bond you want to dump, and the market may or may not want it.

At Fidelity, you're best off calling a Fidelity fixed-income trader and asking that trader to give you a handle on what the bond is worth. You can then go online, place a "Limit Price" order to sell, and you'll very likely get what the Fidelity trader told you you'd get. But here's the catch: Fidelity itself may wind up buying your bond and selling it to someone else at a large markup. I asked a Fidelity supervisor if perhaps Fidelity couldn't be a better advocate for its clients if Fidelity itself didn't bid on the bonds, and what I got in response was a wee bit Orwellian. The answer is yes. Fidelity could be a better advocate for its clients if it weren't also dealing in the bonds its clients are trading. So be it.

Saving money with a full-service broker?

Many people assume that discount and online brokers allow you to trade bonds more cheaply than with full-service brokers, and that can be true sometimes. But it isn't *always* the case, says Kevin Olson, muni-market investment advocate. "Full-service brokers may offer you the best deals on new issues of municipal bonds, especially in those cases where the full-service broker is itself underwriting the bond," he says. If you're going to trade individual munis, Olson suggests having a number of accounts with different brokers, including both discount and full-service brokers. Sometimes, he says, you'll be surprised where you get the best deals. That's true both for new issues of bonds and for the secondary market.

Truth be told, you are likely to pay a high markup anywhere if you sell a bond before its maturity. Charles Schwab is similar to Fidelity in that you tend to pay through the nose when selling, says Dalibor Nenadov, a fee-only financial planner with Northern Financial Advisors in Franklin, Michigan. "The bottom line for the average middle class investor is to build a bond ladder, and hold until maturity. Don't sell before maturity, and don't try to time rates," he says.

Perfecting the Art of Laddering

Bond laddering is a fancy term for diversifying your bond portfolio by maturity. Buy one bond that matures in two years, another that matures in five, and a third that matures in ten, and — presto! — you have just constructed a bond ladder (see Figure 15-3).

Why bother? Why not simply buy one big, fat bond that matures in 30 years and will kick out regular, predictable coupon payments between now and then? Laddering makes more sense for a few reasons, which I explain here.

Protecting you from interest rate flux

The first rationale behind laddering is to temper interest rate risk. If you buy a 30-year bond right now that pays 4.5 percent, and if interest rates climb over the next year to 6.5 percent and stay there, you're going to be eating stewed crow for 29 more years with your relatively paltry interest payments of 4.5 percent. Obviously, you don't want that. (You could always sell your 30-year bond paying 4.5 percent, but if interest rates pop to 6.5 percent, the price you would get for your bond is not going to make you jump for joy.)

Figure 15-3:
A typical
bond ladder.

5.15% March 2015
2.25% November 2020
5.31% January 2025
5.40% April 2030
5.45% November 2035

Illustration by Wiley, Composition Services Graphics

Of course, you don't have to buy a 30-year bond right now. You could buy a big, fat two-year bond. The problem with doing that is twofold:

✔ You won't get as much interest on the two-year bond as you would on the 30-year bond.

✔ You are subjecting yourself to *reinvestment risk:* If interest rates fall over the next two years, you may not be able to reinvest your principal in two years for as much as you are getting today.

If you ladder your bonds, you shield yourself to a certain degree from interest rates rising and falling. If you're going to invest in individual bonds, laddering is really the only option. Do it. Do it!

Tinkering with your time frame

Note that as each bond in your ladder matures, you would typically replace it with a bond equal to the longest maturity in your portfolio. For example, if you have a two-year, a five-year, and a ten-year bond, when the two-year bond matures, you replace it with a ten-year bond. Why? Because your five-year and ten-year bonds are now two years closer to maturity, so the average weighted maturity of the portfolio will remain the same: 5.6 years.

Defining "excessive" in bond markups

You buy a bond from a broker. You pay $10,000. The broker bought the bond that same morning for $9,700. You sell a bond. You get $10,000. You do your research and discover you sold it to a broker who then turned around and sold it for $10,300. Are these fair spreads, or are they excessive?

"There's no hard and fast rule," says Chris Genovese, executive vice president of Advisor's Asset Management, Inc., a nationwide firm that provides advice on bond portfolio construction to investment advisors. "As far as what is excessive, spreads tend to get bigger when you are dealing in high-yield bonds, long-term bonds, thinly traded bonds, and small lots. Deciding on what is an excessive spread really depends on the transaction," he says. "The question of what is an appropriate markup and what is an excessive one is purely a facts-and-circumstances one, not a bright-line test, and many factors must be considered."

True. True. Many factors must be considered, but industry insiders tend to look askance at any markups that exceed 3 percent — and so should you. If your bond deal sees a cut this big, or even close, you should start asking questions.

"Markups, markdowns and commissions have to be fair and reasonable," says Gerri Walsh, vice president for investor education with the Financial Industry Regulatory Authority (FINRA). "Don't hesitate to ask your broker to provide the details about markups, markdowns or any fees or commissions associated with your investment. These costs ultimately impact the overall return on your investment and you have a right to know this information." If you do feel these costs are excessive, you may file a complaint using FINRA's online Complaint Center; go to `www.finra.org/complaint`.

Of course, over the course of two years, your economic circumstances may change, so you may want to tinker with the average weighted maturity. That depends on your need for return and your tolerance for risk: topics I discuss in Part I.

A perfectly acceptable (and often preferable) alternative to bond laddering is to buy a bond mutual fund or exchange-traded fund. This option is the heart of Chapter 16. But whether you ladder your bonds or you buy a bond fund, I would caution you that relying only on fixed income to fund your retirement is probably not the wisest path. You should have a bond ladder or bond funds *and* other investments (stocks, real estate, perhaps commodities) as well. I discuss this subject fully in Part V.

Chapter 16

Picking a Bond Fund That Will Serve You for Life

....

....

*W*hen I was 11, I found a fan belt in the street, undoubtedly fallen from some car engine. I wiped the grease and dirt off on my T-shirt and claimed the 9-inch diameter oval piece of rubber as my prize. One of the other boys in the neighborhood, Brian Callahan, decided that he wanted it as *his* prize. So he lunged at me, grabbed the belt, and started to pull. I pulled back. He slugged me. About a dozen other boys were looking on, so what could I do? I returned the punch. Next thing, the two of us were rolling around in the middle of the busy street, cars hurtling by. One of us, or both of us, might have been killed.

Was it worth risking life itself for a piece of old rubber?

Yup.

In the eyes of an 11-year-old boy, at least in the neighborhood I grew up in, getting run over by a two-ton vehicle was clearly preferable to being labeled a wimp.

And so it is with some bond investors. They cling to the notion that if you hire a fund manager, you are something of a wimp. They'd rather get run over trading individual bonds. Doing so is somehow more manly, more intelligent, more sophisticated than buying a bond fund — despite all evidence to the contrary. Yes, even armed with the valuable tips I provide in the previous chapter, a small investor in individual bonds can wind up with tire treads on his back.

I know bonds . . . and I know dumb. I actually have a 45-year-old fan belt in the memorabilia box in my closet (no kidding!) to prove it. So trust me on this: For the vast majority of individual investors, funds are the way to go. That was true several years ago, and it's even truer today with the advent of dozens of bond exchange-traded funds (ETFs) that allow the small investor ready access to some darned good and ultra low-cost bond portfolios.

There's nothing wimpy about bond funds, and provided you do your homework, they can be as intelligent and sophisticated an investment vehicle as you'll ever find. (Index funds, which include most of the fixed-income ETFs, are seen by some as the wimpiest things under the sky but turn out to be mighty tough themselves.)

In this chapter, I introduce you to the many kinds of bond funds — index, active, mutual funds, ETFs, closed-end funds, and unit investment trusts — and reveal that although none are worth dying for, some may well be worth fighting for.

Defining the Basic Kinds of Funds

With hundreds upon hundreds of bond funds to choose from, each representing a different basket of bonds, where do you start? That part is actually easy: You start with the particular class of bonds you want to own. Treasuries? Corporate bonds? Munis? Long-term? Short-term? Investment-grade? High-yield? A blend of all of the above? The chapters in Part II of this book help you answer that question. But knowing what class of bonds you want in the basket isn't enough. You also need to know what kind of *basket* you want.

Bond baskets (funds) come in five varieties:

- Open-end mutual funds, typically referred to simply as *mutual funds,* are far and away the most common.

- Closed-end mutual funds, usually referred to only as *closed-end funds,* offer comparatively greater return for greater risk.

- Exchange-traded funds (ETFs) are the newer kids on the block, catching on very quickly — for good reason.

- Unit investment trusts are not well known but perhaps worth knowing.

- Exchange-traded notes (ETNs) are sort of bonds within bonds with bells and whistles and their own unique characteristics.

Table 16-1 offers an overview of how these types of funds compare. In the following sections, I provide the details.

Table 16-1	Comparing the Five Kinds of Bond Funds				
Fund Type	How Many Funds Are There?	Do They Offer Diversification?	Active Management or Passive (Index)?	Fee or Commission to Buy or Sell?	Average Yearly Expense Ratio
Mutual funds	1,739	Yes	Most are active	Sometimes	1.01 percent
Closed-end funds	414	Yes	Active	Yes	1.27 percent
Exchange-traded funds	150	Yes	Most are index	Usually	0.30 percent
Unit investment trusts	Varies	Yes	Quasi-active	Yes	0.81 percent
Exchange-traded notes	40	Yes	Passive-leveraged	Yes	0.90 percent

Mining a multitude of mutual funds

When most investors speak of funds, they're talking about mutual funds. And it's no wonder. According to Morningstar, the total number of distinct mutual funds (ignoring different share classes of certain mutual funds) clocks in at an astounding 7,087. Of those 7,087 funds, 1,739 of them — nearly 25 percent — represent baskets of bonds.

Like all funds, a mutual fund represents a collection of securities. You, as the investor, pay the mutual fund company a yearly fee and sometimes a sales charge (called a *load*) to buy the fund. In exchange for your money, the mutual fund company offers you an instant portfolio with professional management.

Most mutual funds are *open-end* funds. This means that the number of shares available is not limited. Within reason, as many people who want to buy into the fund can buy into the fund. As more people buy into the fund, more bonds are purchased. The mutual fund shares then sell at a price that directly reflects the price of all the bonds held by the mutual fund. The interest you receive from the fund is a *pro rata* portion of the total interest received by all the bonds in the basket, minus whatever management fees are taken out.

Mutual fund orders can be placed at any time, but they are priced only at the end of the day (4 p.m. on Wall Street), and that's the price you're going to get. If you place an order to buy after 4 p.m., the trade is executed at the next day's closing price.

Most mutual funds are actively managed, which means that the managers try to beat the broad bond market by picking certain issues of bonds or by trying to time the markets. Other mutual funds are passively run, or *indexed*, which means they are set up to track standard fixed-income indexes. Index funds tend to cost you a lot less in fees than actively managed funds. Which are better? See the sidebar "Choosing between active mutual funds and passive (index) funds" for my thoughts.

Choosing between active mutual funds and passive (index) funds

One of the hottest debates among investors — one that will never end — is whether actively managed investments are any wiser than index fund investments. I'm a huge proponent of index funds. The vast majority of index investors — and I am primarily an index investor — do better than the vast majority of active investors. Although various studies show various results, I know of none that contradicts the basic premise that indexing works, and works very well.

When we look at bond funds in particular, however, things get a bit muddled. On one hand, bond index funds are way cheaper than actively managed bond funds, just as stock index funds are cheaper than actively managed stock funds. But because bond funds tend to yield more modest returns, costs are more important. A fund made up of bonds that collectively yield 5 percent that costs 1 percent to hold suddenly yields 4 percent; that's a difference in *your* return of one-fifth.

But there's another side to the story, explains Matthew Gelfand, PhD, CFA, CFP, managing director and senior economist with Rockefeller Financial. Despite the cost/yield equation, which Gelfand doesn't deny for a second is very important, he argues that active management

of bonds can make sense. In fact, it makes very good sense, says Gelfand, because bonds are so much more complicated than stocks.

"There are many, many more bonds and kinds of bonds than there are stocks on the market," says Gelfand. "The analyst coverage is much more sparse. Although more and more trading now is through electronic markets via the web, trading is still mostly over-the-counter, so bid/ask spreads remain wider than in stock markets. All this makes for a less 'efficient' market and allows for good active managers to add real value," he says. "If you can find a reasonably priced, well-managed active bond fund, it stands a better chance of outperforming a bond index fund."

I agree. There's certainly nothing wrong with passively managed (index) bond mutual funds or exchange-traded funds. In fact, Gelfand and I agree that they can, and often do, make excellent investments. Still, handpicking the right actively managed bond fund, if you do so smartly, can juice the returns of your fixed-income portfolio, with limited additional risk. See the last part of this chapter for some of my favorite funds of both flavors, active and indexed.

Regardless of whether you go with active or passive, choose only those bond mutual funds that have solid track records over several years and are reasonably priced. The average yearly operating expense of a bond mutual fund, per Morningstar, is 1.01 percent. Because total return on bond funds, over time, tends to be less than that of stock funds, the cost ratio is usually a bigger factor. I wouldn't touch anything over 1.0 percent without a very compelling reason to do so. You likely don't need to buy more expensive funds; you have many inexpensive alternatives to choose from, and they tend to offer better performance over time.

Considering an alternative: Closed-end funds

Most mutual funds are open-ended, and some are not. The closed-end funds are a universe unto themselves. Unlike open-end funds, closed-end funds have a finite number of shares. The price of the fund does not directly reflect the value of the securities within the fund. Nor does the yield directly reflect the yield of the bonds in the basket. In investment-speak, the _net asset value_ (NAV) of the fund, or the price of the securities within the fund, may differ significantly from the price of the fund itself.

Supply and demand for a closed-end fund may have more bearing on its price than the actual securities it holds. Closed-end funds tend to have high management fees (almost always more than 1 percent a year), and they tend to be more volatile than open-end funds, in part because they are often leveraged. Closed-end funds are traded like stocks (yes, even the bond closed-end funds), and they trade throughout the day. You buy and sell them through any brokerage house — not directly from the mutual fund company, as you can do with most mutual funds.

All closed-end funds are actively managed. There are 631 closed-end funds, of which 414, or nearly two-thirds, are bond funds. The average yearly fee of these bond funds, per Morningstar, is a relatively chunky 1.27 percent. I suggest that if you do buy a closed-end fund, you choose one selling at a discount to the NAV, not at a premium. Studies show that discounted closed-end funds tend to see better performance (similar to value stocks outperforming growth stocks).

Establishing a position in exchange-traded funds

Although relatively new, exchange-traded funds (ETFs) have caught on big in the past several years. If you read my _Exchange-Traded Funds For Dummies,_

2nd Edition, you'll know that I'm a big fan. ETFs, like closed-end funds, trade on the exchanges like individual stocks. (Yes, even the bond ETFs trade that way.) You usually pay a small brokerage fee ($10 or so) when you buy and another when you sell. But while you own the fund, your yearly fees are very low; they are, in fact, a fraction of what you'd pay for a typical bond mutual fund, closed-end fund, or any other kind of fund.

Unlike closed-end funds, ETFs usually maintain a price that closely matches the net asset value, or the value of all the securities in the portfolio. However — at least at the present time — the vast majority of ETFs are index funds, unlike both closed-end and mutual funds. About 11 percent (150) of all 1,441 ETFs available to U.S. investors are bond ETFs.

There aren't as many fixed-income ETFs relative to mutual and closed-end funds, but I predict that the number will continue to expand. Their popularity is in part due to their super low expense ratio. The average bond ETF charges only 0.30 percent a year in operating expenses, and a good many are less than 0.20 percent.

Stock ETFs tend to be much more tax-efficient than stock mutual funds. In the bond arena, the difference isn't as great. ETFs tend to be lower cost, but you may have to deal with small trading commissions. And at times the net asset value of your ETF's securities may rise above, or fall below, the market price. This flux shouldn't be a major concern to buy-and-hold investors.

Understanding unit investment trusts

A unit investment trust (UIT) is a bundle of securities handpicked by a manager. You buy into the UIT as you would an actively managed mutual fund. But unlike the manager of the mutual fund, the UIT manager does not actively trade the portfolio. Rather, he buys the bonds (or in some cases, bond funds), perhaps 10 or 20 of them, and holds them throughout the life of the bonds or for the life of the UIT.

A UIT, which may contain a mix of corporate bonds, Treasuries, and munis, has a maturity date — it could be a year, 5 years, or even 30 years down the road. Interest payments (or principal payments, should a bond mature or be called) from a UIT may arrive monthly, quarterly, or semi-annually. Management expenses for a UIT range from 0.2 and 1.0 percent, and you also pay a commission when they're bought of about 1 to 3 percent. (You don't pay anything when you sell them.) Contact any major brokerage house if you're interested.

Should you be interested?

"A UIT can give you the diversification of a mutual fund as well as greater transparency by knowing exactly what bonds are in your portfolio," says Chris Genovese, senior vice president of Fixed Income Securities, a nation-wide firm that provides targeted advice on bond portfolio construction to investment advisors. "They are certainly appropriate for many individual investors, whether in retirement accounts or investment accounts." UITs come and go from the marketplace, explains Genovese. "If you are interested in seeing the currently available selection, talk to your broker. Look at the prospectus. As you would with any other bond investment, weigh the ben-efits and the risks of the bonds in the portfolio, and determine if it looks like the right mix for you."

Bond ETFs can also give you the diversification and transparency of a UIT, but only a handful of bond ETFs offer target maturity dates, as UITs do.

Taking a flyer (or not) on an exchange-traded note

Although they sound alike, exchange-traded notes and exchange-traded funds are hugely different. ETNs, which trade just like ETFs or individuals stocks, are debt instruments. The issuer, a company such as Direxion or PowerShares or Barclays (all big players in the ETN game), issues an ETN and promises shareholders a rate of return based on the performance of X. What is X? It could be the price of a commodity, or the value of a certain currency, or the return on a certain bond portfolio.

Unlike ETFs, the underlying investments (bonds, commodities, what have you) are not necessarily owned by the issuer of the ETN.

ETNs have been proliferating of late, with dozens having popped up in the past couple of years. Of these, only three — count 'em, three — are based on any simple and recognizable index of bonds. All the other bond ETNs, currently 37, give you exposure to bonds in a strange, distorted fashion, typically offering you either a doubling or tripling of the bonds' returns or, conversely, the inverse of the bonds' performance. For instance, if Treasuries lose 3 percent tomorrow, some ETNs will go up 3 percent in value. Others may go up 6 percent . . . or 9 percent.

Although bond ETNs have one big advantage over ETFs (they are generally taxed more gingerly), they really are not very good vehicles for bond expo-sure. As I note earlier in this discussion, these are debt instruments. As such, when you buy an ETN issued by, say, PowerShares, you take on double credit risk. You need to worry about the credit worthiness of those who issue the bonds in the portfolio, as well as the credit worthiness of PowerShares itself. This is not the case with ETFs.

More troubling is the nature of the beast itself. Yes, a leveraged ETN may double or triple your money — but read the fine print! The doubling or tripling is done on a *daily* basis. The strange mathematics of daily returns means that you will lose money over the long run. Trust me on this. *You will lose money over the long run.* Your principal will simply be eaten away by the extreme volatility.

If you don't want to trust me, take out your calculator. Imagine you hold a triple-the-daily-return ETN, such as the Direxion Daily 10-year Treasury Bull 3X Shares ETN (TYD). Let's imagine that you invest $1,000. Now let's assume that Treasuries go up 3 percent today, 3 percent tomorrow, and 3 percent on the next day. And let's then assume that Treasuries go down 3 percent a day for each of the next three days. If you were holding real Treasuries, how much would you now have? You'd have $997.30.

And what would you have in your Direxion ETN, which just went up 9 percent for three days running, and then lost 9 percent a day for three days? You'd have $975.90. After a few more weeks or months of super-volatility, you'd have far less. As I said, extreme volatility eats returns.

Knowing What Matters Most in Choosing a Bond Fund of Any Sort

For years, alchemists tried to turn common metals into gold. It can't be done. The first rule to follow when choosing a bond fund is to find one appropriate to your particular portfolio needs, which means finding a bond fund made of the right material. After all, bond fund managers can't do all that much more than alchemists.

Selecting your fund based on its components and their characteristics

It you're looking for a bond fund that's going to produce steady returns with little volatility and very limited risk to your principal, start with a bond fund that is built of low-volatility bonds issued by credit-worthy institutions. A perfect example would be a short-term Treasury bond fund. If you're looking for kick-ass returns in a fixed-income fund, you can start looking for funds built of high-yield fixed-income securities.

One of the main characteristics you look for in a bond is its tax status. Most bonds are taxable, but municipal bonds are federally tax-free. If you want to laugh off taxes, choose a municipal bond fund. But just as with the individual muni bonds themselves, expect lower yield with a muni fund. Also pick and choose your muni fund based on the level of taxation you're looking to avoid. State-specific municipal bond funds filled with triple-tax-free bonds (free from federal, state, and local tax) are triple-tax-free themselves.

Pruning out the underperformers

Obviously, you want to look at any prospective bond fund's performance *vis a vis* its peers. If you are examining index funds, the driving force behind returns will be the fund's operating expenses. Intermediate-term Treasury bond index fund X will generally do better than intermediate-term Treasury bond index fund Y if less of the profits are eaten up by operating expenses.

With actively managed funds . . . guess what? Operating expenses are also a driving force. One study conducted by Morningstar, reported in *The Wall Street Journal,* looked at high quality, taxable bond funds available to all investors with minimums of less than $10,000. More than half of those funds charge investors 1 percent or more. Not surprisingly, almost three-quarters of those pricier funds showed performance that was in the bottom half of the category for the previous year.

Russell's rule: Don't pay more than 1 percent a year for any bond fund unless you have a great reason. And don't invest in any actively managed bond fund that hasn't outperformed its peers — and any proper and appropriate benchmarks — for at least several years. (By "proper and appropriate benchmarks," I am referring to bond indexes that most closely match the composition of the bond fund in question. A high-yield bond fund, given that you can expect more volatility, *should* produce higher yields than, say, a Treasury index. Any comparison of a high-yield fund's return to a Treasury index is practically moot.)

Laying down the law on loads

An astonishing number of bond funds charge loads. A *load* is nothing more than a sales commission, sometimes paid when buying the fund (that's called a *front-end* load) and sometimes paid when selling (that's called a *back-end* or *deferred* load). My advice? NEVER PAY A LOAD. There is absolutely no reason you should ever pay a load of (not unheard of) 5.5 percent to buy a bond fund. The math simply doesn't work in your favor.

Evaluating bond fund advertisements

Some years ago, back in the "wild west" days, bond fund advertisements were often squirrelly tracts of trash. "But regulators have cracked down quite a bit," says Eric Jacobson, director of fixed-income research at Morningstar.

Although we've come a long way, you're still advised to read bond mutual fund advertisements with a critical eye. "As with any and all advertisements, you can assume that what you see puts the product in the best possible light," says Jacobson. "You are not going to get a complete, balanced picture."

A typical fund advertisement, for example, may ballyhoo a fund's performance or Morningstar or Lipper ranking over a limited time period when the fund shined, but fail to show that the fund may not have performed so well over the longer run. There's nothing wrong with casting a quick eye at recent returns or rankings. But,

says Jacobson, "you really need to look beyond that." He likens buying a bond fund to buying a used car. "The sales people will do the best they can to put a shine on the product, and make it look pretty, but you should never buy without examining under the hood."

Keep in mind that a bond fund's performance, which is largely measured by its past yield, can go up or down dramatically moving forward. Bond funds are not bonds, and they aren't CDs. Price of the shares and yields change over time. The riskier bond classes — long-term bonds and high-yield bonds — are especially prone to dramatic change.

Of course, you would know that if you read the very small print at the bottom of each advertisement:

Performance data represents past performance, which does not guarantee future results.

If you pay a 5.5 percent load to buy into a fund with $10,000, you lose $550 up front. You start with an investment of only $9,450. Suppose that the fund manager is a veritable wizard and gets a 7 percent return over the next five years, whereas similar bond funds with similar yearly operating expenses are paying only 6 percent. Here's what you'll have in five years with the load fund, even though there's a wizard at the helm: $13,254. Here's what you'd have with the no-load fund, assuming the manager is merely average: $13,382.

Russell's rule: Buying a load bond fund is plain and simple dumb. Unless you get some kind of special deal that allows for the load to be waived, don't buy load funds. Repeat: Don't buy load funds.

Sniffing out false promises

Although morally dubious, and in some cases even illegal, some brokerage houses and financial supermarket websites have been known to promote certain bond funds over others not because those funds are any better but because a certain fund company paid to be promoted. (In the industry, this is sometimes known as "buying shelf space.") Buyer beware!

"Investors need to fully understand how their broker is being compensated, and if a firm is promoting certain bonds or bond funds, investors should ask if the firm is being compensated for that promotion," says Gerri Walsh, vice president for investor education with the Financial Industry Regulatory Authority (FINRA).

My Picks for Some of the Best Bond Funds

And now for the meat . . . In this section I introduce you to bond funds well worth considering for your portfolio. I lay them out in roughly the same order I introduce you to various kinds of bonds in Part II of this book. I start with very short-term, investment-grade bond funds, sometimes referred to as *near cash.* I then proceed to longer-term Treasuries, corporate bonds (investment-grade and junk), agency bonds, municipal bonds, and international bonds.

If you have a somewhat modest portfolio (less than $50,000), I wrap up this chapter with some recommendations for good blend funds that allow you instant exposure to a variety of bonds. If you have an even more modest portfolio (less than $20,000), I suggest you consider a fund that allows you instant exposure to a variety of both bonds and stocks, and I name several that fit that bill, too.

Please note that under each section, I list my favorite funds alphabetically. If you were to see a bond fund called Aardvark Bonds (you won't, but humor me) followed by a bond fund called Zygote Fixed Income, don't assume that I like Aardvark any more than I do Zygote.

Very short-term, high quality bond funds

These funds are going to pay slightly higher rates of interest than money market funds and CDs but less than longer-term bond funds. They carry very little risk of default and have minimal volatility. Sometimes referred to as *near-cash,* these bond funds are often the best investments for money that you may need to tap within one to three years.

Fidelity Spartan Short-Term Treasury Bond Index Fund (FSBIX)
Contact: 800-544-6666; www.fidelity.com

Type of fund: Actively run mutual fund

Types of bonds: Short-term government bonds

Average maturity: 2.8 years

Expense ratio: 0.20 percent

Minimum investment: $10,000

This is a convenient place to park your short-term money, especially if you're building a portfolio at Fidelity.

State Farm Interim (SFITX)

Contact: 800-447-4930; www.statefarm.com

Type of fund: Actively run mutual fund

Types of bonds: Short-term government

Average maturity: 2.8 years

Expense ratio: 0.16 percent

Minimum investment: $250

Generally, insurance company mutual funds stink; this is a notable exception! I especially like the low minimum investment.

Vanguard Short-Term Investment-Grade (VFSTX)

Contact: 800-662-7447; www.vanguard.com

Type of fund: Actively run mutual fund

Types of bonds: Short-term government and high-grade corporate

Average maturity: 2.7 years

Expense ratio: 0.22 percent

Minimum investment: $3,000

If you have $50,000 to invest in this fund, you are eligible for the Admiral Shares class (ticker VFSUX). You'll be investing in the same fund as VFSTX, but the expense ratio drops to 0.11 percent.

Vanguard Short-Term Bond ETF (BSV)

Contact: 800-662-7447; www.vanguard.com

Type of fund: Index exchange-traded fund

Types of bonds: Short-term government and high-grade corporate

Average maturity: 2.8 years

Expense ratio: 0.11 percent

Minimum investment: None

This fund is also available in mutual-fund form under the tickers VBISX (minimum investment $3,000, with an expense ratio of 0.22 percent) and VBIRX (minimum investment $10,000, with the same expense ratio as the ETF, 0.11 percent).

Intermediate-term Treasury bond funds

U.S. government bonds can be bought on www.treasurydirect.gov without paying a markup. Nonetheless, Treasury bond funds offer instant diversification of maturities at modest cost. Remember that while conventional Treasury bonds are said to carry very little risk of default, they do carry other risks, such as interest-rate risk. And in these days of modest yield, you also run the risk that you may not be able to stay ahead of inflation. You find more on Treasury bonds in Chapter 5.

Fidelity Government Income (FGOVX)

Contact: 800-544-6666; www.fidelity.com

Type of fund: Actively managed mutual fund

Types of bonds: Intermediate government

Average maturity: 6.3 years

Expense ratio: 0.45 percent

Minimum investment: $2,500

This mutual fund, run by one of the largest U.S. asset managers, features an array of government bonds. The fund may use leveraging (borrowing) to juice the yield, which creates a tad bit of risk, but the management team seems careful not to go overboard.

iShares Barclays 7–10 Year Treasury Bond Fund (IEF)

Contact: 800-474-2737; www.ishares.com

Type of fund: Exchange-traded fund

Types of bonds: Intermediate-term Treasury

Average maturity: 8.5 years

Expense ratio: 0.15 percent

Minimum investment: None

As with all ETFs, you generally pay a commission to buy and sell this fund. Comparing the expense ratio of this ETF to very similar mutual funds, you can see why I like (many, but not all) ETFs!

Treasury Inflation-Protected Securities

iShares Barclays TIPS Bond Fund (TIP)
Contact: 800-474-2737; www.ishares.com

Type of fund: Exchange-traded fund

Types of bonds: Treasury Inflation-Protected Securities

Average maturity: 9.3 years

Expense ratio: 0.20 percent

Minimum investment: None

If you want inflation protection in a bond fund, this is an excellent choice. Do, however, note the long maturity of the bonds held by this fund; long maturities mean that there will be some volatility. This is not a fund for money that you may need within the next several months.

Vanguard Inflation-Protected Securities Fund Investor Shares (VIPSX)
Contact: 800-662-7447; www.vanguard.com

Type of fund: Actively run mutual fund

Types of bonds: Treasury Inflation-Protected Securities

Average maturity: 9.4 years

Expense ratio: 0.22 percent

Minimum investment: $3,000

If you have $50,000 to invest, go with the Admiral Shares version of this fund (ticker VAIPX), and the expense ratio drops to a bargain-basement 0.11 percent a year.

(Mostly) high quality corporate bond funds

Investment-grade corporate bonds have a history of returning about a percentage point higher than Treasuries each year. For more on corporate bonds, see Chapter 6.

Dodge & Cox Income (DODIX)
Contact: 800-621-3979; www.dodgeandcox.com

Type of fund: Actively run mutual fund

Types of bonds: Mostly high-grade corporate, plus a few junkier issues

Average maturity: 7.0 years

Expense ratio: 0.43 percent

Minimum investment: $2,500 ($1,000 in an IRA)

A super track record at a fairly reasonable cost.

iShares iBoxx $ Investment Grade Corporate Bond Fund (LQD)
Contact: 800-474-2737; www.ishares.com

Type of fund: Exchange-traded fund

Types of bonds: Investment-grade corporate

Average maturity: 10.2 years

Expense ratio: 0.15 percent

Minimum investment: None

This is the low-cost index leader for corporate investment-grade bond investing.

Loomis Sayles Bond Fund (LSBRX)

Contact: 800-633-3330; www.loomissayles.com

Type of fund: Actively run mutual fund

Types of bonds: Mostly corporate, with a smattering of both government and international

Average maturity: 10.3 years

Expense ratio: 0.92 percent

Minimum investment: $2,500

Over the long run, this fund has outperformed just about every other fixed-income fund on the market. How so, despite its relatively high cost, and whether the outperformance will continue are something of a mystery. The guy at the helm for many, many years, Dan Fuss, is interviewed in Chapter 21.

Junk city: Corporate high-yield funds

High-yield bonds return more than other bonds, but you can lose your money in times of recession when shakier companies start to default on their loans. More on junk bonds in Chapter 6.

iShares iBoxx $ High Yield Corporate Bond Fund (HYG)

Contact: 800-474-2737; www.ishares.com

Type of fund: Exchange-traded fund

Types of bonds: Corporate high yield

Average maturity: 6 years

Expense ratio: 0.50 percent

Minimum investment: None

This fund opened in April 2007. Its first full year in operation, 2008 (a bad year for corporate high-yield bonds), the fund lost 17.19 percent. The next year, it came back with a return of positive 28.74. (The net result after two years was a gain of 6.6 percent.) This is obviously not your typically sedate bond fund.

Vanguard High-Yield Corporate Fund (VWEXH)

Contact: 800-662-7447; www.vanguard.com

Type of fund: Actively run mutual fund

Types of bonds: Junk bonds, but not enormously junky

Average maturity: 5.3 years

Expense ratio: 0.25 percent (although you also face a 1 percent redemption fee if you hold shares for less than one year)

Minimum investment: $3,000

This is a long-time leader in junk bond investing. Since its inception in late 1978, this fund has returned almost 9 percent, but not without some bumps in the road. In 2008, shareholders lost 21.3 percent. If you have $50,000 to invest in this fund, choose the Admiral Shares version (ticker VWEAX), which carries an expense ratio of only 0.13 percent.

Agency bond funds

As far as default risk, agency bonds are almost as safe as Treasury bonds. However, you get a bit of extra kick on the coupon payments. These issues lack the liquidity of Treasury funds, which explains much of the premium. They are also mortgage-backed, which means they are subject to greater volatility (due to prepayment risk) but also offer greater diversification from other bonds, such as corporate bonds. For more on agency bonds, see Chapter 7.

American Century Ginnie Mae (BGNMX)

Contact: 800-345-2021; www.americancentury.com

Type of fund: Actively run mutual fund

Types of bonds: Intermediate-term government agency

Average maturity: 5.6 years

Expense ratio: 0.56 percent

Minimum investment: $2,500

You get better return in the long run than on a Treasury bond of similar maturity, and a tad more volatility.

Fidelity GNMA Fund (FGNMX)

Contact: 800-544-6666; www.fidelity.com

Type of fund: Actively run mutual fund

Types of bonds: Intermediate government agency

Average maturity: 4.6 years

Expense ratio: 0.45 percent

Minimum investment: $2,500 ($500 in an IRA)

This is technically an actively run fund but pretty close to an index fund.

Vanguard GNMA Fund (VFIIX)

Contact: 800-662-7447; www.vanguard.com

Type of fund: Index mutual fund

Types of bonds: Intermediate government agency

Average maturity: 6.0 years

Expense ratio: 0.23 percent

Minimum investment: $2,000

If you happen to have $50,000, invest in the Admiral Shares version of this fund (ticker VFIJX). Your management expenses then drop to a very delightful 0.11 percent.

Vanguard Mortgage-Backed Securities ETF (VMBS)

Contact: 800-662-7447; www.vanguard.com

Type of fund: Index exchange-traded fund

Types of bonds: Intermediate government agency mortgage-backed securities issued by Ginnie Mae, Fannie Mae, and Freddie Mac

Average maturity: 4.7 years

Expense ratio: 0.15 percent

Minimum investment: None

In 2010, Vanguard issued its agency-bond ETF and chose a broad spectrum of bonds using an indexed approach. Among the handful of agency-bond ETFs, this is my favorite.

Municipal bond funds: Taxes be damned

These funds don't give you the yield that taxable corporate bond funds do, but you'll be spared, perhaps entirely, from paying federal income tax. For more on municipal tax-free bonds, see Chapter 8. Note that I've included two high-yield muni funds among my choices. *High-yield* does not mean the same in the world of munis as it does in corporate bonds. Municipal bonds rarely go belly up, and even when they do, you usually get most of your money back — well, that's the way it's been in the past, at least.

Fidelity Tax-Free Bond (FTABX)

Contact: 800-544-6666; www.fidelity.com

Type of fund: Actively run mutual fund, although index-like

Types of bonds: Municipal tax-free, high credit quality

Average maturity: 10 years

Expense ratio: 0.25 percent

Minimum investment: $25,000

This is a well-run bond fund. All the bonds are exempt from the alternative minimum tax (AMT) so it's a good deal for people in higher tax brackets.

T. Rowe Price Tax-Free High-Yield (PRFHX)

Contact: 800-683-5660; www.troweprice.com

Type of fund: Actively run mutual fund

Types of bonds: Municipal tax-free, low credit quality, long maturity

Average maturity: 20 years

Expense ratio: 0.68 percent

Minimum investment: $2,500 ($1,000 in an IRA)

With the modest minimum investment limit, this is a good alternative for people with high incomes but limited wealth. Given the long maturities and the lower credit quality of the bonds, expect a fair deal of volatility. This fund lost 21.49 percent in 2008. Since its inception in 1985, it has seen an annualized return of nearly 7 percent a year.

Vanguard Intermediate-Term Tax Exempt (VWITX)

Contact: 800-662-7447; www.vanguard.com

Type of fund: Actively run mutual fund

Types of bonds: Municipal tax-free higher quality bonds

Average maturity: 5.5 years

Expense ratio: 0.20 percent

Minimum investment: $3,000

Got $50,000 to invest? Then go with the Vanguard Admiral Shares version of this fund (VWIUX), which carries an expense ratio of only 0.12 percent.

Vanguard High-Yield Tax-Exempt (VWAHX)

Contact: 800-662-7447; www.vanguard.com

Type of fund: Actively run mutual fund

Types of bonds: Municipal tax-free high yield (lower credit quality)

Average maturity: 7.0 years

Expense ratio: 0.20 percent

Minimum investment: $3,000

Most, but not all, of the bonds are free from the alternative minimum tax. Although the fund does have high-yield bonds, it also has some higher quality munis. If you have $50,000 to invest, go with the Admiral Shares version of this fund, which carries an expense ratio of 0.12 percent.

International bond funds

These funds feature mostly high quality bonds issued in Japan, Western Europe, and Australia. For more on international bonds, see Chapter 9.

American Century International Bond (BEGBX)

Contact: 800-345-2021; www.americancentury.com

Type of fund: Actively managed mutual fund

Types of bonds: High quality international corporate

Average maturity: 9.4 years

Expense ratio: 0.81 percent

Minimum investment: $2,500

The returns reflect differences in currency exchange rates, as well as interest payments on the bonds, making this a volatile fund by fixed-income standards.

T. Rowe Price International Bond (RPIBX)

Contact: 800-683-5660; www.troweprice.com

Type of fund: Actively managed mutual fund

Types of bonds: Mostly high credit quality international

Average maturity: 8.1 years

Expense ratio: 0.82 percent

Minimum investment: $2,500 ($1,000 in an IRA)

The returns reflect differences in currency exchange rates, as well as interest payments on the bonds.

Emerging market bond funds

If you are willing to deal with the volatility, these bond funds — made up of bonds from countries such as Russia, Brazil, Mexico, and Turkey — offer excellent return potential. For more on emerging market bonds, see Chapter 9.

Fidelity New Markets Income Fund (FNMIX)

Contact: 800-544-6666; www.fidelity.com

Type of fund: Actively run mutual fund

Types of bonds: Emerging market, mostly government, with some corporate issues; the majority are U.S. dollar-denominated

Average maturity: 12.7 years

Expense ratio: 0.87 percent

Minimum investment: $2,500

One of the first emerging market bond funds. In 1998, the fund lost 22.38 percent, and in 2008, it lost 18.24 percent. Most other years, however, the fund has seen impressive returns. Since inception, the annualized return has been slightly greater than 12 percent.

iShares JPMorgan USD Emerging Markets Bond (EMB)

Contact: 800-474-2737; www.ishares.com

Type of fund: Exchange-traded fund

Types of bonds: Emerging market, mostly government, denominated in U.S. dollars

Average maturity: 9.5 years

Expense ratio: 0.60 percent

Minimum investment: None

This fund has been a bit less volatile than the other emerging market ETFs available, which is why my heart warmed to it even though some of the other ETF choices are a wee bit cheaper.

T. Rowe Price Emerging Markets Bond (PREMX)

Contact: 800-683-5660; www.troweprice.com

Type of fund: Actively run mutual fund

Types of bonds: Emerging market, mostly government, mostly dollar-denominated

Average maturity: 10.7 years

Expense ratio: 0.95 percent

Minimum investment: $2,500 ($1,000 in an IRA)

Since 1994, this fund has lost money in only two years: in 1998, when it lost 23.1 percent; and in 2008, when it lost 17.7 percent. Overall, however, the fund has done quite well. Since inception, it has enjoyed an annualized return of just about 12 percent.

All-in-one bond funds

Rather than picking and choosing, perhaps you'd like to buy up a representative sampling of the total bond market? Then consider these options.

T. Rowe Price Spectrum Income (RPSIX)

Contact: 800-683-5660; www.troweprice.com

Type of fund: Actively managed mutual fund

Types of bonds: Anything and everything in bonds, with a smattering (currently 13 percent) in stocks

Average maturity: 7.3 years

Expense ratio: 0.70 percent

Minimum investment: $2,500 ($1,000 in an IRA)

This has been an industry leader since 1990.

Vanguard Total Bond Market ETF (BND)

Contact: 800-662-7447; www.vanguard.com

Type of fund: Exchange-traded fund

Types of bonds: All higher credit quality, both government (about two-thirds) and corporate

Average maturity: 7.2 years

Expense ratio: 0.11 percent

Minimum investment: None

Introduced to the market in April 2007, this fund brings new meaning to low-cost, well-diversified bond investing. "BND is a great core bond holding," says Ron DeLegge, host of the *Index Investing* syndicated radio show and publisher of www.ETFguide.com. If you prefer mutual funds to ETFs, this fund comes in mutual fund version, as well: With $3,000 or more, you can invest in the Vanguard Total Bond Market Index Fund Investor Shares (VBMFX), which carries an expense ratio of 0.22 percent; with $10,000 or more, you can invest in the Admiral Shares class (VBTLX), which carries an expense ratio of 0.10 percent, even lower than the ETF.

All-in-one bond and stock fund

For the total bond market AND the total stock market AND international stocks all rolled up in one, try this.

Vanguard STAR Fund (VGSTX)

Contact: 800-662-7447; www.vanguard.com

Type of fund: This is a fund of funds with a moderate risk allocation

Types of bonds: Across the board

Average maturity: 7 years

Expense ratio: 0.34 percent

Minimum investment: $1,000

For those with limited funds (under $10,000), this Vanguard offering allows for an instant diverse 60/40 portfolio (60 percent diversified stocks; 40 percent diversified bonds). Other funds are available that will do the same, but I really like this one and have recommended it to investors with modest portfolios. It's been around since early 1985 and has returned an average of 9.7 percent a year.

Target-retirement date funds (otherwise known as life-cycle funds)

Another easy option, best if you have limited funds ($10,000 or less) or a real aversion to dealing with your investments (in which case, granted, you are probably not reading this book), is a target-retirement date fund. Like the Vanguard STAR Fund, these funds give you the whole ball of wax. Bonds, stocks, and sometimes commodities are all rolled up into one simple fund. Unlike the STAR Fund, which has a static mix of stocks and bonds, life-cycle funds move you over the years from very aggressive to very conservative, depending on your chosen retirement date.

If you are a typical 30-year-old, or a typical 50-year-old, then a target-retirement date fund may be fine for you. Some of the better ones really aren't bad choices — provided you are typical, with a typical amount of money, a typical projected retirement date, a typical need for return, and a typical stomach for risk. As not everyone is "typical," I can't rave about these funds. They also tend to be a bit more expensive than many other options. Nonetheless, if you think you fit the bill, consider one of the following lineups of funds.

One entire bond fund category to avoid

Bonds are mostly ballast. Bonds are safety. Bonds are not meant to deliver super high performance. That's what equities are for. Please do not jump on the bandwagon-to-self-destruction and buy into any number of short and leveraged bond exchange-traded funds and exchange-traded notes that have lately shown up on the market. These would include such choice offerings as the PowerShares DB 3X Italian Treasury Bond Futures ETN, the Direxion Daily 7–10 Year Treasury Bear 3X Shares fund, and the ProShares UltraShort TIPS fund. These investments are risky, they are expensive, they are largely nonsensical, and, unless you are extremely lucky and manage to get in and out in a hurry, these funds will lose you money.

Note that not only are some pricier than others, but also one lineup can be considerably more aggressive than another.

Fidelity Freedom Index (2020, 2025, 2030, and so on)

Contact: 800-544-8888; www.fidelity.com

Average expense ratio: 0.20 percent

Percent in fixed income for those planning to retire in 10 more years: 50 percent

Minimum investment: $2,500 ($500 for IRA)

iShares S&P Target Date (2020, 2025, 2030, and so on)

Contact: 800-474-2737; www.ishares.com

Average expense ratio: 0.30 percent

Percent in fixed income for those planning to retire in 10 more years: 35 percent

Minimum investment: None

T. Rowe Price Retirement (2020, 2025, 2030, and so on)

Contact: 800-683-5660; www.troweprice.com

Average expense ratio: 0.75 percent

Percent in fixed income for those planning to retire in 10 more years: 30 percent

Minimum investment: $2,500 ($1,000 for IRA)

Vanguard Target Retirement Funds (2020, 2025, 2030, and so on)

Contact: 800-662-7447; www.vanguard.com

Average expense ratio: 0.17 percent

Percent in fixed income for those planning to retire in 10 more years: 35 percent

Minimum investment: $1,000

Alert! Some really ba-a-a-ad bond funds

What are the worst of the worst? They tend to have high expenses and questionable managerial talent. The envelope, please . . .

Oppenheimer Champion Income C (OCHCX)

With a 1.0 percent back-end load and ongoing management expenses of 2.18 percent, you wouldn't expect this fund to be tops on any performance lists. But the quality of management undoubtedly explains why this fund ranks dead last, according to Morningstar Principia, in 10-year average annual returns, adjusted for loads. As of February 29, 2012, that figure was –8.92 percent a year. Your heart has to go out to the investors in this fund.

AMF Intermediate Mortgage (ASCPX)

Losing money in short-term, mostly government bonds, is almost impossible. Yet the manager of the AMF Intermediate Mortgage bond fund has achieved that nearly impossible goal by losing about 3 percent a year over the past decade. The net expense ratio of 0.75 percent isn't ridiculously high, so that points to some other ridiculousness of uncertain nature.

Pacific Advisors Government Securities C (PGGCX)

It takes exceptional talent to lose money in short-term government bonds, and AMF (above) has that talent; Pacific Advisors only comes close. In 2002, investors who bought into this fund "enjoyed" 10-year returns, after paying the back-end load, of 0.50 percent a year. Keep in mind that this was a darned good decade for bonds. In the case of Pacific Advisors, the gross expense ratio of 4.42 percent (net expense ratio of 2.40 percent) explains much of the fund's performance drag.

Part V
Bonds As Replacements for the Old Paycheck

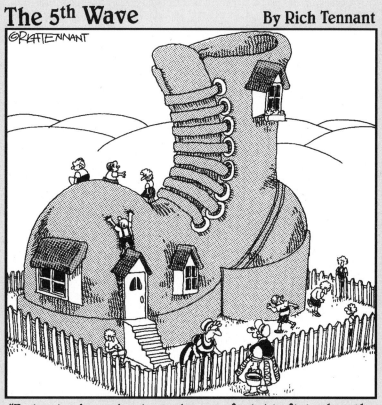

The 5th Wave   By Rich Tennant

"I plan to downsize to a nice, comfortable flat when the kids move out."

In this part . . .

Although I do use the word *retirement* in this part, I really prefer to use *retunement*. Today's retirement has changed so much from a generation ago that the difference is almost as great as between *stationary* and *stationery*, *cats* and *cuts*, *flies* and *fries*.

A generation ago, most people built a small nest egg, retired at 65, got a pension and Social Security, and lived predictably ever after. Today, the pension has vanished for many. Social Security isn't as secure as it was. Savings rates are negligible.

All this has served to blur the line of retirement. Some older Americans can't retire. Some much younger ones can. Some folks are working part-time and using savings for supplemental income (whether they should or not).

This section is for anyone who has begun to take withdrawals from a portfolio or is thinking about doing so. It's about tapping into that portfolio in the most rational manner. It's about using the portfolio to live the life of your dreams, while keeping your nest egg intact just in case you live to 105.

You won't be surprised to find that bonds are an essential part of the picture.

Chapter 17

Fulfilling the Need for Steady, Ready, Heady Cash

In This Chapter

▶ Estimating your future needs for pocket money

▶ Expanding your view of fixed income

▶ Understanding the dancing role of different investments in a retirement portfolio

▶ Introducing the beautiful concept of rebalancing

*W*hen I was young, my father would suit up every morning, get into the car, hit the Long Island Expressway, and battle his way into Brooklyn, among the grittier of New York City's boroughs. There, at 50 Court Street, he would take the elevator to his seventh-story office, make himself a cup of coffee, and turn on the big fan, the one that spit out U.S. dollars, which my father would then collect and stuff into his brown leather briefcase.

For years, that's how I thought my family paid the bills.

I realized at some point that my father's story of how he made money wasn't entirely true. (Nor was he a five-star general in World War II, even though my Uncle Sid, also a five-star general, corroborated the story entirely.)

Today, many youngsters believe that money is produced by ATM machines. (That's probably because with air conditioning, they don't see many electric fans anymore.) But, of course, we mature, educated adults don't harbor such silly fantasies about money. Doooweee?

Yeah, right.

There's a particular fantasy about money and retirement, and it goes something like this: _You work hard for many years, you send holiday cards to the creep of a boss, you invest in stocks all the while, and the stocks grow. Then, when your portfolio has grown enough, you move your money to safe bonds, you no longer have to send holiday cards to the creep of a boss, you retire, you live off the interest from the bonds, you golf, and you do the early-bird specials._

In this chapter, I explain why that line of reasoning may be as silly as thinking money comes from fans — maybe more so. I explain why a diversified portfolio that includes bonds _and_ healthy doses of other investments makes just as much sense to a retiree as it does to working folk. And I explain — in this chapter and the next — how to use your bonds, in conjunction with other investments, to ride steadily and easily into your financial future long after you've given up the day job in Brooklyn (or wherever you happen to toil).

Reaping the Rewards of Your Investments

At this very moment, as I'm typing this very paragraph, I'm feeling rather fortunate. I've had a number of jobs in my life that I didn't particularly enjoy (credit analyst, Maryland National Bank, Baltimore, 1981). But I've also had some that I've enjoyed enormously (yoga instructor, Club Med, Al Hoceima, Morocco, 1978). Luckily, my current job (financial planner and author, Allentown, Pennsylvania) falls into the latter category.

As much as I enjoy my present work, it comforts me greatly to know that in a few more years — and fewer, still, if this book sells a lot of copies! — whether I get up in the morning to work-for-pay or sleep in, volunteer my time for a worthy cause, or phone a friend for a chat, the decision will be completely up to me.

In this section, I help you start thinking about what you need to accomplish financially so you, too, can someday choose for yourself what each day will bring.

Aiming for freedom

What makes work-for-pay optional (other than being born rich, resorting to crime, or marrying a heart surgeon) is a _freedom portfolio_ — a portfolio big enough to produce the income needed to support your lifestyle.

When is a portfolio big enough that employment becomes optional? When it provides enough cash flow to pay the bills: both today's and tomorrow's. The tough part about retirement planning is that you don't know how many tomorrows you're going to have; estimating bills that are years off is tough; and certain ongoing expenses, such as medical bills, may be well beyond your control. In addition, Congress keeps toying with tax rates and such, so you can't even estimate your future IRS bills.

And on top of all *that,* even though a predictable cash flow for you could be arranged, total predictability, with today's pathetic yields on ultra-conservative investments, comes at a heavy price.

Estimating your target portfolio

In Chapter 12, I introduce the *20 times rule*: You figure out how much money you need to live on for a year (being realistic — look at your bills) and multiply that number by 20. That is the very *minimum* most financial professionals, including me, would want to see you have in your portfolio before you permanently quit your day job. Anything less, and you can't have any reasonable assurance that you aren't going to be living off baked beans and homegrown parsley someday. But this rough rule doesn't factor in the price of beans, how many beans you can eat, or any number of other variables over the coming decades.

To do a much better estimation and get a firmer idea of what kind of portfolio you should shoot for, you may want to hire a financial planner with fancy software to create a retirement plan for you. Or you can turn to any number of websites, some of which do a fair (but not great) job at estimating what size portfolio you'll need. Among my favorites is a website called www.firecalc. com; click on the Advanced FIREcalc tab, and take it from there. Just about all brokerage house and financial supermarket websites have calculators, as well.

Although they're better than any rough rule (even mine), the problem with all retirement plans — yes, even the fancy ones done by professionals — is that they're static. Over the course of your life, things change: interest rates, the inflation rate, your portfolio returns, your spending, your health, and those stupid sunset provisions on certain taxes — to name just a few. That said, for the moment we're going to accept the 20x rule (as splintery rough as it is) and move on to the question: Where will your cash actually come from after you are no longer getting a paycheck?

Cash flow, dear reader, is the name of the game. Cash — pure, steady cash — is what you need to quit your paid employment, if that is your goal.

After all, you may have $5 million in net worth, but if that $5 million is in the form of a framed Picasso or a hilltop house with an Olympic-sized pool in the yard, though you're technically a multimillionaire you may not have enough in your wallet to buy yourself lunch at Taco Bell.

Lining up your bucks

The gods of retirement offer you a number of options for putting cash in your wallet. If you're one of those lucky Americans (retired congressmen, senators, executives in the pharmaceutical industry) who can still bank on a solid fixed pension with health benefits, that's great. Social Security, when you're gray enough, can also provide steady cash . . . although at the time of this writing, it seems that Social Security may need to start slashing benefits (not all, but some) within the next two decades or so.

Because this is an investment book, I spend the rest of this chapter, and the next, talking about the money you can tap from your savings. Most of us who are not retired senators will need this money in order to retire, and it can come from one or all of three sources: interest, dividends, and the sale of securities. Your choice among these options (or some combination of the three) will have a great bearing on how big your portfolio needs to be and how much you can safely withdraw.

The best option — *always* — is to adopt a cash withdrawal plan from your portfolio that is flexible and potentially allows for all three sources of cash flow to play into your new paycheckless life. One of the biggest and most common investment mistakes that people make is to lock their sights on one form of cash flow (typically interest income) and ignore the others.

Toward the end of this chapter, I show you how a flexible, sensible, triple-source-of-cash-flow plan works. First, allow me to introduce you to each of the three options just mentioned and explain why the gods of retirement created them, where to find them, and how to maximize them.

Finding Interesting Sources of Interest

All pigs are mammals, but not all mammals are pigs. All bonds are fixed-income investments, but not all fixed-income investments are bonds. Anything that yields steady, predictable interest can qualify as fixed income. That includes not only bonds but also CDs, money market accounts, and a few other not-as-common investments that I address here. Any and all of these may serve as sources of cash, either to boost a preretirement portfolio or help mine cash from a postretirement portfolio.

Certificates of deposit (CDs)

As predictable as the Arizona sunrise, CDs, like zero-coupon bonds, offer your principal back with interest after a specified time frame (usually in increments of three months) for up to five years in the future. Like savings bank accounts, CDs are almost all guaranteed by the Federal Deposit Insurance Corporation (FDIC), a government-sponsored agency, for amounts up to $250,000. Interest rates offered tend to increase with the amount of time you're willing to tie your money up. (If the bank will give you, say, 1.5 percent interest for six months, you can often get 1.75 percent for 12 months.) Take your money out before the maturity of the CD, and you pay a fine, the severity of which depends on the particular issuer.

Because nearly all CDs are federally insured, the security of your principal is on par with Treasury bonds. Interest rates vary and may be higher or lower than you can get on a Treasury bond of the same maturity. (Check www. bankrate.com and your local newspaper for the highest CD rates available.) FDIC-insured Internet banking accounts, which tend to pay higher rates of interest than the corner bank, are also often on a par with one-year to two-year CDs. Often the three investments — CDs, short-term Treasuries, and Internet banking accounts — hug very closely to the same (modest) interest rate. If all three are equal, the CD, a favorite with retirees everywhere, should be your *last* choice. Here are two key reasons:

- ✔ The CD requires you to tie your money up; the FDIC-insured Internet bank account does not.

- ✔ The CD, as well as the bank account, generates fully taxable income; the Treasury bond or bond fund income is federally taxable but exempt from state tax.

Even though there can be blips in time when CDs are great deals, by and large, CDs are vastly oversold. If you're going to settle for a modest interest rate, you generally don't need to have your money be held captive. Some banks of late have been offering more flexible step-up CDs that allow for interest rates to float upward; these are worth some consideration if the initial rate is competitive.

Compared to bonds: Most bonds provide higher long-term returns than CDs and tend to be more liquid (meaning you can cash out easier). However, only Treasury bonds carry the same U.S. government guarantee that a CD has.

Mining the many money market funds

Money market funds are mutual funds that invest in very short-term debt instruments (such as Treasury bills, CDs, and bank notes) and provide (but do not guarantee) a stable price with a very modest return. In essence, a money market is a bond turned inside out. It provides a stable price with a floating interest rate, while a bond provides stable return with a potentially volatile market price (if you sell the bond before maturity). Money market funds are not guaranteed by the federal government, as are most CDs and savings bank accounts, but they're generally quite safe due to the quality of their investments and the short-term maturities.

At rare times in history, when long-term lending pays no more than short-term lending (a *flat yield curve* exists, as I discuss in Part I), money market funds can offer a yield competitive with, or, perhaps even exceeding, short-term bond funds. (*Short-term* means that the bonds held by the fund generally mature in one to three years.) But at most times in history, a money market fund doesn't pay as much as bond funds. Some money market funds, however, may offer yields as high as you can get on any CD.

Money market funds are often used as the *cash* or *sweep* positions at most brokerage houses. Be aware that when you open an account at a brokerage house, the default, if you fail to specify which sweep account you want, may be a very low-yielding money market fund. And simply for the asking, you may have your money moved to a higher yielding money market fund. But you need to ask: "What are my sweep account options?" Some money market accounts, which hold short-term municipal bonds, offer tax-free interest, but the interest rate is usually less than the taxable money market accounts and, therefore, usually makes sense only for those in the higher tax brackets.

In 2008, Charles Schwab offered a short-term bond fund to its customers as a sweep option — sort of like a juiced-up money market. As it turned out, Schwab's YieldPlus fund managers were squeezing that extra juice from some risky mortgage bonds, which wound up defaulting during the mortgage crisis. Schwab investors, who thought their money was safe, lost a bundle. The SEC brought suit against Schwab, and three years later, investors recouped some, but not all, of their savings. Moving forward, my hunch is that brokerage houses will be much more careful about what funds they present as "stable" reservoirs of cash and what funds they offer as sweep options. However, just in case you come across something that looks like a money market fund but is offering to pay considerably higher rates than all the others, make sure to read the prospectus carefully.

To date, only two real money market funds "broke the buck" — returning less principal to shareholders than they invested. In both cases, the principal lost was only about 1 percent (a penny on each dollar invested). And the regulations in place today are a bit tougher than they once were, making such a "break" less likely.

Compared to bonds: Expect most bonds and bond funds to provide higher long-term returns than money market funds. Money market funds, however, offer greater liquidity and (at least historically) a very high degree of safety.

Banking on online savings accounts

FDIC-insured online banks often offer interest rates on savings accounts comparable to CD rates. Of late, www.ally.com consistently pays some of the highest rates. You can shop for rates online (as well as for local bank rates) on either www.bankrate.com or www.moneyaisle.com. Some online banks occasionally offer special enticements, such as a $25 check to anyone opening a new account with at least $250. So why tie up your money in a CD when you don't have to?

Compared to bonds: Expect most bonds to provide higher long-term returns than any savings account. An online savings account, however, may offer fairly handsome rates, with instant liquidity and FDIC insurance.

Prospering (perhaps) with peer-to-peer lending

This is the new kid on the fixed-income block. If you haven't checked out www.prosper.com or www.lendingclub.com, you may want to do so. Even if you decide not to invest, you'll likely find the cybertrip fascinating. These sites are something like eBay for cash. (They have some similarities to Match.com, too.) People go onto the websites in search of loans (trying to look as respectable as possible), and other people choose whether or not to lend them money. The process is called *peer-to-peer* lending. Instead of turning to a credit card company, would-be borrowers go public with their money needs and try to get a better deal. In fact, they often do. And lenders, although charging less interest than Visa and MasterCard (not hard to do), may get a higher return than they would in another fixed-income investment, like bonds.

Both sites say they do credit checks on all borrowers, but credit checks aren't perfect. And some of the borrowers are listed as known bad credit risks. You can choose them or avoid them.

All in all, I find these are promising ventures, although certainly not something to bank on heavily quite yet. Investment-wise I see these as the equivalent to corporate junk bonds, but the return may be higher than you can get by lending to corporations. Only time will tell.

A few caveats if you want to give peer-to-peer lending a whirl:

✔ **Spread your loans out.** Don't lend too much to any one person, regardless of how good his story or credit rating seems.

✔ **Take the aggregate return figures posted by these sites with a big, fat grain of salt.** A lot of wrinkles still need ironing out when it comes to how returns should be calculated on peer-to-peer sites.

✔ **Know that you are taking substantial risk with your money.** I've seen one of Prosper.com's web advertisements, aimed at potential lenders, claiming: "It's Simple, Safe & Secure." BS! It isn't all that simple — it takes some time to get up to speed — and it isn't at all safe and secure. If you want safe and secure, put your money in an FDIC-insured savings account!

Compared to bonds: Expect peer-to-peer lending to generate a yield comparable to high-yield corporate bonds, and perhaps higher. The risk also may be comparable (which is to say considerable) and perhaps significantly higher — especially if you choose to lend to high-risk borrowers in search of higher returns. Interest earned is generally taxed as normal income, although one rep from Lending Tree tried to convince me that dividing up my money into many small loans would allow for some kind of tax loophole . . . I dunno. Tax loopholes exist, for sure, but I prefer to play it kosher with the IRS.

Considering the predictability of an annuity

A cross between an insurance product and an investment, annuities come in myriad shapes and sizes. The general theme is that you give your money to an institution (usually an insurance company or a charity), and that institution promises you a certain rate of return, typically for as long as you live. What's the difference between an annuity and a bond? With an annuity, you don't expect to ever see your principal back. In return for giving up your principal, you expect a higher rate of return.

Some annuities, called *variable* annuities, offer rates of return pegged to something like the stock market. Other annuities, called *fixed* annuities, offer a steady rate of return or perhaps a rate of return that adjusts for inflation.

Some annuities charge a small fortune in fees. Most annuities ask for surrender charges if you try to change your mind.

Be careful out there! A majority of annuities are horrific rip-offs, with all kinds of hidden costs and high surrender charges should you attempt to escape (as many people do when they finally figure out the costs). I'm talking about a very steep penalty here. A typical annuity may charge you, say, 7 percent of the total amount invested if you withdraw your money within a year, 6 percent within two years, and so on, with a gradual tapering off up to seven years.

Most annuities are sold with 78-page contracts that no one, not even lawyers, can understand. (I kid you not. I've had lawyer clients who bought these, then later came to me red-faced, telling me they thought they had been hoodwinked.)

But some good annuity products are out there as well. See *Annuities For Dummies* by Kerry Pechter (Wiley) for advice. I have a strong preference for fixed annuities that adjust with inflation. Among the best providers of those are several insurance companies that have contracted with Vanguard and Fidelity; go to www.vanguard.com or www.fidelity.com and do a search for "fixed annuities" to find out more.

An intriguing form of annuity worthy of consideration is the *deferred income annuity*, often referred to as *longevity insurance*. Only a handful of insurers — including New York Life, Symetra Financial, and Northwestern Mutual — offer these policies. Though they provide a stream of income just as other fixed annuities do, these deferred annuities don't kick in for years to come. If you buy a policy at age 56, you may not see a payoff for another 30 years . . . and only if you're still alive.

Because you may not live to see the eventual payoff — which, thanks to inflation, will be worth a lot less than in today's dollars — and because the insurance company gets to play with your money for 30 years, you don't need to kick in much cash to (potentially) get a lot at the back end. For example, I recently asked several insurers for a quote. If I (age 56) cough up $100,000 today, I can buy an immediate annuity that pays me about $5,800 a year for the rest of my life, with payments starting right away. Or, I can buy a deferred income annuity that gives me about $68,600 a year, with payments starting on my 85th birthday — if I'm still around. Of course, even if I am, with future possibilities of raging inflation, $68,600 a year may be just enough income to keep me stocked up in dental floss.

Longevity insurance reduces the financial risks associated with living a long life for those who have reason to believe they'll be around a very long time. But keep in mind that you have no guarantee of throwing yourself a big birthday party in 30 years, paid for by your deferred income annuity.

Generally, annuities do not belong in tax-advantaged retirement accounts, such as IRAs. A main advantage to an annuity is the ability to defer taxes. Putting an annuity into an IRA, which is already tax-advantaged, makes about as much sense as flapping your arms as you board an airplane.

Compared to bonds: Returns on annuities grow larger the longer you hold off on buying one. (Extreme example: Any insurance company would be more than happy, I would think, to take your money, stick it into an annuity, and pay you 20 percent a year — provided you are 97 years old.) In almost all cases, if you are in your mid-60s or older, you'll get more cash flow than you would by investing in bonds, but you give up your principal, and you may not get more than you would with bonds in the end (I'm talking here about the *end* end). The taxing of annuity income can be very complicated. Talk to your tax advisor.

Hocking your home with a reverse mortgage

These babies have been around for a long while but have exploded in popularity the past several years. You own a home? You're 62 or over? You can sell it back to the bank over time. Each month, you get a check. Each month, you have less equity in your home. Reverse mortgages are complicated. And, like annuities, both good and bad products exist. Do your research. Here are some suggestions:

- ✔ Order the booklet "Home Made Money" from AARP at 1-800-209-8085.

- ✔ Talk to a reverse mortgage counselor. AARP has some on board, or try the nonprofit Consumer Credit Counseling Service in your area. Perhaps your best option is to call the U.S. Department of Housing and Urban Development at 1-800-569-4287 to be referred to a HUD-certified reverse mortgage counselor in your area.

- ✔ Oh, and read *Reverse Mortgages For Dummies* by Sarah Glendon Lyons and John E. Lucas (Wiley).

Compared to bonds: The cash flow you get from a reverse mortgage varies tremendously depending on your age, the equity you have in your home, and the terms of the mortgage agreement. Reverse mortgage income isn't taxable.

Recognizing that Stocks Can Be Cash Cows, Too (Moo)

Stocks can generate returns in two ways:

- ✔ They can appreciate in value.
- ✔ They can pay dividends.

Historically, dividends have actually accounted for the lion's share of stock returns. Not long ago, however, dividends fell out of favor, reduced to a pittance throughout the '80s and '90s. But in the past few years, they've come raging back into vogue. Who can say why? At present, the dividend yield of an average basket of U.S. stocks, per Morningstar, is now about 1.75 percent — nearly, but not quite as much, as you would get on a 10-year Treasury bond.

Stock dividends, by definition, are not fixed in stone, as are interest payments on bonds. However, they can, within a diversified portfolio of stocks, deliver a fairly consistent cash flow. And unlike bond interest, which is generally taxed as income, the majority of stock dividends receive special tax treatment. At least under current laws, taxes would rarely be higher than 15 percent.

Not all stocks are equally likely to cough up dividends. If you wish, you can add stocks to your portfolio that will do just that. You can grab your dividends with either individual stocks or with any number of mutual funds or exchange-traded funds that offer high-dividend paying stocks.

Focusing on stocks with sock-o dividends

Your yearly dividend yield can increase to more than 2 percent with relative ease if you choose your stocks selectively or pick up either a high-dividend stock mutual fund or exchange-traded fund. Investors who usually jump on board new investing trends have been quick to do just that lately. The reasons? Low yields on bonds and good performance on dividend stocks.

But high-dividend stocks won't see high performance every year, or even every decade. High-dividend-paying companies, often categorized as *value* companies (precisely because they pay out higher dividends), tend to invest less in their own growth. Companies that are more miserly with dividends (often called *growth* companies) tend to shovel more into R&D and such. Sometimes that "R&D and such" translates into new products, growth, and greater profits that result in gangbuster stock performance. (Think of the entire 1990s; growth stocks were definitely the place to be.)

There's certainly nothing wrong with dividends, per se, but by focusing on them you may be giving up on absolute return. The best stock portfolios are well diversified: They have both value and growth stocks. I wouldn't want to see you with a stock portfolio of all high-dividend companies, even though the cash flow would be sweet.

Nor would I want to see you with a portfolio too concentrated in a handful of industry sectors. As fate would have it, most high-dividend-paying stocks tend to fall heavily in certain industry sectors, such as utilities, tobacco, pharmaceuticals, and banks. Gear your portfolio too heavily toward high dividends, and you'll be pretty much locking yourself outside of semiconductors, medical equipment, Internet technology, biotechnology, and other sectors that may well turn out to be the superstars of the next decade.

Compared to bonds: The cash flow from interest on bonds is greater and more predictable than the cash flow from stock dividends. Over the long haul, however, expect the *total* return on stocks (which includes both dividends and price appreciation) to be higher. Stocks are also much more volatile than bonds. Whereas bond interest is typically issued semiannually and bond funds usually pay interest monthly, stock dividends are more commonly posted quarterly, although stock funds may issue dividends quarterly, semiannually, or annually.

Realizing gain with real estate investment trusts (REITs)

One particular sector of the stock market, real estate investment trusts (REITs), offers among the highest dividend yields in the land: currently 3.3 percent, says Morningstar. REITs are also slightly different animals from most stocks, in that REITs *must,* by law, pay out at least 90 percent of their earnings as dividends. And the dividends that REITs pay are generally not taxed at 15 percent, as are most other stock dividends, but rather at normal income tax rates.

The real estate sector also shows delightfully low correlation to the rest of the stock market. So whether or not you want the dividends, it may not be a bad idea to plunk 10 to 15 percent of the money you have allocated for stocks into REITs — preferably low-cost, indexed REIT mutual funds or exchange-traded funds, both U.S. and foreign.

Caveat: REIT distributions are not only generally taxed as regular income but also may include return of principal, which can make tax reporting tricky. For this reason, your best bet is to house your REIT holdings in a tax-advantaged retirement account.

Compared to bonds: REITs pay very high dividends by stock standards, and when interest rates are as low as they have been lately, the REIT dividends may even exceed the interest from bonds of equal principal value. REITs experience more volatility than bonds, but they also offer significantly greater potential for appreciation.

Taking a middle ground with preferred stock

Often referred to as a sort of hybrid between a stock and a bond, *preferred stock,* issued by companies both public and private, generally offers greater and more secure dividends than common stock. Preferred stock is also safer than common stock in that if a company goes under, the holders of preferred stock must be paid back before the owners of common stock.

Many variations of preferred stock are on the market with varying degrees of payoff and risk. Generally, preferred stock, like most hybrid kinds of investments, wouldn't be my first choice of investment for most people. I'd prefer to see you have a mix of stocks and bonds, which together provide the same benefit as preferred stock but with more diversification power. If the concept of preferred stock floats your boat, however, feel free to discuss it with your broker. There are worse investments.

Compared to bonds. Preferred stocks' dividends can be just as much as or more than bond interest on a similar amount of money. However, the dividends from the preferred stock may be taxed more gingerly than the interest on bonds. Some preferred stock (convertible preferred) offers an opportunity for substantial capital appreciation. But preferred stock — although safer than common stock — is riskier than most forms of true fixed income.

Introducing a Vastly Better Way to Create Cash Flow: Portfolio Rebalancing

I'd like to start this section with two seemingly short and simple questions. Are you ready?

Question #1: You have $100,000 in your portfolio. You withdraw exactly $10,000. How much do you have left?

I know you know the answer.

Question #2: Does it matter whether the money you withdraw — the $10,000 — comes from this past year's interest payments on your bonds or this past year's appreciation in the value of your stock holdings?

Either way, you still have $90,000 left, riiiight?

Yes. Yes. YES. YESSSS.

And yet, despite the simplicity of these two questions, you'd be amazed at how many people get the second question wrong. Then, when I look at them quizzically, they argue with me.

"But . . . but . . . but . . . Russell . . . If I withdraw the money from bonds, since that represents interest, my principal will still be intact. But if I withdraw the money from stocks, I'm then tapping my principal, and then I'm eating into a productive asset," they argue.

No. That's wrong. Your portfolio, after withdrawing the $10,000, will be worth $90,000. Period. End of story. Argue all you want. This is basic math here. The resulting balance is the same. It doesn't matter whether the sum withdrawn comes from bond interest, stock dividends, stock appreciation, selling the Picasso from the hallway, renting out the pool, or unicorn droppings. It just doesn't matter.

I'm not sure where the *bond-interest-is-okay-to-withdraw-but-stock-appreciation-isn't-okay-to-withdraw* myth ever started. But for the record, there is no such thing as leaving your bond principal intact. In truth, more than half the money that you're ever likely to earn in bonds is simply keeping your principal afloat of inflation. If you withdraw those inflation-neutralizing interest payments from your portfolio, the remainder of your bond holdings won't be "intact" at all. Your bond holdings will slowly but surely lose value due to the steadily rising cost of living, otherwise known as inflation.

Table 17-1 shows what $100 today will be worth in the future, assuming an annual inflation rate of 3 percent (the rate of inflation in the United States over the past several decades). According to these figures, if you have a $100 bond maturing in 20 years and you siphon off all the coupon payments, your "intact" principal will probably be worth only $55 when the bond matures. If you have $100 in stock and you siphon off all the appreciation and dividends over the next 20 years, the stock that remains will probably be worth $55, too.

Table 17-1	The Value of Today's $100 Assuming 3 Percent Inflation
Years in Future	*Value of Today's $100*
5	$86
10	$74
15	$64
20	$55
25	$48
30	$41

When you can see that withdrawing $10,000 means withdrawing $10,000 — regardless of the source — and that there's no such thing as leaving your principal "intact," you are ready to create a portfolio that can handle withdrawals objectively. By "objectively," I am saying that sometimes it makes sense to take your cash flow from appreciated stock, sometimes from stock dividends, and sometimes from bond interest. As I say at the onset of this chapter, the best option for withdrawing cash from a portfolio — *always* — is to adopt a cash withdrawal plan that is flexible and potentially allows for all three sources of cash flow.

Buying low and selling high

Here is the best method, far and away, for extracting cash from a portfolio. For illustration purposes, I'm going to use a very simple portfolio, consisting of Domestic Stock Fund A, Foreign Stock Fund F, Commodity Fund C, Bond Fund B, and Short-Term Cash Fund S.

Your portfolio allocation today, based on careful analysis of your need for return and your stomach for risk (as I discuss in Part III), looks like this:

Domestic Stock Fund A	26%
Foreign Stock Fund F	25%
Commodity Fund C	5%
Bond Fund B	38%
Short-Term Cash Fund S	6%

You've set up your accounts so that all your interest, dividends, and capital gains are reinvested in (rolled directly into) each security as they accrue.

Six months pass. During that time, you've been pulling regularly from your short-term cash fund (which, at 6 percent of your portfolio, is enough to cover a year to 18 months' expenses). The world economy is humming, and stocks are sailing, especially foreign stocks. Your allocations have all gone awry. Your portfolio now looks like this:

Domestic Stock Fund A	30%
Foreign Stock Fund F	32%
Commodity Fund C	5%
Bond Fund B	30%
Short-Term Cash Fund S	3%

What do you do? You *rebalance*. That means you sell off some of your stock funds, and you use the proceeds both to boost your cash position and add to your bond position. Your goal is to bring everything back into alignment so you are once again starting with the same allocation (26 percent U.S. stocks, 25 percent foreign stocks, and so on) you had at the beginning of the year. That allocation (your risk/return sweet spot) changes only if your life circumstances change — if, for example, you inherit $1 million from a rich aunt or, conversely, a rich aunt successfully sues you for $1 million.

Rebalancing not only creates cash flow but also puts your portfolio on anabolic steroids. Every six months (it doesn't have to be six months, but I find that is a good time frame for those making regular withdrawals), you are providing yourself with living expenses and keeping your portfolio where it should be in terms of your personal risk/return sweet spot, *and* you are continually selling high and buying low: the best formula I know — the best formula there is — for long-term investment success.

One more example, yet six months later. During this half-year, the stock market took a face-dive, commodities soared, and bonds did very well. Your portfolio at year-end again is out of alignment. It now looks like this:

Domestic Stock Fund A	22%
Foreign Stock Fund F	20%
Commodity Fund C	9%
Bond Fund B	46%
Short-Term Cash Fund S	3%

At this point, you're going to sell off the bond and commodity portion of your portfolio. And, after you've gotten your cash position back up to where you need it, you may wind up buying more stocks, which are now selling at bargain-basement prices.

Rolling bond interest back in

In Part I of this book, I explain that bonds' main role in your portfolio isn't so much for the income, nice as income is, but to provide ballast, to keep your portfolio afloat when the waters get choppy. Now you can see why I'm of that opinion.

The coupon payments from your bonds, or the interest payments generated by your bond fund, are to be plowed directly back into the bond side of your portfolio. This practice keeps your bond holdings from getting eaten up by inflation. Historically, stocks have returned much more than bonds. If that holds true in the future (if . . . if . . . if), you'll be skimming much more from the stock side of your portfolio during retirement. If the future turns out to be different from the past, those predictable bond coupons could spare you from destitution, just as they may have spared your grandparents during the Great Depression.

Bless bonds. Bless bond income. I only ask that you don't become a slave to that income.

Dealing with realities

In the real world, rebalancing can sometimes be a bit tricky. If your portfolio is in a taxable account rather than a tax-advantaged retirement account, you may have to contend with tax consequences when you sell any security. You may also have to deal with trading costs, depending on your choice of securities and the brokerage house you use to house your portfolio. Trading costs and taxes both can nibble away at a nest egg. You've got to be careful.

Perhaps you feel confident factoring those variables into your rebalancing plan. If not, you should see a financial planner, at least for a single visit, to help you orchestrate and fine-tune your rebalancing strategy.

But before you decide whether to handle it alone, read Chapter 18. In this exciting chapter, I discuss your portfolio allocation during retirement and how to sculpt your portfolio — including putting a certain good percentage in bonds, of course — so as to maximize your withdrawal potential without jeopardizing your nest egg.

Chapter 18

Finding Comfort and Security in Old Age

· ·

In This Chapter

▶ Tapping into the wisdom of actuarial science

▶ Weighing the optimal bond allocation for a post-employment portfolio

▶ Calculating permissible rates of withdrawal

▶ Taking pains not to run afoul of Uncle Sam's rules

· ·

When it comes to old age, common fears include everything from incontinence and impotence to failing eyesight and loose teeth. But on the financial front, the greatest fear, it goes without saying, is running out of money.

For folks who have money in the first place — enough to build a decent portfolio, enough to confidently give up the day job — two basic things can go awry. The first is market volatility; a growling bear market suddenly turns investment dollars to dimes. The second is unexpectedly high inflation, a slow and steady drain of spending power.

If you fear market volatility most, you may tend to err on the side of what is traditionally seen as investment conservatism. You probably love predictable investments: CDs, money markets, savings bonds, annuities, and such. If your big fear is inflation, you likely tend to err on the side of what is traditionally seen as investment aggressiveness. You're going for maximum return with stocks, commodities, real estate investments, and perhaps even high-yield or leveraged bonds.

In this chapter, I present the views of both camps (financial liberals and conservatives), blend them together, and present the view that I believe makes the most sense. Together, you and I figure out the best mix of retirement investments to weather both market volatility *and* inflation. As for incontinence, impotence, and loose teeth . . . let's leave all that for another book, shall we?

Looking Ahead to Many Years of Possible Portfolio Withdrawals

Lifespans have increased. If you are now 65, there's better than a 50/50 chance that either you or your spouse will still be alive at age 90. If you plan to retire at age 65, that means you need a portfolio that can provide cash flow for at least 25 more years. Two and a half decades is a long time. It allows for inflation to eat up a good bit of your savings. (Consider how much gasoline, a chocolate bar, or a loaf of bread cost 25 years ago.)

Table 18-1 shows the odds that you'll still be alive and kicking at age 80, 90, or 100 (15, 25, or 35 years beyond the traditional age of retirement). It's based on figures from the Society for Actuaries.

Table 18-1	Your Chances of Longevity Beyond 65			
Age	*Husband*	*Wife*	*Both of You*	*Either of You*
80	65%	75%	49%	91%
90	24%	37%	9%	52%
100	2%	4%	0.1%	6%

What that added longevity means, all things being equal, is that it behooves you to invest a wee bit more aggressively than did your grandparents. How aggressively? That depends on many factors and whom you ask. There is, unfortunately, no firm consensus among financial professionals. Just like the amateurs, we each have a certain bias.

Knowing Where the Real Danger Lies: The Risk of Being Too Conservative

Most financial pros have moved well beyond the old adage, held dearly for years, that the percent of your portfolio held in bonds should be equal to your age. (By age 60, you should be 60 percent in bonds; by age 70, 70 percent; and so on.) Some say, as do I, that the formula is as antiquated as the crossbow — and, potentially, just as dangerous. In this section, I introduce you to some newer ways of thinking about how much of a retirement portfolio belongs in bonds.

Considering an aggressive approach

"The real risk to most people's portfolios is, paradoxically, not taking enough market risk with higher-returning but more volatile investments, like stocks and commodities," says Steve Cassaday, CFP, president of Cassaday & Company, Inc., an investment management and financial planning firm in McLean, Virginia. "Given what most people have saved by retirement, and the average lifespan today, a more aggressive portfolio is the only choice if people are going to maintain their lifestyles."

Cassaday has researched the returns of various kinds of investments over the past 35 years and has concluded that a portfolio of 15 percent bonds and 2.5 percent cash, with the rest in more aggressive but very well-diversified investments like stocks and commodities, actually offers the greatest degree of absolute safety to the average investor. In other words, he opts to put his retired clients in portfolios that are over 80 percent equities, including U.S. stock, foreign stock, REITs, and commodities.

Cassaday's views were published in the *Journal of Financial Planning* and created quite a stir among professional financial types, many of whom are skeptical, at best, of Cassaday's conclusions.

I know, as the author of a book on bonds, you wouldn't expect me to agree with Cassaday. However, I've seen his number crunching, and I'm impressed. Although I don't buy into his strategy completely, I don't think the guy is too far off the mark. His aggressive portfolios, when *back-tested* (using computers to simulate how they would have done over history), have held up remarkably well through both bull markets and bears. Sure, they dip when the stock market is down, but they come back — at least to date they have.

Easing back toward your comfort zone

The aggressiveness of Cassaday's approach may not be right for all investors. I say that not because I doubt his numbers but for two other reasons:

- ✔ The future of the stock market may be not quite as rosy as the past.
- ✔ A portfolio of more than 80 percent equity is subject to huge dips in bad times. People tend to panic and sell their fallen angels just when they should be holding them the most. The stock and commodity markets are like giant rubber bands: After the biggest down stretches, you tend to see the strongest snap-backs, and vice versa (although giant rubber bands tend to be more predictable than the stock market).

Keep in mind that a portfolio of 80 percent stocks and 20 percent bonds *will* have short-term setbacks, some of them major. According to data compiled by Vanguard, such a portfolio has seen negative annual returns in 23 of the past 86 years. But the average annual return has been a very impressive 9.4 percent.

"The tradeoff for occasional annual returns below the long-term average has historically been long-term returns well above what is possible with a more stable portfolio," says Cassaday. "Our guidance to clients has always been to hold on to the side of the kayak when things get rough. Declines have always become recoveries, and as long as you do not need all of your money in one lump sum and any given point (very few ever do), then it has always paid to wait."

Not every investor can "hold on to the side of the kayak." For those who can't, a somewhat less aggressive portfolio than Cassaday advises will probably work best. (Cassaday himself amends his portfolio for his clients who can't emotionally handle a lot of volatility.)

Another colleague of mine, William P. Bengen, CFP, wrote a book for other financial planners called *Conserving Client Portfolios During Retirement* (FPA Press). His book suggests something of a compromise between Cassaday's portfolio and the traditional age-based portfolio. Most financial planners I know are much more in line with Bengen's thinking than with Cassaday's.

Setting your default at 60/40

Bengen, like Cassaday, crunched the numbers backwards and forwards. His conclusion: Yes, tweak your portfolio as you approach retirement to include more bonds and less stock, but don't tweak it too much. "Given that stock returns have historically creamed bond returns, you may need those stock returns if your portfolio is going to last as long as you do," says Bengen.

For most people, says Bengen, 40 percent nonvolatile, safe investments is probably enough. If you want to get more conservative than that, Bengen suggests that you subtract your age from 120 and allocate that amount to the safe and nonvolatile. For example, at age 60, you might give yourself a 60/40 split (stocks/bonds), and at age 65, you might give yourself a 55/45 split.

"I wouldn't update asset allocation every year — only every fifth year, on a birthday divisible by five," says Bengen. Our 65-year-old above might then, at age 70, go for a 50/50 split.

Bengen's formula is not as far from Cassaday's as it may initially seem. The stocks part of the equation may include any investment with a potentially high yield but also potential volatility: commodities, investment real estate, junk bonds, and even 30-year Treasuries. The bond side of his portfolio would include any kind of truly nonvolatile investment, including short- and intermediate-term high-quality bonds, annuities, and CDs.

And to some degree, investors should tweak the percentages in accordance with economic conditions. Keep an eye out for extreme changes in market conditions (such as those I discuss next) and tweak as needed. "Don't be wooden," says Bengen.

Allowing for adjustments to suit the times

One of the few constants in the world of investing is the tendency for investment returns to revert to their mean. What this means is that if a particular kind of investment (stocks, bonds, what-have-you) typically returns X percent a year, but for the past several years has returned considerably more than X, you have a better than 50/50 chance that the returns are in for a slowdown. If, conversely, the investment has been producing returns in the past several years far less than X, you have a better than 50/50 chance that the returns are about to improve. This rule, appropriately enough, is called *reversion to the mean.*

Stock returns are popularly calculated by what is referred to as the *P/E ratio.* The "P" stands for price. The "E" stands for earnings. When the average price of all stocks is divided by the average earnings of all companies, you typically come up with a number somewhere around 20. In other words, if the average price of the average stock is $10, then companies are by and large making about ($10 × 20) $200 a year for every share of stock they've issued.

 Studies going back decades show that whenever the P/E has risen far north of 20 (such as it did in 1999), stock returns usually start to sputter, and they sputter for a good while. When the P/E drops far below 20 (as it did in 2008), stock returns usually heat up for the next few years.

Not long ago, a Yale economist named Robert J. Shiller adjusted the P/E to reflect not only earnings of the past year (as the P/E typically measures) but earnings over the past 10 years, taking inflation into consideration. Testing of the data seems to indicate that the Shiller P/E (which can be found on the website www.multpl.com — the P/E ratio is often called the *multiple*) may be a somewhat more accurate predictor of future stock performance than the old-fashioned P/E. (This topic is currently an area of hot debate.)

 The old-fashioned P/E ratio is published in many places. The easiest way to find it is to go to www.vanguard.com, search for the Vanguard Total Stock Market ETF (VTI), and check the current P/E ratio in the fund's description. Click on the "Portfolio & Management" tab. When I last checked, the P/E was about 17, slightly under the historical norm. The Shiller P/E, however, was riding at about 23, above its historical mean of 16.5.

You don't want to go crazy with this stuff, but if both P/E ratios were to fall well behind historical norms, it may be a good time to beef up on stocks . . . perhaps adding 5 percent or so to your normal allocation. If the ratios rise well above historical norms, you may want to beef up on bonds . . . perhaps taking your normal allocation up 5 percent and reducing your stock holdings accordingly.

I offer a concrete example, using myself as the guinea pig, next.

Choosing my and your ultimate ratio

Unless my circumstances change, my personal retirement portfolio — which I already have planned! — will be about 60/40: 60 percent stock (and other high-return investments) and 40 percent bonds (and other low-return, low-volatility investments). If, at some point, stock prices seem cheap (low P/E ratios), I may move my portfolio toward a more aggressive 65/35 allocation. If the situation is reversed, with seemingly expensive stocks (high P/E ratios), I may move my holdings to a more conservative 55/45. I don't think I would ever get more conservative than that, even if I live (as I hope to) to a very old age.

But I can emotionally stomach more volatility than most people. I know I won't sell if the market takes a flop. If the market sours badly and I need to supplement my portfolio income, I, fortunately, have the kind of career that easily allows me to pick up a few bucks working part-time. Otherwise, I'd aim for a somewhat more conservative retirement position for myself, as I do for some of my clients.

I'll note, too, that upon giving up my day job, I will likely (depending on rates at the time, and my health) buy myself a fixed annuity. I'll be guaranteed an income stream, which, combined with Social Security, will ensure that I'll always have enough money to eat and pay the rent. I'm probably looking at perhaps 15 to 20 percent of my retirement portfolio being handed over to an insurance company or two. Fixed annuities are discussed in Chapter 17.

Obviously, retirement planning is a very personal process.

Bottom (mushy) line: Most people living off their portfolios are advised to have very well-diversified portfolios. A diversified portfolio should contain U.S. stock, foreign stock, small cap and large cap stock, and value and growth securities. It's also good advice to include 30 percent to 60 percent fixed income: investment-grade bonds, fixed annuities, and cash. Only a very conservative investor will want 70 percent fixed income. If you go beyond that, your hankering for safety may very well backfire, and your "safe" portfolio could wind up risking your lifestyle as inflation takes its steady toll.

What about the house?

If — and that's a *big* if — you have sizeable home equity *and* you think you'll be able to downsize to something cheaper at a certain point in the future, you can factor your home equity into your retirement portfolio. Most people these days, however, seem to have a hard time downsizing, in which case, your home equity is nice to have but won't provide you with any needed cash. Not now. Not later. If you want to give up your day job, the two empty rooms upstairs won't help you have cash to pay for groceries. Of course, if you're willing to sell the ranch and move into an apartment or retirement facility, the home equity you've built up can play a very important role in your sunset years.

Calculating How Much You Can Safely Tap

Earlier in the book, I present the *20 times rule*: a thumbprint that gives you a very rough guide of how big a portfolio you need before you retire. In short, figure out how much you need in a year, subtract whatever retirement income you have outside of investment income (such as Social Security), and multiply the remainder by 20. So if you need $50,000 a year and Social Security will provide $20,000, you should build a portfolio of ($30,000 × 20) $600,000, at the very minimum, before you kiss your office colleagues good-bye forever.

That rough rule, like all rough rules, is the product of a few assumptions. Foremost, it assumes that you have a diversified portfolio returning enough so you can not only keep up with inflation but also withdraw 4 to 5 percent a year without denting your principal.

 That allowable withdrawal amount depends on a whole slew of factors, such as the actual rate of inflation, your tax hit, market conditions, and — a biggie — your life expectancy and current age. (At age 97, it's probably okay to see a slow dwindling in your portfolio size.) A lot of those variables, such as your lifespan, can be controlled to only a limited extent (eat carrots). What you can control *entirely* — and what will have great bearing on how much you can withdraw — is the allocation of your portfolio, especially the ratio of stocks to bonds.

Revisiting risk, return, and realistic expectations

How realistic is a 4 to 5 percent withdrawal rate? According to figures from Vanguard, a retirement portfolio with an allocation of 50 percent bonds and 50 percent stocks has about an 85 percent chance of lasting 30 years, provided the initial withdrawal is limited to 4 percent and then adjusted for inflation. The number would be 74 percent over 30 years if using the 5 percent withdrawal rate. I don't know about you, but I find those numbers a bit depressing. It means that you need $800,000, or preferably $1 million, to generate just $40,000 a year, and even then you could still go broke before you die.

According to Steve Cassaday, if you are willing to deal with the volatility that comes with a portfolio of 80 percent equities, you should be able to withdraw up to *7 percent* a year and be safe for 30 years and beyond. Those numbers are much less depressing: You would need, to generate $40,000 a year, a portfolio of considerably less, about $570,000.

If you go that route, know that at times your portfolio will sink, and sink hard, and you'll be wondering whether you're going to run out of money next month. Although I like Cassaday's figure (who wouldn't?), I'm not sure how many people could sit tight and deal with the kind of volatility that would be inevitable with such a market-risk-laden portfolio. Also, if the future is considerably different from the past, things could turn out ugly.

Basing your retirement on clear thinking

Although history rarely repeats, I'm not the first to say that it often echoes. The long-term return on large stocks — at least over the past century or so — has been just a bit shy of 10 percent a year. Small stocks (prone to greater price sways) have returned about 12 percent a year. The long-term return on bonds has been about 5.5 percent. And the inflation rate moving forward, most economists agree, will probably stay somewhere close to its present 3 percent. Based on these numbers, and your final portfolio allocations, you can best judge whether a 3 percent withdrawal, a 7 percent withdrawal, or something in between can be sustained.

My own 60 percent equity/40 percent bond retirement portfolio (once it's in place) should fairly safely allow me to withdraw up to 5 percent a year for at least 30 years. If the markets don't cooperate, I realize that I may have to tighten my belt. I'm willing to do that, if necessary.

But that's me. You need to devise your own plan based on your own expected longevity, stomach for risk, and the other factors I describe earlier in this chapter. I would only ask you not to think pie-in-the-sky and, as William Bengen says, "Don't be wooden." Allow yourself some flexibility to adjust your cash flow after you begin to withdraw. No retirement plan should be fixed in stone, or wood.

Of the many books and articles I've read on retirement planning, one that makes particular sense is *Work Less, Live More* by Bob Clyatt (Nolo). The author suggests something he calls the "95% Rule." It starts with a retirement plan that incorporates a reasonable rate of withdrawal: Clyatt conservatively says 4 percent, maybe 4.5 percent of your initial portfolio ($24,000 to $27,000 a year on a $600,000 portfolio), adjusted each year for inflation. However, if the markets turn sour in any particular year or years, you economize a bit over that time period by withdrawing no more than 95 percent of what you withdrew the previous year. "You'll tighten your belt somewhat, but you won't turn your world upside down," writes Clyatt.

Clyatt purports that following the 95% Rule, a portfolio of stocks and bonds (50/50) with a 4.5 percent yearly withdrawal (plus adjustments for inflation) has a 92 percent chance of lasting 30 years. Those aren't bad odds at all.

Making the Most Use of Uncle Sam's Gifts

The Internal Revenue Service, in cahoots with Congress, gives the U.S. investor two basic kinds of tax-advantaged retirement accounts:

- ✔ Plans that allow for the deferral of income tax until the money is withdrawn (IRAs, SEP-IRAs, 401k plans)
- ✔ Plans that, provided you follow certain rules, allow for tax-free withdrawals after reaching age 59½ (Roth IRAs, Roth 401k plans)

I won't get into the many rules and regulations and the amount that you can stash in each kind of account. That information is readily available elsewhere, and it strays a bit from the focus of this book. Instead, I want to discuss in which account you should place your bond allocation and, should you be in the withdrawal phase of your investing career, from which account you should yank your cash.

Minimizing income is the name of the game

Interest payments from bonds or bond funds (other than municipal bonds, as I discuss in Chapter 8) are generally taxable as normal income. In contrast, the money you make off stocks, whether dividends or capital gains, is usually taxed at 15 percent (although this rate is always subject to change). It makes sense, especially if you are in a tax bracket that's higher than 15 percent, to keep your bonds in a tax-advantaged retirement account. Even if you are in the 15 percent bracket, this plan still makes sense because bond income, regular and steady, is taxed regardless of whether you withdraw it or not. Stock appreciation (capital gains) is taxed only when you sell, although stock held in mutual funds may incur capital gains when the fund sells, even if you don't.

When allocating your portfolio, keep in mind at all times that money in your 401(k) or IRA will eventually be taxed as regular income. Say you decide that you want a 30 percent allocation to bonds, and all of those bonds are in your IRA. If you are within four or five years of withdrawing some of that money, you may want to make the actual allocation of bonds somewhat higher. I can't give you an exact figure because I don't know your tax bracket and I don't know what kind of capital gains taxes you'll pay when you cash out of your taxable accounts. But you may, for example, allocate 35 percent or 45 percent of your portfolio to bonds.

If you have various retirement accounts with more space than you need for just your bond allocation, put the bonds in the tax-deferred accounts and put potentially higher-yielding assets, like stocks, in your tax-free accounts, such as your Roth IRA. That's because the Roth IRA does not require you to start taking minimum required distributions at age 70½, so you may as well fuel up your Roth with assets that can really grow over the years.

Lowering your tax bracket through smart withdrawals

At age 70½, you have to start taking something from your 401(k) or your regular or rollover IRA; it's the law. (See the sidebar "Missing the minimum required distribution — don't!") But prior to that age, and to a certain degree after that age, whether your cash comes from your 401(k), IRA, Roth IRA, or taxable account is up to your discretion.

How to best use that discretion?

WARNING!

Missing the minimum required distribution — don't!

I'm very happy to live in a country where people who break the law are given due process and, if found guilty of a crime, they'll neither have their limbs removed, nor will they be stoned to death. Yet we have the minimum required distribution (MRD) on 401(k) plans as well as regular and roll-over IRAs. And woe is you if you miscalculate! No, you won't be stoned, but your finances will certainly be pummeled hard.

Of course, the calculation is easy — says the IRS! You simply take your retirement account's starting balance as of December 31 the prior year and divide that number by your "life-expectancy factor" (which is found in IRS publication 590, available on the IRS website www.irs.gov).

Don't get it wrong! The penalty for taking less than your minimum required distribution is brutal. If you withdraw less than the required minimum amount, the IRS can nail you for a sum equal to 50 percent of the MRD not taken.

MRDs generally begin at age 70½. If you feel uncomfortable doing the calculation yourself, a retirement specialist at the brokerage house where you have your account will help you, or you can ask your tax guru.

Caution: There is an entirely different table for MRDs on inherited IRAs. Lots of people mess up there, with potentially expensive consequences.

TIP

Balance, Grasshopper, balance. Most likely, you want to pull from your tax-deferred retirement accounts only to the point that doing so doesn't push you into a higher tax bracket. At that point, supplement that cash with money from your Roth account or your taxable brokerage account.

For example, if you are a single guy or gal withdrawing $40,000 a year from your portfolio, you most likely want to take at least the first $8,700 of that amount from your 401(k) or traditional IRA. You'll be taxed only 10 percent on that money. You may want to consider taking as much as $35,350 from one of these accounts. That amount (according to the 2012 federal tax schedule), and no more, will keep you squarely in the 15 percent tax bracket. Show any more incremental income, and you'll be taxed at 25 percent — a two-thirds increase in tax! Solution: Withdraw the remaining $4,650 ($40,000 – $35,350) from either your Roth or your taxable brokerage account, and you'll keep yourself in the 15 percent bracket.

Having retirement money that is both taxable and tax-free is known in the financial planning world as *tax diversification*. It makes a lot of sense.

Caveat: If you have mucho bucks — more than the federal estate tax exemption (which varies year to year) — the rules change. Your heirs will generally fare much better inheriting money outside of your IRA or 401(k) than money within. It may make sense, in your case, to well exceed your minimum required distributions, take the tax hit, but spare your heirs from having to pay a hefty estate tax plus income tax. Talk to an estate planning attorney, tax accountant, or financial planner before setting up your withdrawal strategy.

Oh, and Roth money is a great gift for your heirs.

Part VI
The Part of Tens

The 5th Wave

By Rich Tennant

"I've always used historical data analysis to rebalance my assets, but lately it's been pretty much hysterical data analysis that I've been working with."

In this part . . .

You have now arrived at The Part of Tens, a classic feature in all *Dummies* books that offers fun and practical lists chock full of takeaway information. I begin with the ten most common misconceptions about bonds — some of them rather huge misconceptions that I've seen carried even by some very experienced investors. I then present ten mistakes that bond investors often make, some potentially quite costly. And I wrap up this section with ten Q&As with Dan Fuss of Loomis, Sayles & Company, without any question one of the most successful bond managers of our age.

Chapter 19

Ten Most Common Misconceptions about Bonds

. . . .

In This Chapter

▶ Deciphering the jargon

▶ Debunking some myths

▶ Recognizing gross oversimplifications

. . . .

A scoop of lake water in your hands, clear and cloistered, unmoving, looks like the very essence of simplicity. And yet, a dab under the high-powered microscope reveals an entire world of complex organisms wiggling and squiggling about in your palms.

A bond selling for 100 and paying 5 percent looks like the clearest, most easy-to-understand investment possible. Yet it is, in reality, a much more complex organism. Scoop through these ten common bond misconceptions, and you'll no doubt see what I'm talking about.

A Bond "Selling for 100" Costs $100

Welcome to the first complexity in bonds: *jargon*! When a bond broker says that he has a bond "selling for 100," it means that the bond is selling not for $100, but for $1,000. If that same bond were "selling for 95," it would be on the market for $950. If it were "selling for 105," you could buy it for $1,050.

Ready for more jargon?

The *par value* or *face value* of a $1,000 bond is $1,000. But the *market value* depends on whether it's selling for 95, 100, 105, or whatever. In addition, that $1,000 face bond may be said to "pay 5 percent," but that doesn't mean you'll get 5 percent on your money! It means you'll get 5 percent on the par value: that is, 5 percent on $1,000, or $50 a year, which may mean a yield of greater or less than 5 percent to you. If you paid 105 for the bond (that's called a *premium*), you'll actually be making less than 5 percent on your money. If you paid 95 for the bond (that's called a *discount*), you'll be making more than 5 percent on your money.

Confused? Turn to Chapter 4.

Buying a Bond at a Discount Is Better Than Paying a Premium, Duh

Duh, yourself. Sometimes, you get what you pay for.

Discounted bonds sell at a discount for a reason; premium bonds sell at a premium for a reason. Here's the reason: Those premium bonds typically have higher coupon rates than prevailing coupon rates. Discount bonds, in contrast, typically have lower coupon rates than prevailing coupon rates. Both in theory and in practice, two bonds with similar ratings and similar maturities, all other things being equal, will have similar yields-to-maturity (the yield that really matters) whether sold at a premium or a discount.

Example: Bond A, issued in 2005, has a coupon rate of 6 percent. Bond B, issued in 2010, has a coupon rate of 4 percent. Everything else about the bonds is the same: same issuer, same maturity date (let's say 2025), same callability. Currently, similar bonds are paying 5 percent. You would fully expect Bond A to sell at a premium and Bond B to sell at a discount. In both cases you would expect their yields-to-maturity to be roughly 5 percent.

A Bond Paying X% Today Will Pocket You X% Over the Life of the Bond

A bond paying a coupon rate of 5 percent may (if the bond is purchased at a discount) be yielding something higher, like, say, 6 percent. But each six months, as you collect that 6 percent on your money, you'll either spend it or reinvest it. If you reinvest it at an even higher rate of interest (suppose interest rates are going up) — say 8 percent — then your *total return* on your money, over time, will be higher than both the coupon rate of 5 percent and the current yield of 6 percent. If you sell the bond before maturity, the price you get for it (the market value of the bond at the time) will also be factored into your total return.

In sum, the total return on the money you invest in bonds is often unknowable. Bonds are not at all as predictable as they seem at first glance!

Rising Interest Rates Are Good (or Bad) for Bondholders

In general, rising interest rates are good for *future* bondholders (who will see higher coupon payments); for those who *presently* own bonds, rising interest rates may not be so good because rising interest rates push bond prices down. (Who wants to buy your bond paying 5 percent when other bonds are suddenly paying 6 percent?)

On the other hand, rising interest rates allow present bondholders to reinvest their money (the coupon payments that arrive twice a year) for a higher return.

In the end, however, what matters most for bondholders both present and future is the *real* rate of interest, after tax. The real rate of interest is the nominal rate minus the rate of inflation. You'd rather get 6 percent on a bond when inflation is running at 2 percent than 10 percent on a bond when inflation is running at 8 percent — especially after taxes, which tax the nominal rate and ignore inflation.

Certain Bonds (Such as Treasuries) Are Completely Safe

Our national government has been spending money like a drunken sailor on payday. But the U.S. government can also print money and raise taxes. So there isn't much chance of Uncle Sam having to default on his debt — that's true. Treasuries are not completely safe, however. They are still subject to the other risks that bonds face. I'm talking about inflation risk and interest-rate risk.

There's also the risk that some future bevy of government leaders may find the government so much in debt, and the thought of raising taxes or risking inflation so intolerable, that they decide to pay 90 cents on the dollar to bondholders. Other governments have done this.

Although the United States doesn't seem likely to follow that lead, you'd better read Chapter 10 before plunking your entire savings into Treasury bonds.

Bonds Are a Retiree's Best Friend

Rely on an all fixed-income portfolio to replace your paycheck, and you'd better have an awfully big portfolio or you risk running out of funds. Bonds, unfortunately, have a long-term track record of outpacing inflation by only a modest margin. If you plan on a long retirement, that wee bit of extra gravy may not be enough to get you through the rest of your life without resorting to an awfully tight budget. The retiree's best friend is a *diversified* portfolio that has stocks (for growth potential) *and* bonds (for stability) *and* cash (for liquidity), with maybe some real estate and a smattering of commodities mixed in.

For further discussion on shaping your post-paycheck portfolio for maximum longevity, see Part V.

Individual Bonds Are Usually a Better Deal than Bond Funds

Some of the newer exchange-traded funds offer an instant diversified bond portfolio with a total expense ratio of peanuts — in the case of iShares, Schwab, SPDR, and Vanguard bond ETFs, you're looking at 0.10 to 0.15 percent per year. (That's 15 percent of 12 percent a year or less.) These ETFs are excellent ways to invest in bonds. Many other bond funds offer professional management with reasonable expenses and impressive long-term performance records.

Buying individual bonds may be the better route for some investors, but the decision is rarely a slam-dunk, especially for those investors with bond port-folios of, say, $350,000 or less. Less than that, and it may be hard to diversify a portfolio of individual bonds. Plus, the markups you pay on your modest buys and sells may be significantly more than you would pay for a bond fund — especially if you wind up not keeping the bond till maturity. Despite popular myth, individual bonds do not offer up all that much more predictability than do bond funds. More, yes. Much more, no.

Chapter 14 provides greater insight into the question of individual bonds versus bond funds.

Municipal Bonds Are Free of Taxation

Most income from municipal bonds is free from federal income tax. But the income from many municipal bonds is taxed at the local and state level, especially if you buy bonds that were issued outside of your own backyard. If you see a capital gain on the sale of a muni or muni fund, that gain is taxed the same way any other capital gain would be. And some municipal-bond income is subject to the Alternative Minimum Tax (AMT), designed so that those who make six figures and more can't deduct their way out of paying any tax.

Do municipal bonds make sense for you? The tax question is the primary one. Unfortunately, it isn't as straightforward as it looks.

Don't invest in munis, which generally pay lower rates of interest than do taxable bonds, without having the entire picture. Crunch the numbers. Talk to your tax guru. Always diversify. Read Chapter 8.

A Discount Broker Sells Bonds Cheaper

Often, a discount broker has the best deals on bonds, but sometimes not. That's especially true for new offers on municipal bonds and corporate bonds when a full-service broker may actually be packaging the bond for the public. It always pays to shop around. When buying Treasuries, don't go to any broker; shop direct on www.treasurydirect.gov.

The Biggest Risk in Bonds is the Risk of the Issuer Defaulting

Even in the world of corporate junk bonds, where the risk of default is as real as dirt, I'm still not sure if actual default qualifies as the biggest risk that bond-holders take. Maybe sometimes. But investors in general focus too much on default risk. A bond can also lose plenty of market value if the issuing company is simply downgraded by one of the major credit ratings agencies. Most commonly, however, a bond's principal crashes if interest rates soar. No matter how creditworthy the issuer, a swift rise in interest rates will cause your bond's value to dip. That's not an issue if you hold an individual bond till maturity, but you may be less than thrilled to be holding a bond that is paying 5 percent when all other bonds are paying 8 percent.

Chapter 20

Ten Mistakes That Most Bond Investors Make

*I*nvesting in bonds is easy. Investing well in bonds is hard. The hard part, in good measure, is that some very hungry middlemen out there are more than willing to share in your profits. In addition, bonds, by their very nature, can be more complicated than they appear. It's easy to get bamboozled, easy to make dumb mistakes. But if you watch out very carefully for the following ten do's and don'ts, you'll be far ahead of the game.

Allowing the Broker to Churn You

Bond brokers generally make their money when you buy and sell bonds. They rarely make anything while the bonds are simply sitting in your account, collecting interest. Largely for that reason, your broker may find many reasons to call you with special deals, and perhaps reasons that a bond issue he sold you last year is — ooops! — no longer worth holding.

In truth, it rarely, rarely happens that a bond you were sold last year is no longer worth holding. Company was downgraded by the major ratings agencies? You probably already lost whatever money you're likely to lose; selling the bond now will result in your locking in that loss. Why not hold the bond till maturity, if that was your original plan? Interest rates have risen or fallen?

Yeah, so? Don't they always? Bond B has a more favorable tax status than Bond A? Well, why weren't you told that when you bought Bond A?

I won't say that you'll *never* encounter a good reason to swap one bond for another. But you are almost always going to be better off as a buy-and-hold-till-maturity investor than you are riding the bond merry-go-round. If your broker calls with reasons to buy or sell, ask lots of questions and make sure you get clear answers as to why it is to *your* benefit, not his, to start trading.

Not Taking Advantage of TRACE

Buying and selling bonds is more transparent than ever before. That means that lots of information is available, if you know where to look. Until just a few years ago, a bond broker could charge you any kind of markup her heart desired, and you would have no idea what that markup was. Now, with a system called TRACE (the Trade Reporting and Compliance Engine), you can go online and within moments (often) find out how much your broker paid for the bonds she's now offering to sell you. If you can't, you can find out how much very similar bonds are selling for. Conversely, if your broker sells some bonds for you, you can find out how much she sold them for. You have a right to know.

At the same time you're checking TRACE to see what the broker is looking to score, you'll be able to compare the yield on a prospective bond purchase with the yields of comparable bonds. In fact, the better yield on comparable bonds often results from a lesser markup by the middleman. The two are closely intertwined.

See Chapter 15 for complete instructions on checking a bond's price history and the yield on comparable bonds.

Choosing a Bond Fund Based on Short-Term Performance

A bond fund's performance figures, especially going back for any period of less than, say, three years, can often look very impressive, but it may not mean squat. In most cases, a fund's performance, especially over such a short time period, has more to do with the kind of bond fund it is than with any managerial prowess. If, for example, high-yield bonds have had a great year, most high-yield bond funds — even the lousy ones — will see impressive performance. If foreign bonds have had a great year, foreign-bond funds will rally as a group. If interest rates have recently taken a nosedive, *all* bond funds will likely look good.

What matters most isn't raw performance but performance in relation to other similar funds and performance over the very long haul — five, six years and beyond. See Chapter 16 for more tips on choosing the best bond fund or funds for your portfolio.

Not Looking Closely Enough at a Bond Fund's Expenses

Bonds historically haven't returned enough to warrant very high management expense ratios on bond funds. But that certainly hasn't stopped some bond-fund managers from slapping on high fees. If you look at the performance of bond funds in the long run, the least expensive funds typically do the best. Don't pay a lot for a bond fund. You don't need to. The recent advent of exchange-traded funds has brought fund fees down dramatically.

Going Through a Middleman to Buy Treasuries

Through the U.S. government's own website — www.treasurydirect.gov — you can buy any and all kinds of Treasury bonds without paying any markup or fees whatsoever. You don't need a broker. The website is easy to navigate, and everything (including the bond holding itself) is electronic. See Chapter 5 for more on investing in Treasury bonds.

Counting Too Much on High-Yield Bonds

High-yield (*junk*) bonds look sweet. Historically, they offer higher returns than other bonds. But the return on high-yield bonds is still much less than the return you can expect on stocks. It may not be worth the added risk of getting an extra couple of percentage points to hold high-yield bonds.

The main role of bonds in a portfolio is to provide ballast. That's not to say that the interest payments from bonds aren't important — they certainly are. But, above all, bonds should be there for you if your other investments, including stocks, have a bad year or few years. Unfortunately, junk bonds don't provide that ballast. When the economy sours and stocks sink, junk bonds typically sink right along with all your other investments. Investment-grade bonds, such as Treasuries, agency bonds, most munis, and high-quality corporates, usually hold their own and may even rise in value when the going gets rough.

Paying Too Much Attention to the Yield Curve

At times, short-term bonds, even money market funds (built on very short-term debt instruments), yield as much as intermediate or long-term bonds. During these times, the yield curve is said to be *flat*. Flatness in the yield curve entices many people to move their money from long-term to short-term bonds. In a way, it makes perfect sense. Why tie your money up and take the greater risk that comes with long-term bonds if you aren't getting compensated for it?

But I would argue that longer-term bonds still belong in your portfolio, even when the yield curve is flat — heck, even when the yield curve becomes *inverted* (meaning short-term bonds yield more than long-term bonds), as happens on rare occasion. Remember that the main point of bonds in your portfolio isn't to provide kick-ass returns. That's the job of stocks. The main job of bonds is to provide your portfolio some lift when most of your holdings are sagging. If the economy hits the skids (hint: an inverted yield curve can be a sign of impending recession) and stocks suddenly plummet, chances are good that a lot of money will be funneled into long-term, high quality bonds. Interest rates will drop; long-term, investment-grade bonds will soar; and you'll wish you were there.

Conversely, when the yield curve is *steep,* and long-term bonds are yielding much more than short-term bonds, you may be tempted to load up on 20-year bonds. Resist. If interest rates pop, your bonds will be hurt badly. It pays to have a well-diversified bond portfolio — regardless of market conditions.

Buying Bonds That Are Too Complicated

Floating-rate bonds, reverse convertible bonds, catastrophe bonds, leveraged and inverse bond exchange-traded notes . . . many bonds and bond byproducts out there promise far more than simple interest. But in the end, many (if not most) investors who get involved wind up disappointed. Or crippled.

Keep it simple. Really. There's no such thing as a free lunch, and any bond or bond package that promises to pay you more than plain vanilla bonds is doing so for a reason. Some risk is involved that you may not see unless you squint really hard — or until that risk pummels your savings.

Ignoring Inflation and Taxation

If you're making 5 percent on your bonds, and you're losing 3 percent to inflation, you're about 2 percent ahead of the game . . . for a brief moment. But you'll likely be taxed on the 5 percent.

Inflation and taxation can eat seriously into your bond interest payments. That's not a reason not to invest in bonds. But when doing any kind of projections, counting your bond returns but ignoring inflation and taxation is like visiting Nome in winter and trying to ignore the snow.

Relying Too Heavily on Bonds in Retirement

If this were a chapter on the ten most common mistakes that *stock* investors make, I would advise readers that they must invest in bonds as well as stocks. But this is a chapter on the ten most common mistakes that *bond* investors make, so I must caution that an all-bond portfolio rarely if ever makes sense.

Stocks offer a greater potential for long-term return and a better chance of staying ahead of inflation than bonds. They also tend to move in different cycles than bonds, providing delicious diversification. They help dampen volatility and smooth out a portfolio's long-term returns, thereby potentially boosting long-term returns. Stocks and bonds complement each other like spaghetti and sauce.

Chapter 21

Ten Q & A's with Bond Guru Dan Fuss

The Loomis Sayles Bond Fund has returned more than 10 percent a year over the past 20-plus years — about 3 full percentage points above the return for the entire bond world during this same period. At the helm of the fund since 1991 (joined by co-manager Kathleen Gaffney in 1997) sits Dan Fuss, who is also vice chairman of the Boston-based Loomis, Sayles & Company. He has been managing investments for more than half a century. I thought it appropriate that this final chapter of *Bond Investing For Dummies*, 2nd Edition offer a few words from a guy who obviously knows fixed income . . . perhaps better than anyone.

Q. Dan, to what do you attribute your incredible success as a bond investor?

A. As you head to work in the morning and look around you, you get a sense for what season it is. Just as the calendar has seasons, there are also seasons of the economy, what one can also refer to as "cycles." These can greatly affect bond returns. One advantage I have is being older than the hills . . . I've seen a good number of seasons, and I can perhaps recognize them a little better or quicker than most. While I'm looking out for changes in the seasons, I also look at individual bond issuers and how the change of seasons is likely to affect them. "Breezy-Weezy Widget Company," for example, might do better in a hot season than cold.

Q. What would you say is the most common mistake that bond investors make?

A. If we're talking about investors in individual bonds, the most common mistake is not diversifying enough. I don't think it is even *possible* to diversify adequately unless you have a bond portfolio of considerable size . . . $100,000 for Treasury bonds, $200,000 for municipals, and if you're investing in corporate bonds, you'd better have at least $1 million to invest — *and* lots of time to invest in research, *and* a broker you really know and trust. Otherwise, you're bound to take too much risk on individual issues, and you're going to get eaten alive with fees.

Q. And what about investors in bond funds? What do you see as their most common or most fatal mistake?

A. There, I'd say the greatest mistake is buying an undifferentiated, general market-correlated fund — almost a "closet" index fund — with high expense ratios. If you're going to be paying a bond manager to manage your bond portfolio, you want that manager to really *manage*. You don't want that manager simply buying the market, because the market is full of terrible bonds that might make perfect sense for the companies issuing them and the brokerage houses selling them, but make no sense for investors.

Q. Many investors today are nervous about both stocks and bonds — stocks because of the great volatility we've been seeing, and bonds because interest rates are so low. Are these fears warranted? What is your prediction as to what the total return on bonds and stocks will be over the next ten years?

A. Prediction? Let's not use that word! My *guess* is that both bonds and stocks will return about 7 percent a year over the next decade, but stock returns will bounce around a lot more than bonds.

Q. So you're saying that bond returns are likely to be considerably higher than their historical average, and stock returns will be considerably lower. On what are you basing those predictions, er, guesses?

A. Mostly on the growing U.S. federal deficit. That will require greater borrowing by the Treasury, which will tend to force up interest rates. In the long term, such as ten years, rising interest rates will be a good thing for bond investors and not such a good thing for stock investors. But I'm looking at other factors, too, including the currently reasonable valuations of most U.S. companies.

Q. You're talking nominal returns, right? How much of these investment gains do you see being eaten away by inflation over the next decade?

A. Yes, I'm talking nominal returns. My best guess for inflation would be about 4 to 5 percent a year. It will be slower at first and then we'll see a crescendo toward the end. Hopefully, it won't be like the second half of the 1970s . . . hopefully!

Q. So if you reckon that stocks and bonds are going to return about the same in future years, and bonds are going to be much less volatile, are you then advocating all-bond portfolios?

A. I like bonds, but a diversified portfolio with both bonds and stocks still makes sense! First, my guesses about returns could be totally wrong. Second, stock and bond returns will likely continue, as they have in the past, to move up and down in different cycles. Third, if you know what you're doing, you can add a whole lot more return on the stock side by focusing on specific risks.

Q. What is the best place to invest right now for people who are most concerned with safety?

A. There are no completely safe places in the bond market. The risk of capital loss is minimal if you invest in short-term Treasuries, but you have maximum reinvestment risk. If you invest in 30-year Treasury zero-coupons, there is no reinvestment risk, but there is certainly a lot of risk to the value of your principal. With corporate bonds, of course, there are all kinds of additional risks. The greatest safety, now and always, can be found in diversification.

Q. What tips do you have for someone shopping for a bond fund . . . other than choosing Loomis Sayles, of course!

A. The expense ratio needs to be reasonable: less than 0.5 percent for a Treasury fund . . . not much more than 1.0 percent for anything else. There should be limited turnover. Turnover costs you money — I'd be wary of any kind of flipping over 80 percent a year. Look for a fund with a long-term positive track record, and make sure that the same manager or team that earned that track record is still the one running the show. Perhaps most importantly, make sure you know what you're buying. For most investors, multi-sector bond funds will make the most sense. Beware that there are many so-called "strategic income" funds out there that sound like multi-sector bond funds, but they may really be balanced funds with exposure to equity as well as fixed-income investments. Read the prospectus!

Q. You've talked of diversification and you've used the word "multi-sector." How diversified should investors be? And how "multi" is "multi" where bonds are concerned?

A. A diversified portfolio will have both equity investments and bonds. If munis make sense from a tax vantage point, I like to see a good array of municipal issues. If taxable bonds make more sense, I like to see a mix of Treasuries, corporate bonds, agencies, mortgage-backed, and international. Each category will do better at different times. As much as everyone likes to make predictions, you never know what's coming around the corner.

Appendix

Helpful Web Resources for Successful Bond Investing

・・

1 designed this book so that much of the information is perennial, but some of it will certainly go out of date. Following are a number of websites that will change with the times and help to keep you up to speed on changes in the world of bond investing. Of course, many, many websites offer financial information — and misinformation. I handpicked the ones listed here as the best of the lot. Nearly all are entirely free, and they're chock full of good stuff. Some serve as portals that allow you to buy and sell bonds. Others provide you with data unavailable anywhere else.

Bond-Specific Sites

http://finance.yahoo.com/bonds/composite_bond_rates: A great snapshot of the entire bond market, and a logical place to start any bond-shopping expedition.

www.bondbuyer.com: Would you believe there's a daily newspaper about municipal bonds?

www.emma.msrb.org: Information galore on municipal bonds, including official statements, annual financial statements, and other juicy disclosures about municipal bond issuers. EMMA reports every trade in municipal bonds. For fun and profit, check to see your broker isn't ripping you off with an excessive markup.

www.investinginbonds.com: Scads of information on bonds and bond investing from the Securities Industry and Financial Markets Association. This website is also a portal to TRACE, the system that allows you to see what your broker paid for the bond that he's now trying to sell you.

www.munimarket.com: Trying to become the eBay for bonds.

www.muniadvocate.com: Consumer advocate Kevin Olson warns of consumer deceptions and fraud in the selling of tax-exempt bonds.

General Financial News, Advice, and Education

`http://finance.yahoo.com`: Navigate your heart away . . . tons of information on financial markets.

`www.bankrate.com`: Compare rates on all sorts of fixed-income investments.

`www.bloomberg.com`: Rather hardcore financial data.

`www.cnnfn.com`: Get your daily fix of everything money related.

`www.dinkytown.com`: Calculators of all sorts.

`www.sec.gov/edgar.shtml`: The official government repository for information about corporations that have issued publicly traded securities, including bonds and bond funds.

`www.moneychimp.com`: For the more advanced investor. Don't let the silly name fool you.

`www.morningstar.com`: Exclusive ratings of funds, and more.

`www.socialinvest.org`: A wealth of information on investing for social good.

Financial Supermarkets

Otherwise known as large brokerage houses, here are some places where you can buy, sell, and house your bonds or bond funds — as well as other investments, such as stocks.

`www.fidelity.com`: Or telephone Fidelity at 1-800-544-8888.

`www.schwab.com`: Or telephone Charles Schwab at 1-866-232-9890.

`www.tdameritrade.com`: Or telephone TD Ameritrade at 1-800-454-9272.

`www.troweprice.com`: Or telephone T. Rowe Price at 1-800-638-5660.

`www.vanguard.com`: Or telephone Vanguard at 1-800-662-7447.

Bond Issuers and Bond Fund Providers

If you're in the market for Treasury bonds (see Chapter 5), go to www. treasurydirect.gov.

To check out agency bonds (see Chapter 7), start with these sites:

- ✔ www.fanniemae.com
- ✔ www.freddiemac.com
- ✔ www.ginniemae.gov

If a bond fund is in your future, check out these sites:

- ✔ www.allianzinvestors.com
- ✔ www.americancentury.com
- ✔ www.barclaysglobal.com
- ✔ www.dodgeandcox.com
- ✔ www.doubleline.com
- ✔ www.fidelity.com
- ✔ www.hussmanfunds.com
- ✔ www.loomissayles.com
- ✔ www.paxworld.com
- ✔ www.payden-rygel.com
- ✔ www.pimco.com
- ✔ www.schwab.com
- ✔ www.troweprice.com
- ✔ www.vanguard.com

Best Retirement Calculator

How large a portfolio are you going to need to retire in style? How much are you going to have to sock away, and what kind of rate of return do you need to get there?

www.fireseeker.com: *Fire* stands for *financial independence/retire early.* If you didn't realize it, there is an entire movement devoted to financial independence. Use this website as your entry point. You find what is arguably the best retirement calculator on the web, along with an Early Retirement Forum where other *Fire* fans passionately discuss their strategies.

Regulatory Agencies

www.sec.gov: This is the website of the U.S. Securities and Exchange Commission. Click on <u>Funds and Advisers</u>, <u>Investor Info</u>, and <u>Check Out Brokers and Advisors</u> to make sure a financial planner is fully licensed. You'll also find out if your candidate has any disciplinary history for unethical conduct.

www.finra.org: This is the website of the Financial Industry Regulatory Authority (FINRA), formed in July 2007 when the National Association of Securities Dealers (NASD) merged with the New York Stock Exchange Member Regulation. Find scores of information on bond yields, prices, and trends, as well as — naturally — all kinds of regulatory stuff.

Where to Find a Financial Planner

www.cambridgeadvisors.com: Alliance of Cambridge Advisors is a national network of *fee-onlies* (financial people who work for a straight fee rather than commissions) who are eager to work with middle-class folk.

www.cfainstitute.org: CFA Institute is where you want to go to find a Chartered Financial Analyst (CFA), which is not as well-known but very similar to a Certified Financial Planner (CFP).

www.cfp.net: The Certified Financial Planning Board of Standards lists Certified Financial Planners (CFPs) nationwide. The CFP designation assures that the person has a fair amount of education and experience, and passed a wicked 10-hour exam.

www.fpanet.org: The Financial Planning Association is the nation's largest organization of financial planners. It doesn't take much to join.

www.garrettplanningnetwork.com: Garrett Planning Network is a community of more than 300 financial advisors who charge for services on an hourly, as-needed basis. Average cost per hour: $200. Average length of engagement: 7.5 hours.

www.napfa.org: The National Association of Personal Financial Advisors is the association for fee-onlies. About four out of ten financial planners are fee-onlies, and that includes the author of this book.

Yours Truly

www.globalportfolios.net or www.russellwild.com: Both URLs will take you to the same place: the author's own fashionable website.

Index

• C •

• D •

Apple & Mac

iPad 2 For Dummies,
3rd Edition
978-1-118-17679-5

iPhone 4S For Dummies,
5th Edition
978-1-118-03671-6

iPod touch For Dummies,
3rd Edition
978-1-118-12960-9

Mac OS X Lion
For Dummies
978-1-118-02205-4

Blogging & Social Media

CityVille For Dummies
978-1-118-08337-6

Facebook For Dummies,
4th Edition
978-1-118-09562-1

Mom Blogging
For Dummies
978-1-118-03843-7

Twitter For Dummies,
2nd Edition
978-0-470-76879-2

WordPress For Dummies,
4th Edition
978-1-118-07342-1

Business

Cash Flow For Dummies
978-1-118-01850-7

Investing For Dummies,
6th Edition
978-0-470-90545-6

Job Searching with Social
Media For Dummies
978-0-470-93072-4

QuickBooks 2012
For Dummies
978-1-118-09120-3

Resumes For Dummies,
6th Edition
978-0-470-87361-8

Starting an Etsy Business
For Dummies
978-0-470-93067-0

Cooking & Entertaining

Cooking Basics
For Dummies, 4th Edition
978-0-470-91388-8

Wine For Dummies,
4th Edition
978-0-470-04579-4

Diet & Nutrition

Kettlebells For Dummies
978-0-470-59929-7

Nutrition For Dummies,
5th Edition
978-0-470-93231-5

Restaurant Calorie Counter
For Dummies,
2nd Edition
978-0-470-64405-8

Digital Photography

Digital SLR Cameras &
Photography For Dummies,
4th Edition
978-1-118-14489-3

Digital SLR Settings
& Shortcuts
For Dummies
978-0-470-91763-3

Photoshop Elements 10
For Dummies
978-1-118-10742-3

Gardening

Gardening Basics
For Dummies
978-0-470-03749-2

Vegetable Gardening
For Dummies,
2nd Edition
978-0-470-49870-5

Green/Sustainable

Raising Chickens
For Dummies
978-0-470-46544-8

Green Cleaning
For Dummies
978-0-470-39106-8

Health

Diabetes For Dummies,
3rd Edition
978-0-470-27086-8

Food Allergies
For Dummies
978-0-470-09584-3

Living Gluten-Free
For Dummies,
2nd Edition
978-0-470-58589-4

Hobbies

Beekeeping
For Dummies,
2nd Edition
978-0-470-43065-1

Chess For Dummies,
3rd Edition
978-1-118-01695-4

Drawing For Dummies,
2nd Edition
978-0-470-61842-4

eBay For Dummies,
7th Edition
978-1-118-09806-6

Knitting For Dummies,
2nd Edition
978-0-470-28747-7

Language &
Foreign Language

English Grammar
For Dummies,
2nd Edition
978-0-470-54664-2

French For Dummies,
2nd Edition
978-1-118-00464-7

German For Dummies,
2nd Edition
978-0-470-90101-4

Spanish Essentials
For Dummies
978-0-470-63751-7

Spanish For Dummies,
2nd Edition
978-0-470-87855-2

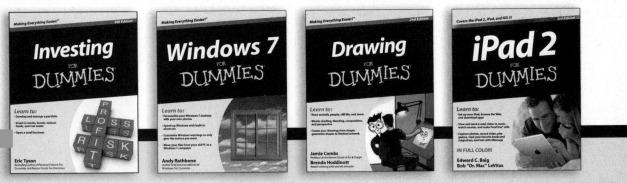

Available wherever books are sold. For more information or to order direct: U.S. customers visit www.dummies.com or call 1-877-762-2974.
U.K. customers visit www.wileyeurope.com or call (0) 1243 843291. Canadian customers visit www.wiley.ca or call 1-800-567-4797.

Connect with us online at www.facebook.com/fordummies or @fordummies

Math & Science

Algebra I For Dummies,
2nd Edition
978-0-470-55964-2

Biology For Dummies,
2nd Edition
978-0-470-59875-7

Chemistry For Dummies,
2nd Edition
978-1-1180-0730-3

Geometry For Dummies,
2nd Edition
978-0-470-08946-0

Pre-Algebra Essentials
For Dummies
978-0-470-61838-7

Microsoft Office

Excel 2010 For Dummies
978-0-470-48953-6

Office 2010 All-in-One
For Dummies
978-0-470-49748-7

Office 2011 for Mac
For Dummies
978-0-470-87869-9

Word 2010
For Dummies
978-0-470-48772-3

Music

Guitar For Dummies,
2nd Edition
978-0-7645-9904-0

Clarinet For Dummies
978-0-470-58477-4

iPod & iTunes
For Dummies,
9th Edition
978-1-118-13060-5

Pets

Cats For Dummies,
2nd Edition
978-0-7645-5275-5

Dogs All-in One
For Dummies
978-0470-52978-2

Saltwater Aquariums
For Dummies
978-0-470-06805-2

Religion & Inspiration

The Bible For Dummies
978-0-7645-5296-0

Catholicism For Dummies,
2nd Edition
978-1-118-07778-8

Spirituality For Dummies,
2nd Edition
978-0-470-19142-2

Self-Help & Relationships

Happiness For Dummies
978-0-470-28171-0

Overcoming Anxiety
For Dummies,
2nd Edition
978-0-470-57441-6

Seniors

Crosswords For Seniors
For Dummies
978-0-470-49157-7

iPad 2 For Seniors
For Dummies, 3rd Edition
978-1-118-17678-8

Laptops & Tablets
For Seniors For Dummies,
2nd Edition
978-1-118-09596-6

Smartphones & Tablets

BlackBerry For Dummies,
5th Edition
978-1-118-10035-6

Droid X2 For Dummies
978-1-118-14864-8

HTC ThunderBolt
For Dummies
978-1-118-07601-9

MOTOROLA XOOM
For Dummies
978-1-118-08835-7

Sports

Basketball For Dummies,
3rd Edition
978-1-118-07374-2

Football For Dummies,
2nd Edition
978-1-118-01261-1

Golf For Dummies,
4th Edition
978-0-470-88279-5

Test Prep

ACT For Dummies,
5th Edition
978-1-118-01259-8

ASVAB For Dummies,
3rd Edition
978-0-470-63760-9

The GRE Test For
Dummies, 7th Edition
978-0-470-00919-2

Police Officer Exam
For Dummies
978-0-470-88724-0

Series 7 Exam
For Dummies
978-0-470-09932-2

Web Development

HTML, CSS, & XHTML
For Dummies, 7th Edition
978-0-470-91659-9

Drupal For Dummies,
2nd Edition
978-1-118-08348-2

Windows 7

Windows 7
For Dummies
978-0-470-49743-2

Windows 7
For Dummies,
Book + DVD Bundle
978-0-470-52398-8

Windows 7 All-in-One
For Dummies
978-0-470-48763-1